CIA
and the
Vietnam Policymakers: Three Episodes 1962-1968

by Harold P. Ford

History Staff
Center for the Study of Intelligence
Central Intelligence Agency
1998

To Jo and John

Foreword

This volume is part of the Center for the Study of Intelligence's continuing effort to provide as clear a record of CIA activities as possible within the constraints of overall national security concerns. We believe it is important for the American public to be aware of and to understand the Agency's crucial mission. The CIA is committed to a degree of openness that not only documents its activities but also informs the US public of the historical successes and shortcomings of the Intelligence Community.

This recently declassified study by former CIA officer Dr. Harold P. Ford reviews the Intelligence Community's analytic performance during the chaotic Vietnam era, with particular focus on the efforts of CIA analysts. It offers a candid view of the CIA's intelligence assessments concerning Vietnam during three episodes between 1962 and 1968 and the reactions of senior US policymakers to those assessments. Without ignoring or downplaying the analysts' problems and errors, Dr. Ford argues persuasively that, for the most part, the Agency's analysis proved remarkably accurate. His study shows that CIA analysts had a firm grasp of the situation in Vietnam and continually expressed doubts that heightened US military pressure alone could win the war. Contrary to the opinions voiced by then Secretary of Defense Robert McNamara and others, Dr. Ford strikingly illustrates the substantial expertise CIA officers brought to the Vietnam question.

Dr. Ford was uniquely qualified to undertake this in-depth study of the Agency's performance on Vietnam. After graduating from the University of Redlands, he served as a naval officer in the Pacific during World War II. He earned a Ph.D. in history at the University of Chicago and was a postdoctoral scholar at Oxford University. He joined the CIA's Office of Policy Coordination in 1950 and transferred in 1951 to the Agency's Office of National Estimates where he served for most of his Agency career. He drafted many National Intelligence Estimates concerning Vietnam and participated in several of the inter-Agency Vietnam working groups discussed in this study. He later served as a CIA station chief abroad. Dr. Ford retired from CIA in 1974 and subsequently worked for the Senate Select Committee on Intelligence. He returned to the Agency in 1980 to help form the National Intelligence Council (NIC). At the time of his retirement in 1986 he was the NIC's Acting Chairman.

Gerald K. Haines
Chief, CIA History Staff

This publication is prepared for the use of US Government officials, and the format, coverage, and content are designed to meet their specific requirements. US Government officials can obtain additional copies of this document directly or through liaison channels from the Central Intelligence Agency.

Other requesters can obtain subscriptions to publications similar to this one by addressing inquiries to:

Documents Expediting Project (DOC EX)
ANA Division--Government Documents Section
Library of Congress
101 Independence Ave., S.E.
Washington, DC 20540-4172
Phone: (202) 707-9527
Fax (202) 707-0380

or: **National Technical Information Service**
5285 Port Royal Road
Springfield, VA 22161
Phone: (703) 605-6000 or 1-800-553-6847
Fax: (703) 321-8547

Queries on the availability of this publication may be directed to the DOC EX Project or the NTIS Office of Customer Services at the respective addresses or phone or fax numbers indicated above. Publications are not available to the public from the Central Intelligence Agency.

This document will be available on the Internet at www.odci.gov/csi.

This publication contains copyrighted material. Do not reproduce or disseminate without permission.

All opinions expressed in this study are those of the author. They do not necessarily represent the views of the Central Intelligence Agency or any other component of the US Intelligence Community.

Contents

Preface

This study uses three episodes in the interplay of intelligence with policymaking on Vietnam (1) to examine the information and judgments the Central Intelligence Agency provided presidents and senior administration officials; (2) to assess the impact these inputs had or did not have on policy decisions; and (3) to reflect on why the policy and intelligence outcomes developed as they did. Focusing on CIA intelligence analysis in Washington in the 1960s, the study is intended to complement other History Staff publications on Vietnam treating the Agency's operational performance in the field.

The particular focus of this study takes nothing away from the fact that CIA assessments on Vietnam were an important part of the policymaking process in the years before and after these three episodes. In the earlier years, CIA Headquarters judgments had been consistently pessimistic, holding that the French would almost certainly not be able to prevail in Vietnam. As the US commitment to South Vietnam progressively increased, CIA-produced assessments of the military-political outlook there remained more doubtful than those of US policymakers. Until 1962, CIA's senior officers had focused their attention on field operations, intelligence collection, and the routine supply of finished intelligence to Washington policymakers. That situation changed with the advent of Director of Central Intelligence (DCI) John A. McCone in late 1961. Until early 1965 McCone played an active role in many matters of policy formulation affecting the Vietnam war and broader world issues, though late in 1964 he and President Johnson began to differ on optimum military measures to pursue in Vietnam.

During the brief tenure of McCone's successor, Adm. William F. Raborn, a position of Special Assistant to the DCI for Vietnam Affairs (SAVA) was created to coordinate and focus CIA efforts in support of administration policy. When veteran CIA operations officer Richard Helms replaced Raborn as DCI, he was for the most part less aggressive than McCone in dealing with top policymakers, was generally more responsive than initiative-taking, and gave the White House and the Pentagon vigorous Agency support with respect to Vietnam. In 1967-68, however, he did give President Johnson some remarkably frank reports from CIA officers that went far beyond strictly intelligence matters. It was Helms's Special Assistant for Vietnam Affairs at that time, George A. Carver, Jr., who played an especially influential role in the policy arena, notably in early 1968 when the Tet Offensive forced the Johnson administration to reexamine its policies. Thereafter, however, as the Johnson and Nixon administrations constricted the circle of advisers on Vietnam, CIA contributions focused more on the execution and monitoring of policy than on its formulation.

Contrasted to the narrower opportunities CIA had for influencing policy decisions prior to 1962 and following 1968, the three episodes chosen for this study were cases where US policymakers faced critical points in the evolution of US involvement in Vietnam, and where CIA assessments and senior Agency personalities had at least the potential for significantly affecting the policy decisions taken.

In the first of these episodes, 1962-63, a policy wish intruded on the formulation of intelligence, with DCI McCone playing a key role. This intrusion stemmed from sharply differing views of what was happening in the liberated colonies of former French Indochina. Policymakers believed the positions of US-supported governments in South Vietnam and Laos were improving vis-a-vis the aggrandizement of Communist North Vietnam—so much so, they felt, that the United States could consider withdrawing some of its 10,000 advisory military personnel then in Vietnam. To Washington's working-level intelligence officers, the situation appeared to be getting worse, not better. In the event, in the spring of 1963 things suddenly did get much worse in Indochina, shattering policymakers' optimism and sending them scurrying for new ways to try to save South Vietnam.

The story of that policy search and its interplay with intelligence constitutes the second episode. First came the conviction, championed especially by certain senior State Department officials, that the Ngo Dinh Diem government was incapable of leading the struggle against North Vietnam's aggression and subversion and must be replaced. When Diem's successors proved even less effective, a dominant general view evolved out of the debates among Washington policymakers that South Vietnam could be rescued only by committing US combat forces in the South and systematically bombing the North. Despite the persistent contention at the time by most CIA analysts that such measures by themselves would not save the South, the Johnson administration eventually decided to "go big" in Vietnam, while John McCone, differing with Lyndon Johnson on what military tactics to pursue there, lost his close relationship with the President and resigned his DCI post.

The final case, covering the period 1967-68, treats (1) the circumstances and political pressures that resulted in an estimate of enemy troops in South Vietnam that was considerably lower than the actual total force available to the Communists; (2) the response CIA officers made to those pressures; (3) the alerts which Agency (and other) intelligence officers gave—or did not give—prior to the 1968 Tet holiday that the enemy was likely to launch an unprecedented offensive; and (4) the role CIA inputs played in President Johnson's response to the Tet Offensive. We will see that in this third episode much of CIA's input to the President's policy advisers was made by or through the Director's Special Assistant for Vietnam Affairs, George Carver. This CIA officer enjoyed extraordinary Cabinet-level entree, did not restrict himself to intelligence matters, and, until shortly after the Tet Offensive, usually voiced a more optimistic view of Vietnam than did most of his CIA colleagues.

In evaluating the quality and impact of CIA's input to policymaking in the three episodes examined, we will find a mixed picture in which, numerous historians tell us, CIA's judgments proved prescient much of the time but found little receptivity. At other times during 1962-68, the Agency's intelligence found favor with policymakers but turned out to be wrong. Despite this mixed performance, as this study will find, the intelligence on Vietnam that the Agency provided decisionmakers was for the most part better than that of other official contributors, while within CIA the most acute judgments were generally those of its working-level officers.

A Note on Sources and Perspective: The sources of this study include formerly classified documents largely from CIA files; personal interviews of participants; documents and other materials already in the public domain; and the author's own experience in certain of the episodes under review. Research of CIA records covered the offices of the Director of Central Intelligence (including his Special Assistant for Vietnam Affairs), the Inspector General, the Deputy Directors for Intelligence and Operations, CIA's History Staff, and the former Office of National Estimates (O/NE) and its files of National Intelligence Estimates. All the Agency documents cited in this study come from specific files of the respective CIA offices.

The study is colored and, it is hoped, illuminated by the author's personal experience as a senior analyst of Indochina questions, on and off, beginning in 1952. During the first two episodes covered, he was successively the chief of O/NE's Far East Staff and then chief of the O/NE Staff; throughout these episodes he was concurrently a CIA representative to various interagency consultative bodies and policy working groups concerned with Vietnam. During the third episode he was otherwise engaged as a CIA Chief of Station abroad. Since his retirement from CIA in 1986, at which time he was Acting Chairman of the National Intelligence Council (the successor to O/NE), he has prepared studies on Vietnam and other subjects for CIA's History Staff.

The author recognizes that his personal involvement in some of the historical events reviewed here constitutes a hazard to scholarship. Let it be said at the outset that, having already limited himself to three exemplary episodes from a longer historical period, he will not always represent or reflect every shade of opinion or judgment on the matters addressed. It should be noted, also, when the judgments of National Intelligence Estimates are cited, that they represented the views not only of CIA but also the entire Washington Intelligence Community. Not least, the author does not intend this work to be a paean to CIA analysis: while he examines situations where he considers CIA judgments proved prescient, he also cites instances where CIA analyses and national estimates proved wide of the mark or were too wishy-washy to serve the policymaking process well.

The author wishes to thank those who consented to be interviewed, and those who have pointed out errors or omissions in earlier drafts and have suggested additions and improved language. These latter experts include Lt. Gen. Robert E. Pursley (USAF, Ret.); CIA History Staff Chiefs J. Kenneth McDonald, L. Kay Oliver, and Gerald Haines; former CIA officers William Colby, George Allen, Richard Lehman, Bob Layton, R. Jack Smith, James Hanrahan, and—especially—Richard Kovar; and CIA officers Henry Appelbaum, Teresa Purcell, Marti Spaulding, and Russell Sniady.

The views expressed in this study do not necessarily represent those of CIA; the author alone is responsible for the views expressed and for any errors or omissions that remain. This study was completed in mid-1997.

Episode 1, 1962-1963
Distortions of Intelligence

The struggle in South Vietnam at best will be protracted and costly
[because] very great weaknesses remain and will be difficult to surmount.
Among these are lack of aggressive and firm leadership at all levels of
command, poor morale among the troops, lack of trust between peasant
and soldier, poor tactical use of available forces, a very inadequate intelligence system, and obvious Communist penetration of the South Vietnamese military organization.

> From the draft of NIE 53-63, "Prospects in South Vietnam"
> submitted by the Intelligence Community's representatives
> to the United States Intelligence Board, 25 February 1963[1]

We believe that Communist progress has been blunted and that the situation is improving. . . . Improvements which have occurred during the past
year now indicate that the Viet Cong can be contained militarily and that
further progress can be made in expanding the area of government control
and in creating greater security in the countryside.

> From that NIE's final version, 17 April 1963

Throughout 1961 President Kennedy had been under mounting
pressure from his military and political chiefs to send US troops to Laos
and South Vietnam to stem a floodtide of Communist military successes
and shore up the faltering Government of South Vietnam (GVN).
Finally, late in the year, Kennedy had gambled that a substantial increase
in the allocations of US advisers, trainers, and equipment to the South
Vietnam armed forces would stiffen South Vietnamese resistance and
reverse the tide.

By early November 1963, however, two years after his decision to
expand the US commitment in Vietnam, it had become clear that the situation there had gone from bad to worse, and that his gamble had gone
awry: his administration had sanctioned the overthrow of Saigon's president, Ngo Dinh Diem, who had been murdered, and the first in a series

---

[1] Matthias, Willard, "How Three Estimates Went Wrong," *Studies in Intelligence*, Vol. 12, Winter
1968, p. 27.

of coups and even less effective Saigon regimes had been ushered in. Contributing to that result had been distortions of US intelligence reporting from the field, and of intelligence analysis in Washington.

During the two-year period following President Kennedy's decision in late 1961 to up the ante in Vietnam, much of the reporting from the military and political missions in Saigon continued in the overly optimistic vein that marked most of the French and American experience in Indochina from 1945 to 1975.[2] In 1962-63, the period examined in this study's first episode, senior US decisionmakers came to believe that American military participation in Vietnam might be completed by the end of 1965 and that, as a first step, some 1,000 US military personnel could be withdrawn by the end of 1963. It did not quite work out that way.

In Washington, a significant distortion was, paradoxically, contributed by the Director of Central Intelligence himself, John A. McCone, who had not been notably optimistic about the initial results of President Kennedy's venture. As we will see, in February 1963 he sharply criticized the pessimistic conclusions of his Board of National Estimates, even though it had already diluted the even-darker working-level judgments of the Office of National Estimates (O/NE) staff and the Intelligence Community's representatives. McCone remanded their draft National Intelligence Estimate (NIE) and directed them to seek out the views of senior policymakers in a revised NIE. The revisions made to the final version of that Estimate conveyed a markedly more optimistic forecast of the effectiveness of US and Vietnamese efforts, so described by McCone himself when he later told President Kennedy that the NIE had "indicated we could win."[3]

That reworking of intelligence exacted a steep price. By so altering the tone of the NIE's judgments and producing an authoritative but misleading Estimate, McCone's Office of National Estimates, supposedly above the fray of policy dispute, confirmed the expectations of progress that senior policymakers had long entertained but would soon have to abandon. As the authors of *The Pentagon Papers* later concluded, "The

---

[2] See examples in Annex I, "Expectations," and in Annex II, "Distortions of Intelligence."
[3] McCone, Memorandum for the Record, "Meeting with the President, 10 September 1963." CIA Inspector General's report, November 1964 (TS). CIA files, Job No. 73-B-567, DCI - Inspector General, Box 2, "Surveys," document 185214, p.15 (Hereafter CIA/IG Report). Also cited by Walter Elder (McCone's former Executive Assistant) in "John A. McCone as Director of Central Intelligence," manuscript history, revised edition, 1973, p. 631 (S). CIA files, Job No. 8701032R (Box 4). There are several versions of Elder's history: (1) the one cited above, (2) a 1983 version, and (3) a 1986 version revised by Dr. Mary S. McAuliffe. All are in CIA files, Job No. 8701032R, and all are classified Secret.

intelligence and reporting problems during this period cannot be explained away. . . . In retrospect [the estimators] were not only wrong, but more importantly, they were influential."[4]

The Effort To Begin Withdrawing US Military Personnel From Vietnam

> At the Honolulu conference in July 1962 Defense Secretary McNamara once again asked MACV [Military Assistance Command, Vietnam] commander General Paul Harkins how long it would take before the Viet Cong could be expected to be eliminated as a significant force. In reply [the MACV commander] estimated about one year from the time Republic of Vietnam Armed Forces (RVNAF) and other forces became fully operational and began to press the VC in all areas. . . . The Secretary said that a conservative view had to be taken and to assume it would take three years instead of one, that is, by the latter part of 1965.
>
> *The Pentagon Papers*[5]

The hubris that marked much of President Kennedy's entourage was never more evident than in their approach to Vietnam during 1962 and early 1963. Apparently believing that they had solved the difficult problem of whether and how to expand the American commitment there, having finessed a negotiated settlement in Laos, and having become entranced with the cure-all of "counterinsurgency," many of the Kennedy team members at the outset of 1962 were confident that their managerial know-how could produce victory in South Vietnam. Dean Rusk, Robert McNamara, the Joint Chiefs of Staff (JCS), the Commander in Chief Pacific (CINCPAC), and McGeorge Bundy—all the king's men—were so convinced there was sufficient "light at the end of the tunnel" that in mid-1962 they began fashioning plans to start phasing out most of the 10,000 or so US military advisory personnel then in Vietnam.

Such optimism was by no means new; it had characterized numerous pronouncements by senior US officials since at least 1953.[6] The confidence of the Kennedy team prevailed through the early months of

---

[4]Department of Defense, *United States–Vietnam Relations, 1945-1967*, (*The Pentagon Papers*) Book 3, IV-B-4, "Phased Withdrawal of U.S. Forces in Vietnam, 1962-1964," p. vii. (Hereafter *Pentagon Papers* [DoD ed.])
[5]Gravel edition, Boston: (Beacon Press, 1971) Vol. II, pp. 164, 175. (Hereafter *Pentagon Papers* [Gravel ed.])
[6]See examples at Annex I: "Expectations."

1963—even after South Vietnamese Army (ARVN) units, supported by US helicopters, had failed to destroy a far smaller Viet Cong force in the ARVN's first pitched battle, 3 January 1963, at Ap Bac.[7]

With one notable exception, the prevailing view at senior levels during these months was one of optimism. For example, in May 1962, on one of his many visits to Vietnam, Secretary of Defense McNamara assured newsman Neil Sheehan that "Every quantitative measure we have shows we're winning this war."[8] Two months later, drawing on a study provided him by MACV, McNamara told high-level officials at a Honolulu conference that "conservatively speaking," the Viet Cong would be eliminated as a significant force "by the latter part of 1965."[9] In his 1963 State of the Union speech, four weeks after Ap Bac, President Kennedy assured the nation that "the spearpoint of aggression has been blunted in South Vietnam."[10] Two weeks later, CINCPAC Adm. Harry Felt predicted that South Vietnam would win the war within three years.[11] In April, Secretary of State Rusk told a New York audience that morale in the South Vietnamese countryside had begun to rise and that the Viet Cong looked "less and less like winners."[12] In May, according to participant William E. Colby (then Chief of the CIA Operations Directorate's Far East Division—C/FE), MACV chief Gen. Paul Harkins assured yet another Honolulu conference that, militarily speaking, the Viet Cong would have its back broken within another year.[13] And even as late as October 1963, amid riots in South Vietnam (and just one month before President Diem's overthrow and murder), JCS Chairman Gen. Maxwell Taylor

---

[7]This was the first major engagement in which US attack helicopters were employed on a significant scale. Observers agree that at Ap Bac the ARVN also enjoyed an enormous numerical advantage, but their estimates vary widely: from four to ten times as many troops as the Viet Cong had. See Col. Dave Richard Palmer, *Summons of the Trumpet: US-Vietnam in Perspective* (San Francisco, Presidio Press, 1978), pp. 27ff.; Chester L. Cooper, *The Lost Crusade: America in Vietnam* (New York: Dodd, Mead & Co., 1970), pp. 199-201; Stanley Karnow, *Vietnam: A History* (New York: Viking Press, 1983), pp. 259-262; Neil Sheehan, *A Bright Shining Lie: John Paul Vann and America in Vietnam* (New York: Random House, 1988), pp. 269-283; and Peter Arnett, *Live From the Battlefield* (New York: Simon & Shuster, 1994), pp. 96-98. According to Arnett, Lt. Col. Vann told newsmen shortly after the Ap Bac battle that it had been a debacle, "a damn shame," whereas MACV chief Gen. Paul Harkins told them that "We've got them [the enemy] in a trap and we're going to spring it in half an hour." Arnett, p. 97.
[8]Sheehan, *A Bright Shining Lie*, p. 290. Arthur Schlesinger also cites this remark of McNamara's: *A Thousand Days: John F. Kennedy in the White House* (Boston: Houghton Mifflin Co., 1965), p. 549.
[9]*Pentagon Papers* (Gravel ed.), Vol. II, p. 175.
[10]*The New York Times*, 15 January 1963.
[11]*The New York Times*, 31 January 1963.
[12]As cited in Schlesinger, *A Thousand Days*, p. 986.
[13]Colby, Memorandum for the Record, "Secretary of Defense Conference on Vietnam, 8 May 1963." (S) CIA/DDP files, Job No. 78-597, DDO/ISS, Box 1, Folder 8.

DCI John McCone

told President Kennedy that the Viet Cong insurgency in the northern and central areas of South Vietnam could be "reduced to little more than sporadic incidents by the end of 1964."[14]

A senior dissenter to such optimism in 1962 had been DCI John McCone. In June, upon returning from his first trip to Vietnam, he gave Secretary McNamara a pessimistic estimate of its future. According to Richard Helms, who was CIA's Deputy Director for Plans (now Operations) at the time and who was present at their meeting, the Director told McNamara that "he was not optimistic about the success of the whole United States program. . . . He said he did not think that [the various American efforts] would succeed over the long run, pointing out that we were merely chipping away at the toe of the glacier from the North."[15] Two days later McCone warned Washington's Special Group (Counterinsurgency) that Viet Cong forces were developing new techniques, including larger units with heavier weapons, which might overwhelm South Vietnamese strategic villages before ARVN troops could respond.[16] Given his pessimism, one of the most intriguing events in John McCone's tenure as DCI, discussed below, occurred some eight months later when he insisted that the Intelligence Community's sober draft estimate of Vietnam's future was too pessimistic.

Meanwhile, considerations other than optimism about the course of events in Vietnam supported the Kennedy White House's desire to begin phasing out US military personnel there. Primary were the demands of crises elsewhere in the world and the administration's reluctance to commit US forces to a land war in Asia. Secretary McNamara summed up such concerns in March 1962 when he told Congress that US strategy was to assist indigenous forces in Third World crises rather than commit US forces to combat there. Avoiding direct participation in the Vietnam war, he said, would not only release US forces for use elsewhere, but

---

[14] *Pentagon Papers* (DoD ed.), Book 3, "Phased Withdrawal of U.S. Forces," p. 20.

[15] Helms, Memorandum for the Record, "Director's Meeting with the Secretary of Defense," 18 June 1962 (S). CIA/DCI files, Job No. 80B01285A, "DCI/McCone," Folder 2. Such pessimism as existed at the time among policymakers was confined for the most part to certain State Department officers. For example, these remarks were attributed to Sterling J. Cottrell, Director of State's Vietnam Task Force, 3 May 1962: "Mr. Cottrell summed up the situation by stating that in his opinion, we have reached bottom in South Vietnam, and that he is not sure whether we have made the upturn yet." Meeting of Special Group (Counterinsurgency), Department of State, *Foreign Relations of the United States, 1961-1963, Vol. II, Vietnam*, p. 373. (Hereafter cited as *FRUS*). Also, Joseph Mendenhall, former Political Counselor, Embassy Vietnam, 16 May 1962: ". . . we cannot win the war with the Diem-Nhu methods, and we cannot change those methods no matter how much pressure we put on them." Mendenhall, Memorandum for the Deputy Assistant Secretary of State for Far Eastern Affairs [Rice], *FRUS*, p. 598.

[16] DDP officer's Memorandum for the Record, "Minutes of Meeting of Special Group (CI), 19 June 1962," 29 June 1962 (S). CIA/FE/VCL files, Job No. 72-233R, Box 1, Folder 6, "Switchback Main Folder."

would be the most effective way to combat Communist subversion and covert aggression in Vietnam: "To introduce white [*sic*] forces, US forces, in large numbers there today, while it might have an initial favorable military impact would almost certainly lead to adverse political and in the long run adverse military consequences."[17]

Planning for the phasing out of US military personnel from Vietnam began in mid-1962 with a Presidential request that Secretary McNamara reexamine the situation there and address himself to its future. McNamara quickly convened a full-dress conference at CINCPAC Headquarters in Honolulu on 23 July—the same day, incidentally, that the 14-nation neutralization agreement on Laos was being formally signed at Geneva. Proceeding from optimistic views of Vietnam voiced by McNamara and MACV chief General Harkins, the Honolulu conference charged CINCPAC Adm. Harry Felt with overseeing development of plans for the gradual scaling down of USMACV over the next three years, eliminating US units and detachments as Vietnamese were trained to perform their functions. (When reintroduced under President Nixon, such a policy was specifically stressed as "Vietnamization.") Admiral Felt gave General Harkins the assignment to draw up such a plan, based on the assumption that "The insurrection will be under control at the end of three years (end of CY 65)."[18] The authors of *The Pentagon Papers* later termed this withdrawal planning "absurd" and "almost Micawberesque."[19]

In May 1963, following almost a year of phaseout planning, McNamara called another conference at CINCPAC Headquarters. Upon returning from that meeting he instructed the Defense Department's International Security Affairs bureau (DoD/ISA), together with the Joint Staff, to finish plans for replacing US forces "as rapidly as possible," withdrawing the first element of "1,000 troops by the end of 1963." It should be noted that the date of that McNamara directive was 8 May 1963, the very day that antigovernment riots in Hue signaled the start of the slide of events which culminated so tragically in November.

The planning for the phased withdrawal of US military personnel limped on into the autumn of 1963, even though Communist attacks and civil instability in South Vietnam had reached crisis proportions by that time, and coup plotters against President Diem had received quiet indications of US approval. Some 1,000 US military personnel would actually be pulled out in December 1963, the last bloom of the Kennedy administration's desire to cut back the US troop commitment in Vietnam.

[17] As cited in *Pentagon Papers* (DoD ed.), Book 3, "Phased Withdrawal of U.S. Forces," pp. 1-2.
[18] As above, p. 12.
[19] (DoD ed.), Book 3, "Phased Withdrawal," p. v.

Distortions of Intelligence

From my earliest associations with Vietnam (1951) I have been concerned about US handling of information from that area. . . . This included deliberate and reflexive manipulation of information, restrictions on collection and censorship of reporting. The net result was that decisionmakers were denied the opportunity to get a complete form of information, determine its validity for themselves, and make decisions . . .

> Lt. Col. Henry A. Shockley, Former Chief, Collection and
> Liaison, Defense Attache Office, Saigon, 1975[20]

Army Chief of Staff General Wheeler was also asked to comment on the estimate's judgment: "There is a serious lack of firm and aggressive leadership at all levels of [ARVN] command." . . . This judgment was overstated, he felt, and must be heavily qualified. The US advisory team was very sensitive on this topic.

> O/NE Memorandum for the Record, "Meeting with
> Gen. Earle G. Wheeler [on NIE 53-63 draft],"
> 27 March 1963[21]

It is abundantly clear that statistics received over the past year or more from the GVN officials and reported by the US mission on which we gauged the trend of the war were grossly in error.

> DCI John McCone, 21 December 1963[22]

In the Field

From the outset of America's post–World War II engagement in Indochina, consistently overoptimistic reporting from the field denied Washington's decisionmakers an accurate picture of developments there. As this study and its annex spell out, there were countless examples of such reporting over the years, especially so on the part of US military commands and the US Mission. Reporting by CIA's Saigon Station was in the main somewhat more objective because successive Chiefs of Station imposed stricter requirements on sourcing and accuracy.

---

[20] Shockley, memorandum given to the House Select Committee on Intelligence, 1975, attachment to George Carver, Memorandum for the Director, "Lt. Col. Shockley's Critique of Intelligence on the ARVN," 29 November 1975 (S). CIA files, Job No. 80R01720R, O/D/NFAC, Box 1, Folder 9. See fuller account of Col. Shockley's remarks at Annex, Section II, "Distortions."
[21] CIA/ONE files, Job No. 79R01012A, O/D/NFAC, Box 240, "NIE 63-63 through NIE 53-2-63," Folder 2.
[22] McCone, "Memorandum of Conversations Held in Saigon, 18-20 December 1963," 21 December 1963. CIA/IG Report, p. 43.

Distortions took many forms and were variously motivated. The almost always rosier judgments dictated by senior military and civilian mission officers doubtless resulted simply from their own more optimistic perceptions of "the big picture." But the record is replete with instances where supervisors and field commanders, the men charged with demonstrating operational progress in the programs assigned to them, overrode their subordinates' negative facts and judgments. In many cases supervisors did not send information and intelligence reports directly to Washington intelligence agencies from their J-2 or embassy political offices, but filtered them through J-3 (military operations) or the Ambassador's front office. Dissenting junior officers were urged to "get on the team," and on occasion were frozen out or moved out by their superiors.

Reporting from outside the chain of command was dealt with in other ways. Special targets for official pressure were outspoken members of the press in Saigon, especially Homer Bigart, Neil Sheehan, Malcolm Browne, David Halberstam, and Peter Arnett. For example, according to Arnett, some six weeks after Ap Bac, Ambassador Nolting publicly rebuked the Saigon press corps in these terms: "[they should put an end] to idle criticism, from snide remarks and unnecessary comments and from spreading allegations and rumors which either originate from Communist sources or play directly into Communist hands."[23] These newsmen's appraisals proved in the end to have been more accurate than those of successive Ambassadors and MACV chiefs, largely because they were receptive to the first-hand observations and views of lower-level US military and mission officers frustrated by the proclivity of their supervisors to quash or water down their reports and assessments.

Complaints against official managing of information became so marked that subcommittees of the House of Representatives investigated this situation in the spring of 1963. The Report of the House Committee on Government Operations highlighted an exemplary press guidance cable that Carl Rowan, Deputy Assistant Secretary of State for Public Affairs, had sent out in early 1962. It instructed the field that newsmen there should be advised that "trifling or thoughtless criticism of the Diem government" would make it difficult to maintain cooperation between the United States and the GVN, and that newsmen "should not be transported on military activities of the type that are likely to result in undesirable stories."[24] Some years later, former National Security Council (NSC)

---

[23] Arnett, *Live From the Battlefield*, p. 98. Arnett later commented, "The authorities wanted to fight the war in private and we wouldn't let them." p. 98.

[24] *United States Information Problems in Vietnam*, Eleventh Report of the Committee on Government Operations, House of Representatives, 88th Congress, 1st Session, (Washington, D.C.: Government Printing Office, 1963), pp. 2-3.

staff officer Chester L. Cooper characterized the situation in 1962-63 as having been one where the administration was confronted with "two undeclared wars, one with the Viet Cong, the other with the American press, while in Saigon [Diem's controversial sister-in-law] Madame Nhu was calling American newsmen there 'worse than Communists.'"[25]

The longstanding skepticism in CIA's Office of National Estimates about claimed progress in Vietnam was heavily influenced by its officers' awareness of slanted official reporting. For example, commenting in February 1963 on an earlier (1961) NIE on Vietnam, O/NE held that much of the reporting from the field seemed designed to convey the most encouraging picture possible: "Progress is highlighted and difficulties are often depreciated." Information from opponents or critics of the GVN "is frequently prefaced by comments denigrating its source." Summary introductions to lengthy studies from the field "reflect an optimism not supported by the details in the accompanying text." A clearer view of what is happening in South Vietnam could be derived, said O/NE, "if the field would let the facts in intelligence reports speak for themselves—whether or not they speak in consonance with present US policies and objectives."[26] O/NE officers were not alone. In May 1963, for example, several working-level Pentagon intelligence officers told them that they, too, were disturbed over the field's reporting. Secretary McNamara had recently ordered that MACV henceforth was to send in only finished intelligence reports to Washington; therefore, confided these Pentagon officers, MACV's appreciations and estimates "are becoming unassailable, since no one in Washington has access to the raw facts on which they are based."[27]

There were many reasons why senior US (and, earlier, French) officers did not share such concerns on the part of their subordinates. A basic factor always at work was operational enthusiasm, the natural tendency to get caught up in the progress of a given operation or policy, once that course has been set. Another concern was regard for one's position in the chain of command, which inhibited courageous reporting and induced efforts to stay on "the team." Another propensity in the field was that of soft-pedaling evidence of South Vietnamese lack of progress, for fear Washington superiors would feel that field commanders were not doing their training jobs successfully. Also, much of the reporting passed

[25] Cooper, *The Lost Crusade: America in Vietnam*, pp. 196-197.
[26] O/NE memorandum, "Postmortem on NIE 43-61, 'Prospects in South Vietnam,'" 14 February 1963, (S). CIA files, Job No. 79R01012A, O/D/NFAC, Box 240, Folder 1.
[27] O/NE Memorandum for the Record, "Meeting with General Earle G. Wheeler, [14 March 1963]," 27 March 1963, (S). CIA files as above, Folder 2. According to then Defense Intelligence Agency (DIA) officer George Allen, DIA directed its analysts simply to publish MACV's reports, without adding any DIA interpretation. Allen, comment to author, December 1995.

upward originated with South Vietnamese officials, many of whom fabricated intelligence or put the best face on matters. Then, too, pride also contributed to clouded reporting: the certainty felt by many US officials that American know-how must and would carry the day.

Yet another prime source of unfounded expectations was a generally widespread American ignorance about Vietnam and the Vietnamese. Many decisionmakers did not have a good appreciation of what had gone before in Indochina, and of why the various Vietnamese players behaved as they did.[28] As characterized by a later study commissioned by the US Army's Historical Office, there was a "massive and all-encompassing" ignorance of Vietnamese history and society.[29] For the most part, US policymakers greatly underestimated the enemy's skill, staying power, resourcefulness, and pervasive political and intelligence assets throughout the South. Not least, because of crisis situations elsewhere in the world in 1962, especially Cuba, Berlin, and Laos, US decisionmakers were not focusing their attentions on Vietnam to the degree they were soon to do. Nor, except for conducting clandestine operations in Vietnam, were DCI McCone and the Agency.

Driving the many pressures on senior military and administration figures to paint Vietnam developments in positive terms was the knowledge that their presidents were personally committed to American success in Southeast Asia, were convinced that other "dominoes" would fall there if South Vietnam did, and feared the political consequences of "losing" Vietnam to the Communists. Hence, senior officers of the Kennedy and Johnson administrations brushed aside and at times demeaned those few prominent officials—Mike Mansfield, Chester Bowles, George Ball, J. William Fulbright, Wayne Morse, and Johh Kenneth Galbraith—who in 1962 and early 1963 openly doubted the wisdom of US actions in South Vietnam and questioned the accuracy of ever-optimistic reporting.

There was yet another cause of the upbeat reporting from Vietnam in 1962: the fact that some military progress was actually being registered at the time, the result of the ARVN's receipt of improved US weapons and training and, especially, of the effective commitment of large

---

[28] This was one reason Secretary Robert McNamara later commissioned the compilation of what became known as *The Pentagon Papers*.

[29] Ronald H. Spector, *Advice and Support: The Early Years of the United States Army in Vietnam, 1941-1960*, rev. ed. (New York: The Free Press, 1985), pp. x, xi. Spector's fuller statement deserves notice: "Added to this propensity to try to make something out of nothing was an American ignorance of Vietnamese history and society so massive and all-encompassing that two decades of federally funded fellowships, crash language programs, television specials, and campus teach-ins made hardly a dent. . . . If there is any lesson to be drawn from the unhappy tale of American involvement in Vietnam in the 1940s and 1950s, it is that before the United States sets out to make something out of nothing in some other corner of the globe, American leaders might consider the historical and social factors involved."

numbers of US-piloted combat helicopters to direct-support roles. But the ARVN debacle at Ap Bac in January 1963—where five US helicopters were destroyed and nine were damaged—punctured the illusions of ARVN improvement held by some officers, even though many of their superiors continued to cling to their visions of steady progress and to report them as if they were real.

These misinterpretations of reality are important to this study because they proved instrumental in helping produce a definitive but inaccurate National Intelligence Estimate in April 1963. This might not have mattered so much if, as on so many occasions, officers high in the chains of command had paid scant attention to the NIE; the distorting problem this time would be that top policymakers *did* embrace NIE 53-63's flawed judgments because they so validated their own certainties.

In Washington

DCI John McCone's sudden, surprising overturning of the estimative process on Vietnam occurred when the finished draft of NIE 53-63, "Prospects in Vietnam," came before the United States Intelligence Board (USIB, now NFIB—the National Foreign Intelligence Board) for deliberation. The representatives of the various agencies who approved the draft had differed for the most part over mere shadings; the Department of State stood alone in the view that the estimate was overly pessimistic. At the USIB meeting on 27 February 1963, before a room packed with Intelligence Community principals and staffers, DCI McCone upbraided O/NE Director Sherman Kent and his officers for having prepared an NIE whose judgments differed so widely from those of "the people who know Vietnam best." McCone named a number of such officials (almost all of them senior policy advisers), and directed O/NE to see that their views were considered in a new, revised NIE.[30]

O/NE had long held fairly pessimistic views of prospects in Vietnam. As far back as March 1952, for example, two years before the climactic French defeat at Dien Bien Phu, O/NE had produced an NIE which held that the probable outlook in Indochina for the coming year

---

[30]In 1962-1963, the author of the present History Staff study was chief of O/NE's Far East Staff. He initiated NIE 53-63, wrote its first drafts (together with then O/NE staffer George Carver), and was a participant at the 27 February 1963 USIB meeting. Also, see Willard C. Matthias (who had been the Board of National Estimates Chairman for NIE 53-63), "How Three Estimates Went Wrong," *Studies in Intelligence*, Vol. XII, No. 1 (Winter 1968), pp. 31-35. Also, Matthias, to author, 12 February 1990; George Carver, to author, 8 January 1990; and Sherman Kent, to author, 3 May 1990. CIA files, Job No. 90B00336R, Box 4, Folder 4, "Harold P. Ford Interviews."

Dr. Sherman Kent, with DCIs Allen Dulles (l.) and
Richard Helms (r.)

was one of "gradual deterioration of the Franco-Vietnamese military position," and that, unless present trends were reversed, the long-term prospect included possible French withdrawal from Indochina.[31] Over the years, O/NE's officers voiced doubts about the domino thesis, emphasized the lack of indigenous strength and cohesion in South Vietnam, and questioned whether US or other external military assistance could produce a viable society there. And in June 1962, in its most recent views on Viet-

[31] NIE 35/1, "Probable Developments in Indochina Through Mid-1953," 3 March 1952. *FRUS, 1952-1954, Vol. XIII, part 2, Indochina*, pp. 54-55. At the time this NIE was produced, its views gathered considerable support in the Pentagon. See DoD draft Memorandum, "A Cold War Program to Save Southeast Asia for the Free World," 3 April 1952: "As pointed out in NIE 35/1, [France's difficulties in supporting simultaneous major efforts in Europe and East Asia] will adversely influence France's will to continue resistance in Indochina. It is even more probable that, in the long run, the rising tide of Asian nationalism will make it impossible or too costly to preserve Indochina as a conspicuous remnant of western colonialism in the Far East." *FRUS*, p. 119. Note also this *FRUS* footnote statement, "This memorandum apparently represented the views of the Secretaries of the Army, the Navy and the Air Force." *FRUS*, p. 119. Why the thinking of the Joint Chiefs of Staff on Vietnam changed so radically between the early 1950s and a decade later is a question that still demands close historical scrutiny.

13

nam prior to NIE 53-63, the Board of National Estimates had disagreed with Director McCone as to the basic source of South Vietnam's troubles. To the DCI, that source was China: writing Secretary McNamara on 18 June, he told him that US efforts in Vietnam were "merely chipping away at the toe of the glacier from the North." To Sherman Kent, writing McCone that same day, it was "incorrect to describe US policy in South Vietnam as merely nibbling at the edges of the real threat. The real threat, and the heart of the battle, is in the villages and jungles of Vietnam and Laos." Said Kent:

> That battle can be won only by the will, energy, and political acumen of the resisting governments themselves. US power can supplement and enlarge their power but it cannot be substituted. Even if the US could defeat the Communists militarily by a massive injection of its own forces, the odds are that what it would win would be, not a political victory which created a stable and independent government, but an uneasy and costly colony.[32]

These differences of view went to the heart of the matter and of the US dilemma over Vietnam, differences which continued for some years to divide decisionmakers from many of Washington's intelligence officers. As of 1963, McCone shared the view of Secretary Rusk and many top policymakers that the Communist threat in Indochina was an integral part of the expansionist aims of the USSR and Communist China, whereas O/NE—and many of the Intelligence Community's working-level officers—argued that the chief villain was Hanoi, not Moscow or Beijing, and that the struggle for Vietnam was essentially a military and political civil war.

The NIE 53-63 story began in September 1962 when the O/NE Staff, convinced that behind the signs of some outward improvement lay profound adverse trends, persuaded a reluctant Board of National Estimates to undertake a new NIE on Vietnam.[33] Even though the Board of National Estimates somewhat softened the pessimism of the Staff's initial drafts, the coordinated text that went to USIB in late February 1963 voiced definite alarm about the situation in Vietnam. Following McCone's rejection of that text, and responsive to his remanding directive, O/NE officers proceeded to seek the views of the officials McCone had termed the "people who know Vietnam best." These included the Army's Chief of Staff, Gen. Earle Wheeler; CINCPAC Adm. Harry Felt; MACV's Gen. Paul Harkins; the American Ambassador in Saigon, Frederick Nolting; Defense's Special

---

[32] These documents are in CIA Files Job No. 79R00904A, O/D/NFAC, Box 8, Folder 2.
[33] The author's personal experience. Also, Carver, to author, 3 January 1990; Matthias, to author, 13 February 1990; and Sherman Kent, to author, May 1990.

Assistant for Counterinsurgency and Special Activities, Maj. Gen. Victor Krulak (US Marine Corps); State's Director of Intelligence and Research (INR), Roger Hilsman; and NSC staffer Michael Forrestal.[34]

These "people who knew Vietnam best" were universally critical of the draft NIE. In their view, it was simply wrong in judging that the Viet Cong had not yet been badly hurt. It dwelt too much on South Vietnam's military and political shortcomings and did not sufficiently stress examples of progress. It emphasized frictions between South Vietnamese and American advisers rather than acknowledging that marked improvements were being made. Nor did the draft NIE recognize the progress being reported in the GVN's keystone defensive effort, the strategic hamlet program. All in all, the NIE's assessments were much too bleak.

According to O/NE files, MACV's General Harkins wanted the draft to acknowledge that the GVN was making "steady and notable progress." It was gaining more support from the population at large. The strategic hamlet program was going well. In his view, barring an increase in support to the enemy from outside, the coming year would "see a reduction in the VC's capabilities and a further separation of the people from the VC." Now, two months after the ARVN's defeat at Ap Bac, Harkins assured O/NE that an aggressive South Vietnamese attitude was "becoming more apparent," and that ARVN offensive operations had "shown a marked increase in scope, tempo, and intensity; armed VC attacks are diminishing."[35]

O/NE files record that General Krulak told the Board of National Estimates that, although the number of Viet Cong–initiated incidents had increased over the past few weeks, they remained "well below 1962 levels," and that South Vietnamese military capabilities had "increased markedly," whereas those of the Viet Cong had "probably not increased correspondingly."[36]

[34] McCone directed Kent to solicit responses also from William Colby (Chief of CIA's Far East Operations) and his chief of station (COS) in Saigon, and he sent O/NE officer Chester Cooper to Saigon to look the situation over personally for him. O/NE officers met directly with Wheeler, Krulak, Hilsman, Forrestal, and Colby and obtained the views of the others by cable. Kent, Memorandum for the Director, "NIE 53-63, Prospects in South Vietnam," 15 April 1963 (S). CIA/DDI files, Job No. 79R01012R, O/D/NFAC, Box 240, Folder 3.

[35] CINCPAC cable to DIA, 200426Z, 20 March 1963; appended as Annex to Sherman Kent, Memorandum for the Director, "CINCPAC's Response to the DIA Request for Comments on the Draft NIE re South Vietnam" 25 April 1963 (S). CIA/DDI files, Job No. 79R00904A, O/D/NFAC, Box 9, Folder 2.

[36] O/NE Memorandum for the Record, "Meeting with Major General Victor H. Krulak, USMC, on South Vietnam," 8 March 1963 (S). CIA/DDI files, Job No. 79R01012R, O/D/NFAC, Box 240, Folder 3.

General Wheeler gave O/NE an assessment a senior Joint Chiefs' team had made, shortly after Ap Bac. In part it read, "The team wishes particularly to emphasize that, in sum, the preparations of 1962 have led to the development of the human and material infrastructure necessary for the successful prosecution of the war," and that barring Viet Cong escalation, "the principal ingredients for eventual success have been assembled in South Vietnam."[37]

The DCI's special detailee to Saigon, Chester Cooper, felt that the Estimate took too pessimistic a view of the strategic hamlet program, which he held was making "very good" progress. With US help at approximately existing levels and barring a deterioration along the frontiers of South Vietnam, Cooper believed that "the GVN can probably defeat the Viet Cong militarily"; except in certain portions of the Delta, this would "probably take place within about three years."[38] Cooper later revised his views markedly. After transferring to the NSC Staff and witnessing further deterioration in Vietnam, he became a doubter, later acknowledging that as of 1962–early 1963 "the fact was that the war was *not* going well, the Vietnamese Army was *not* taking kindly to American advice, and Diem was *not* following through on his promises to liberalize his regime or increase its effectiveness."[39]

What most bothered these critics of the NIE, however, was its criticisms of the ARVN, particularly its detailing of ARVN depredations among the rural population and their undermining effects on South Vietnam's war effort. O/NE files record General Wheeler as saying that he "had received no such reports; neither had General Harkins." Further, as noted above, Wheeler said the NIE's assertion that there was "a serious lack of firm and aggressive leadership at all levels of ARVN command" was "overstated" and "must be heavily qualified. The US advisory team was very sensitive on this topic."[40] For his part, General Krulak explained that in East Asia it was to be expected that "the soldier will kick the peasant as he goes by." Krulak had no doubt such offenses were being committed, "but South Vietnam was not 14th and F Streets"; also, he argued, brutality accepted by Asians "would naturally make an impression on inexperienced and youthful American officers."[41] The cruelest cut of all,

[37] O/NE Memorandum for the Record, "Meeting with General Earle G. Wheeler, Chief of Staff, US Army, on South Vietnam," 27 March 1963 (S). CIA/DDI files as above.

[38] Cooper, dispatch, Saigon to DCI, "Comments on Draft NIE 53-63: 'Prospects in South Vietnam,'" 29 March 1963 (S). CIA/DDI files, Job No. 79T01148A, NFAC, Box 9, Folder marked "Policy: GLC: Oct '62-Dec '64.".

[39] Cooper, *The Lost Crusade: America in Vietnam*, p. 196. (Emphasis in the original).

[40] O/NE Memorandum for the Record, "Meeting with General Earle G. Wheeler, Chief of Staff, US Army, on South Vietnam," 27 March 1963. CIA/DDI files, Job No. 79R01012A, O/D/NFAC, Box 240, Folder 2.

[41] O/NE Memorandum for the Record, "Meeting with General Victor H. Krulak, USMC, on South Vietnam," 8 March 1963, (S). CIA/DDI files as above.

however, was levelled at the draft NIE by CINCPAC Admiral Felt: "Charges of [ARVN] rape, pillage and outright brutality are made by Radio Hanoi. We should not parlay them."[42] Two months previously, Felt had publicly stated (four weeks after Ap Bac) that South Vietnam would defeat the Viet Cong "within three years."[43]

The O/NE Staff stuck to its guns despite these attacks on the NIE by senior officers. Of especial note is a defense of the draft that O/NE staffer George Carver gave Sherman Kent on 7 March 1963. According to Carver, the Staff's position on the question of ARVN depredations was supported by the private observations of recent visitors to Vietnam who had talked with US officers in the field. And in Washington, the working-level military intelligence representatives, those officers who had coordinated on the draft estimate, "advise that our judgments [are shared] . . . by practically every field-grade returnee they have had occasion to interview though, of course, the observations of such officers on this topic are seldom reflected in official correspondence from MACV."[44]

In the end, however, the views of O/NE's staff members did not prevail. Over their objections the Board of National Estimates bowed to the pressure of the DCI and the draft's policymaking critics. On 17 April the Board produced a revised, final version of the Estimate whose first sentence flagged the change in tone which McCone's remanding had accomplished: "We believe that Communist progress has been blunted and that the situation is improving."

Some months later, the situation in South Vietnam having gone from bad to worse, McCone admitted he had been wrong; he apologized to Kent for having had senior program officers impose on a draft NIE

---

[42]CINCPAC cable to DIA, commenting on draft NIE 53-63, 12 March 1963, appended as Annex to Sherman Kent, "Memorandum for the Director, "CINCPAC's Response to the DIA Request for Comments on the Draft NIE re South Vietnam," 25 April 1963 (S). CIA/DCI files, Job No. 79R0090A, Box 9 Folder 2. CIA was not the only recipient of strong Pentagon pressures on its analysts to shape up. According to the authors of *The Pentagon Papers*, when State's Bureau of Intelligence and Research published a study on 22 October 1963, detailing downward military trends in Vietnam, this "occasioned controversy and no little recrimination. . . . The outcome was a personal memorandum from the Secretary of State to the Secretary of Defense on 8 November, amounting to an apology for the incident. The Secretary of State stated ' . . . it is not the policy of the State Department to issue military appraisals without seeking the views of the Defense Department. I have requested that any memoranda given inter-departmental circulation which include military appraisals be coordinated with your Department.'" (DoD ed.), Book 3-IV-B-4: "Phased Withdrawal of U.S. Forces." p. 24. That episode has also been treated by former INR Director Thomas Hughes, "Experiencing McNamara," *Foreign Policy*, Vol. 100 (Fall 1995) pp.155-171; and by former INR officer Louis Harris in a letter to the editor,"McNamara's War and Mine," *The New York Times*, 5 September 1995. Both were commenting on the then recently published book by Robert S. McNamara (with Brian VanDeMark), *In Retrospect: The Tragedy and Lessons of Vietnam* (New York: Times Books, 1995).
[43]*The New York Times*, 31 January 1963.
[44]Carver, Memorandum for Kent, "Consultation with General Krulak on South Vietnam in Connection with NIE 53-63" (S). CIA/DDI files, Job No. 79R01012A, O/D/NFAC, Box 240, Folder 3.

optimistic judgments about their own operational progress, and he promised he would not do it again.[45] But why had McCone insisted that a more optimistic Estimate be produced in early 1963, when just seven months earlier he had given President Kennedy some decidedly pessimistic personal judgments concerning South Vietnam's prospects? Several factors no doubt contributed to his turnabout.

First and foremost was the fact that in the interim, between McCone's mid-1962 trip to Vietnam and his sharp criticism of the draft NIE at USIB the following February, O/NE had produced a flawed estimate of historic consequence. Examining the evidence then available concerning the possible emplacement of Soviet offensive missiles in Cuba and finding it lacking, the Board had judged that Soviet practice argued against Moscow's taking such a step.[46] Almost certainly, McCone's later torpedoing of the draft NIE on Vietnam was directly related to the heavy fire he was taking at the time from the White House, and particularly from the President's Foreign Intelligence Advisory Board (PFIAB), for having released so mistaken an NIE the preceding September on a subject so crucial for US security interests. McCone had almost certainly lost some confidence in his Board of National Estimates, and now, in the spring of 1963, it was asking him to issue a definitive NIE on Vietnam that differed sharply from the views of the leading Presidential advisers and their staffs. Going against so many senior decisionmakers without taking a second look would certainly not endear him to the White House or impress a skeptical PFIAB.[47]

Also, McCone was an intimate of many of the senior critics, Gen. Victor Krulak in particular. At the time Krulak was the Pentagon's chief counterinsurgency officer and an outstanding officer who many observers believed would shortly become USMC Commandant; he was close to President Kennedy and, not least, a fast friend of John McCone. The DCI and Krulak often golfed together, and McCone also was deeply engaged at the time in the activities of the Special Group (Counterinsurgency), the White House's senior planning body for covert activities, in which Krulak was a primary participant. Krulak was a true believer that progress was being registered in Vietnam. He continued to hold this view as late as 10 September 1963 when, amid a rapidly deteriorating situation there, he is reported to have assured President Kennedy that "the

[45]The author's personal knowledge. Also, Sherman Kent, to author, 3 May 1990; George Carver, to author, 8 January 1990; Willard Matthias, to author, 12 February 1990; and Matthias, "How Three Estimates Went Wrong," *passim*.

[46] It was subsequent U-2 aerial photography that revealed that Soviet offensive missiles had in fact been deployed in Cuba.

[47] A carefully researched CIA study of DCI McCone's tenure by another History Staff author reaches similar conclusions on McCone's thinking in early 1963.

shooting war is still going ahead at an impressive pace."[48] On that same occasion, Foreign Service Officer Joseph Mendenhall, who like Krulak had just returned from a trip to Vietnam, gave the President a far more pessimistic appraisal, prompting Kennedy to ask, "You two did visit the same country, didn't you?"[49]

Another reason McCone remanded the draft NIE almost certainly was his respect for the views of his close friend, former President Dwight Eisenhower. Presidents Kennedy and Johnson having designated McCone as an official liaison with Ike, the DCI visited him fairly often during 1962-64, in Gettysburg and elsewhere. The former President believed that progress was being made in Vietnam and that, in any case, a strong US course there was necessary to avoid a larger disaster. McCone recorded that on 10 May 1962, for instance, Eisenhower warned him that the consequences would be dire if South Vietnam were lost: "Nothing would stop the southward movement of Communism through Indonesia and this would have the effect of cutting the world in half."[50]

Just three weeks after the revised NIE 53-63 was published, its judgments were called into question by the outbreak of serious antigovernment riots at Hue and the rapid spread of open disaffection in much of South Vietnam. These events produced sharply differing reactions among the senior policymakers whose optimism had been reflected in the Estimate. As this study's next episode discusses in detail, some of them shifted to despair and came quickly to believe that President Diem's regime must be replaced if South Vietnam was to survive. By contrast, other senior US officials continued to cling to their earlier optimism. Admiral Felt, for example, reported on 23 July that MACV commander General Harkins was talking about a "white Christmas" in the belief that by that time "the entire country would be brought to a 'white' or controlled situation."[51] On 10 September General Krulak gave President Kennedy his report of "impressive" progress in the war. On 2 October the President announced that "most" of the 14,000 US military personnel then in South Vietnam could be withdrawn "by the end of 1965," and

---

[48] CIA/IG Report, p.15. Journalist Neal Sheehan considers Krulak to have been "a genius," even though Sheehan criticizes him for distorting reality: "Despite the warning flares of Ap Bac, [Krulak] clung to his preconceptions and helped to implant them in the other members of the Joint Chiefs' mission [which had been sent out to investigate the Ap Bac battle]." Sheehan, *A Bright Shining Lie*, p. 293. Several authors observe that Krulak disdained civilian experts, claiming they had no right to make judgments on military matters. Among such critics is CIA's George Allen, who states that in 1963 he was directed to prepare a military map of Vietnam at Krulak's request; Krulak thought the map was great until he learned that Allen was a civilian, whereupon he trashed the map. Allen, "The Indochina Wars," pp. 208-210.

[49] *Pentagon Papers* (Gravel ed.), Vol. II, p. 244.

[50] McCone, Memorandum for the Record, 10 May 1962 (s). CIA/DCI files, Job No. 80B01285A, DCI/McCone, Box 2, Folder 2.

[51] Felt, statement to McCone as cited in Elder manuscript, CIA History Staff files.

that 1,000 men "might be able to leave" by the end of 1963.[52] At a Honolulu policy conference on 6 November, a few days following the overthrow and murder of Diem, McCone recorded that General Harkins was still insisting that the military situation was going fairly well.[53]

Inevitably, NIE 53-63's relative optimism helped bolster the mistaken confidence of its consumers, especially since its judgments were at the time widely accepted as authoritative. *The Pentagon Papers* later recorded that Secretary McNamara had been told in 1962 that "tremendous progress" had been achieved during the preceding six months, and that "this theme was re-echoed in April of 1963 by [the MACV commander] and an NIE"; and that in retrospect, the intelligence evaluators and assessors "were not only wrong, but more importantly, they were influential."[54]

Retrospect

[The situation in Vietnam since early 1962] was watched carefully by our CIA Station. . . . A number of estimates and a great number of reports and appraisals were issued, each one warning that the deterioration of the regime's popularity gave rise to serious questions concerning the future trend of the war. . . . A review of our reporting over 18 months and resulting estimates bears out that the Agency consistently warned of the deteriorating situation and the possible consequences.

From a review of CIA's intelligence performance
issued by DCI McCone, 21 September 1963[55]

Clearly, CIA did not perform well in the NIE 53-63 episode. Neither the DCI nor the Board of National Estimates covered themselves with glory, with McCone inviting policy managers to press their judgments on the Board, and the Board bowing to those pressures and issuing an NIE that did not accurately reflect existing evidence. Moreover, the Board continued to defend the NIE for some weeks thereafter, assuring McCone on 6 June that "the current [post-Hue] Buddhist difficulties do not render invalid the judgments of NIE 53-63."[56] A month later O/NE

---

[52]*The New York Times*, 3 October 1963.
[53]McCone, present at that conference, recorded that Harkins's remarks had made a "poor impression." CIA/IG Report, pp. 38-40.
[54](DoD ed.), Book 3, "Phased Withdrawal of U.S. Forces, " pp. vi, vii.
[55]As cited in Walter Elder manuscript, pp. 680-681. CIA/DCI files, Job No. 8701032R, Box 4. There is no mention in CIA executive files of McCone's involvement in NIE 53-63 or his changing attitudes toward it.
[56]Sherman Kent, Memorandum for the Director, "NIE 53-63, Prospects in South Vietnam in Light of the Current Buddhist Crisis" (S) CIA/DDI files, Job No. 79R00904A, O/D/NFAC, Box 9, Folder 3.

and McCone did approve an update of NIE 53-63 which predicted that disorders in South Vietnam would increase and judged that the chances of a coup or of assassination attempts against President Diem would "become better than even." But the revised Estimate also held that the Communists would not necessarily profit if Diem were overthrown, and that, given continued US support, a successor regime "could provide reasonably effective leadership for the government and the war effort."[57]

By September, however, the situation had so deteriorated in South Vietnam that McCone began to despair of the prospects there. In a 10 September meeting with President Kennedy, the DCI stated that "victory is doubtful if not impossible."[58] A little later, according to Clark Clifford (at the time Chairman of Kennedy's PFIAB), "the normally cautious and conservative" McCone told his board that the situation had become so bad in Vietnam "that we might have to pull out altogether."[59] And in an Eyes Only letter to Ambassador Lodge, the DCI noted that "I am more disturbed over the situation which has developed in South Vietnam than any recent crisis which has confronted this government."[60] On 21 November, three weeks after Diem had been overthrown, McCone was quoted as having told another Honolulu policy conference that he was returning "more discouraged about South Vietnam than ever in the past, and that he sensed that McNamara and [McGeorge] Bundy have the same impression."[61] And on 6 December McCone told the intelligence subcommittee of the House Appropriations Committee that he was extremely worried about the situation in South Vietnam: "The war effort had not been improved by the new government, and Viet Cong activities had increased."[62]

Further, on 21 December, on the occasion of introducing CIA's new Station Chief (Peer DeSilva) to Ambassador Lodge in Saigon, McCone told the Ambassador there was "no excuse for the kind of reporting" that had been received on difficulties in Long An Province.[63] That same day, en route home from Vietnam, McCone wrote: "It is abundantly clear that statistics received over the past year or more from the GVN officials and reported by the US Mission on which we gauged the trend of the war were grossly in error" and that "the future of the war remains in doubt."[64] Immediately thereafter, back in Washington,

---

[57] SNIE 53-2-63, "The Situation in South Vietnam," 10 July 1963 (S).

[58] Memorandum for the Record by William Colby, who was present at that White House meeting. CIA/IG Report, p. 15.

[59] Clark Clifford and Richard Holbrooke, "Annals of Government, The Vietnam Years," Part I, *The New Yorker*, 6 May 1991, p. 45.

[60] Elder manuscript, p. 672. CIA History Staff files, Job No. 8701032R, Box 4.

[61] Memorandum by CIA officer E. Henry Knoche, 21 November 1963. CIA/IG Report, p. 38.

[62] CIA/IG Report, p. 39.

[63] CIA/IG Report, p. 42.

McCone joined Secretary McNamara in briefing President Johnson on the situation in Vietnam. The DCI and McNamara agreed that there had been a "complete failure of reporting," McCone adding that, while he might not be quite as pessimistic as McNamara, he did foresee "more reasons for concern as to the outcome than not."[65]

By late 1963, then, the complexities of the Vietnam situation had profoundly impressed themselves on McCone. Even so, as reflected in his memorandum of 21 December quoted above, McCone confined the blame for the intelligence failure to America's heavy dependence on *Vietnamese* reporting. He was not alone in this blame-fixing; on the same day, according to CIA files, Secretary McNamara wrote President Johnson that, "since July," the situation in the South Vietnamese countryside had been deteriorating "to a far greater extent than we realized because of our undue dependence on distorted Vietnamese reporting."[66]

Similarly, three weeks later, one of McGeorge Bundy's NSC officers aptly summed up the damage distorted intelligence had done:

> As you are aware, the great difficulties we had to live through last August and September resulted largely from a nearly complete breakdown of the Government's ability to get accurate assessments of the situation in the Vietnamese countryside. The more we learn about the situation today, the more obvious it becomes that the excessively mechanical system of statistical reporting which had been devised in Washington and applied in Saigon was giving us a grotesquely inaccurate picture. *Once again it is the old problem of having people who are responsible for operations also responsible for evaluating the results.* (Emphasis added.)

The author was Michael Forrestal, who 11 months before had been one of the principal critics of the pessimistic assessments the Intelligence Community's working-level officers had made in their February draft of NIE 53-63.[67]

Looking back on these events a decade later, CIA author Anthony Marc Lewis termed the NIE 53-63 episode a "lesson" in how senior CIA officers adjusted to the perceptions of their superiors: "The system by which national intelligence at the highest level is produced led to rejection of some O/NE staffers' perceptions that had been remarkably accurate." Lewis added, "One may easily speculate that those perceptions, had

[64] CIA/IG Report, p. 43.
[65] CIA/IG Report, pp. 43-44.
[66] McNamara, Memorandum for the President, "Vietnam Situation," 21 December 1963, as cited in CIA/IG Report, pp. 43-44.
[67] Forrestal memo to Bundy, "Reporting on the Situation in South Vietnam," 8 January 1964, *FRUS, 1964-1968, Volume I, Vietnam 1964*, p. 7.

they been reflected in the published Estimate, might have aroused serious second thoughts among American policymakers on Vietnam in mid-1963."[68] A nice tribute, if overstated.

The NIE 53-63 episode should have provided a valuable lesson in some of the many ways intelligence can be distorted. Yet these experiences of 1962-63 did not lead to any significant improvements in the estimative processes or in military and mission reporting from the field. Distortions of reality, some wishful, some more deliberate, persisted until the expulsion of the American presence in Vietnam 12 years later—and definitely contributed to that outcome.

[68] Lewis, "Re-examining Our Perceptions on Vietnam," *Studies in Intelligence*, Vol. XVII, No. 4 (Winter 1973) p. 51.

President Johnson—with Mrs. Johnson and their infant
grandchild—reviewing the daily intelligence report.

Episode 2, 1963-1965
CIA Judgments on President Johnson's Decision To "Go Big" in Vietnam

I received in this meeting the first "President Johnson tone" for action [in Vietnam] as contrasted with the "Kennedy tone." Johnson definitely feels that we place too much emphasis on social reforms; he has very little tolerance with our spending so much time being "do-gooders" . . . .

DCI John McCone, 25 November 1963[1]

In early 1965 the Johnson Administration decided to "go big" in Vietnam—to begin sustained bombing raids against the North and to commit US combat troops in the South. This Presidential order to engage the Communist enemy directly came after an agonizing two-year search for a policy expedient that would save South Vietnam from collapsing. The search began in mid-1963 when the headlined political and military failures of the Saigon government abruptly destroyed the long-held illusions of most senior US policymakers that steady progress was being made toward South Vietnamese self-sufficiency. Their subsequent attempt to find a saving formula first produced from the Kennedy administration a decision to accept the overthrow of President Ngo Dinh Diem by a junta of South Vietnamese military officers. Then, when that coup introduced only a series of even-weaker Saigon governments, President Johnson's administration finally came to embrace the assumption that South Vietnam could be saved by systematically bombing the North and committing US troops to combat in the South.

This study focuses on the role that CIA intelligence production and senior CIA officers played, or did not play, in these policy evolutions. As we will see, White House decisions to allow a coup and, later, to go big in Vietnam, were made with little regard for CIA Headquarters' efforts to inform or modify US policy.

[1]McCone, Memorandum for the Record (of a Presidential meeting, 24 November 1963). *FRUS, 1961-1963, Vol. IV, Vietnam, July-November 1963*, p. 637. This meeting, held two days following the assassination of President Kennedy, was Lyndon Johnson's first Vietnam policy outing.

Prelude: The Overthrow of Ngo Dinh Diem[2]

By early 1963, Washington was in a mood of euphoria about Vietnam.

Saigon Ambassador Frederick E. Nolting, Jr.[3]

We are now launched on a course from which there is no respectable turn-ing back: the overthrow of the Diem government . . . . there is no turning back because there is no possibility, in my view, that the war can be won under a Diem administration.

Ambassador Henry Cabot Lodge, Jr., 29 August 1963[4]

Although the product of many causes, the US Government's action in 1965 to engage its forces openly and directly in Vietnam can be said to have evolved from mid-1963, when cumulative mistakes by the Ngo Dinh Diem government caused a precipitate decline in South Vietnam's already-shaky performance against its Communist adversary, the Viet Cong. The shock this reversal produced in Washington was magnified all the more because most top policymakers until that time had believed and proclaimed that the outlook in South Vietnam was fairly bright. The shock led these policymakers to decide, haphazardly as we will see, that Saigon's fragile position might best be strengthened by getting rid of the obdurately autocratic President Diem.

The possibility that he might be overthrown was by no means new, nor was the idea that he be eased out by US pressure. Unsuccessful coup attempts had been launched by dissident South Vietnamese military offic-ers in 1960 and 1962, and various US officials had been voicing arguments for getting rid of Diem for at least that long. For example, in September 1960 US Ambassador in Saigon Elbridge Durbrow had cabled Washing-ton that "If Diem's position in-country continues deteriorate as result fail-ure adopt proper political, psychological, economic and security measures, it may become necessary for US Government to begin consid-eration alternative courses of action and leaders in order achieve our objective." Earlier that year, Durbrow had observed that the regime's many failings and derelictions were "basically due to [the] machinations of Diem's brother [Ngo Dinh] Nhu and his henchmen."[5] By 1962, such

---

[2]This study restricts itself to the Washington scene. Other CIA History Staff studies examine events in the field.
[3]Nolting, *From Trust to Tragedy: The Political Memoirs of Frederick Nolting, Kennedy's Ambas-sador to Diem's Vietnam* (New York: Praeger, 1988), p. 95.
[4]EmbTel 375. *FRUS, 1961-1963, Vol. IV, Vietnam*, p. 21.
[5]EmbTel 624, 16 September 1960. *FRUS, 1958-1960 Vol. I, Vietnam*, p. 579.

arguments had become more bald. In August of that year Durbrow's political counselor, Joseph Mendenhall, returned to Washington to report that "we cannot win the war with the Diem-Nhu methods, and we cannot change those methods no matter how much pressure we put on them. *Recommendation*: get rid of Diem, Mr. and Mrs. Nhu and the rest of the Ngo family."[6]

Dissatisfaction with the governing style of Ngo Dinh Diem and his family went back a long way and prompted constant but fruitless cajoling and nagging from a succession of US ambassadors and CIA station chiefs. By early 1963 Diem had become even more resistant to US advice, more autocratic in his governance, more obsessed with conserving his regular army from combat to ward off coup attempts, more callous in sacrificing ill-trained rural militiamen against increasingly widespread Communist attacks, and more coercive in his suppression of all dissent. His brother Nhu had become a virtual law unto himself, attracting, as did Nhu's flamboyant wife, the opprobrium of US officials and correspondents in Saigon.

It was in this atmosphere that US Ambassador Frederick Nolting, one of President Diem's staunchest supporters within US officialdom, set out on 5 April to impress on his client the need for civil, financial, and military reforms as the price of US funding of the government's counterinsurgency program. He found Diem "courteous but immovable" in his opposition to US proposals and Nolting's personal advice. "Gravely concerned and perplexed," Nolting reported, he told Diem that Saigon's obstinacy would result in a "downward spiral of Vietnam-American confidence" and a "curtailment of U.S. aid," and might well force "a change in the policy of the U.S. Government towards Vietnam."[7]

Nolting's despairing report to Washington of his fruitless three-and-a-half-hour session with Diem helped prime those at home who saw Diem as an obstacle rather than a tool for stemming Communist advances in Southeast Asia. Shortly thereafter Diem and brother Nhu embarrassed their Washington patrons and deepened their domestic unpopularity with a series of affronts to Vietnam's Buddhist population. The flaring domestic crisis fueled by the regime's increasingly harsh treatment of the Buddhists throughout the spring and summer of 1963 dismayed top US policymakers and swept away much of their remaining confidence in the Diem government's abilities.

[6] Mendenhall, Memorandum for Deputy Assistant Secretary of State for Far Eastern Affairs Edward E. Rice, "Vietnam—Assessments and Recommendations," 16 August 1962. *FRUS, 1961-1963, Vol. II, Vietnam, 1962*, p. 598. Mr. and Mrs. Ngo Dinh Nhu were considered by most US officials to be prime sources of Diem's obstinacy and of the Diem regime's most repressive measures.
[7] EmbTel 888, 7 April 1963. *FRUS, 1961-1963, Vol. III, January-June 1963*, pp. 208, 212, 213.

Debating Diem's Fate

Pro-coup sentiment now began building among certain senior Department of State officials. On 23 May, seven weeks after his confrontation with Diem, Ambassador Nolting signed off on a Washington draft of a contingency plan for the US role in the event of a change of government in Vietnam, then took off for a holiday in the Aegean Sea on his way back to Washington on home leave.[8] Public reaction to Diem's continued repression of the Buddhists grew, and on 11 June the Department cabled the Embassy in Saigon that "If Diem does not take prompt and effective steps to reestablish Buddhist confidence in him we will have to reexamine our entire relationship with his regime."[9] Nolting's charge d'affaires was then advised to consider improving the Mission's contacts with "non-supporters of GVN," but "only if you feel our (covert or overt) contacts with those who might play major roles in event of coup are now inadequate."[10]

On 21 June, a paper floated by State's Bureau of Intelligence and Research opined that, although a coup would pose real dangers of major internal upheaval and a serious slackening of Saigon's war effort, there nevertheless was sufficient alternative leadership available in South Vietnam that, "given the opportunity and continued support from the United States, could provide reasonably effective leadership for the government and the war effort."[11] Meanwhile, President Kennedy, caught unawares by the sudden eruption of antiregime protests in Vietnam while his Ambassador there was on vacation, decided to replace Nolting with Henry Cabot Lodge, who had no record of sympathy for Diem.

CIA Station and Headquarters officers had for some years not only scouted closely the possibility of a coup against Diem's faltering rule, but also had from time to time debated the pros and cons of replacing him—without, however, coming to an agreement among themselves about the efficacy of a coup. In February 1961, for example, an Office of National Estimates Staff Memorandum had argued that because the Diem regime was losing the war, had such a narrow base of popular support, and could not be threatened or cajoled into changing its ways, thought should be given to measures which would lead to Diem's replacement. The Director of the Office of National Estimates, Sherman Kent, killed that staff document, ruling it a clear trespass of the policy

---

[8] Nolting, letter to Assistant Secretary of State for Far Eastern Affairs Roger Hilsman, 23 May 1963. *FRUS*, as above, pp. 316-317. This plan warned that although a coup might be pulled off so quickly as to bridge the gap of political power, it was "more than likely that even if coup leaders went so far as to kill Diem, there would be dissension and confusion." *FRUS*, p. 322.
[9] DeptTel 1207, *FRUS*, as above, p. 383.
[10] Newman, John M., *JFK and Vietnam: Deception, Intrigue, and the Struggle for Power* (New York: Warner Books, 1992), p. 335.
[11] Department of State, S/P Files: Lot 70 D 199, Vietnam 1963. *FRUS*, as above, pp. 405-409.

area. By early 1963, however, CIA officers were being drawn into policy analysis by their activist new director, John McCone, and the idea of getting rid of Diem was again being raised. A cautious proposal came from Chester L. Cooper, a senior O/NE officer then detailed to policy liaison duties (and later to the NSC Staff as a Vietnam policy adviser), who wrote McCone in April 1963 that "Diem must step (or be pushed) out, and to that end we should develop a plan for the replacement of Diem (or Nhu) with a man of our own choosing at a time of our choosing."[12] Cooper suggested a target date of April 1966, "because Diem's present term of office will end on 1 April 1966 and because the military phase of the struggle is likely to be largely completed at that time." As we will see, even more explicit pro-coup sentiment welled up within CIA as 1963 wore on, but virtually all of CIA's senior officers—including O/NE's Sherman Kent, DDP Far East Division Chief William Colby, senior DDI officers Huntington D. Sheldon and R. Jack Smith, DDCI Marshall S. Carter, and, most important, DCI John McCone—continued to urge caution about the idea of overthrowing Diem.

The attitude of senior Vietnam policy advisers at State, however, hardened toward Diem's family as the Buddhist crisis gathered momentum through the summer amid reports of restiveness among Diem's generals. The storming of Buddhist pagodas on 21 August by forces directed by Ngo Dinh Nhu crystallized the "Diem must go" convictions, and on Saturday, 24 August, at a time when President Kennedy, National Security Adviser McGeorge Bundy, Secretary of Defense McNamara, Secretary of State Rusk, and DCI McCone happened to be out of town, a small group of strategically placed senior State Department officials smoked a fateful Top Secret/Operational Immediate cable past interagency coordinators to a receptive Ambassador Lodge. In effect, that cable told the Ambassador to advise Diem that immediate steps must be taken to improve the situation—such as meeting Buddhist demands and dismissing his brother. If Diem did not respond promptly and effectively, Lodge was instructed to advise key Vietnamese military leaders that the United States would not continue to support his government. The directive was intended to shake up Diem, neutralize Nhu, and strengthen the hands of a group of generals who opposed the two brothers' coercive

---

[12]Cooper, Memorandum for the Director, "Some Aspects of US Policy with Respect to President Diem," 11 April 1963 (S). CIA/DDI Files, Job No. 79T01148A, O/D/NFAC, "Policy Files," Box 9, Folder "Policy: CLC: Oct 62-Dec 64." In that memo, Cooper acknowledged that "we do not yet really understand the fundamentals of Asian societies or peoples," and that "it is one thing to advocate a course of action leading to the removal of Diem; it is another to proceed on such a course, confident that what would emerge will be better than what we have."

policies and deplored their counterinsurgency tactics. The directive proved crucial two months later, in effect giving a green light to a coup against Diem.[13]

The point man of this fast shuffle was Roger Hilsman, a hard-charging officer who at the time was State's Assistant Secretary for Far Eastern Affairs. His chief colleagues in this affair were Averell Harriman, Under Secretary of State for Political Affairs, and Michael V. Forrestal, a centrally influential NSC staff member and Harriman protege. George Ball, the ranking State Department officer in town, cleared the cable for transmission.

Reading the cable only after it had been sent, virtually all of Washington's top officials were critical of the manner in which Hilsman, Harriman, and Forrestal had acted, and in a series of White House meetings the next week the President himself expressed second thoughts about the faults and virtues of the Ngo brothers and the merits of a military coup. Summing up White House discussions in which he participated during the last days of August 1963, CIA's Far East Division chief, William Colby, recorded that the President and the Attorney General "were apparently appalled at the speed with which the State decision was reached on Saturday afternoon, 24 August, and felt that more thought, analysis, and preparation should have preceded the instruction to Lodge."[14] Vice President Lyndon Johnson, who attended a White House meeting on Vietnam the following weekend, was reported to have had "great reservations with respect to a coup, particularly so because he had never really seen a genuine alternative to Diem."[15]

When he was apprised of the cable's contents, JCS Chairman Gen. Maxwell Taylor told Marine Corps Gen. Victor Krulak that the cable reflected "the well-known compulsions of Hilsman and Forrestal to depose Diem," that had McGeorge Bundy been present the cable would

[13]The text of this cable may be found in *FRUS*, as above, pp. 628-629.
[14]Colby, Memorandum to Walt Elder, at the time Director McCone's Special Assistant. Quoted in CIA/IG "Report on Vietnam," November 1964, p.12. IG files, Box 73-B-567, DCI/Inspector General, Box 2 of 2, "Surveys."
[15]Victor H. Krulak (Maj. Gen, USMC, at the time the JCS Special Assistant for Counterinsurgency and Special Activities), Memorandum for the Record, 31 August 1963. *Pentagon Papers* (Gravel ed.), Vol. II, p. 743. DDCI Pat Carter and FE Division chief Bill Colby were present at that meeting. There State Department Southeast Asia expert Paul Kattenburg made a scathing criticism of the Diem government and of Washington policymakers' lack of understanding of the situation. As he later recalled, "There was not a single person there that knew what he was talking about . . . and I thought, 'God, we're walking into a major disaster,' and that's when I made what essentially was a very imprudent and also presumptuous remark, in a way. And the reaction to it was sort of what I had invited. They all just disregarded it or said it was not backed by anything." Kattenburg, remarks to historian William Conrad Gibbons, 16 February 1979. Gibbons, Part II, p.161. The State Department subsequently gave Mr. Kattenburg Siberia-like assignments.

not have been sent, and that the message "had not been given the quality of interdepartmental staffing it deserved."[16] Four days later, General Taylor wired MACV chief Gen. Paul Harkins that the Hilsman cable had been "prepared without DOD or JSC participation," and that Washington authorities "are now having second thoughts."[17] Years later General Taylor said of the 24 August weekend that "a small group of anti-Diem activists picked this time to perpetrate an egregious 'end run' in dispatching a cable of the utmost importance to Saigon without obtaining normal departmental clearances."[18] Similarly, Lyndon Johnson later termed the dispatching of the cable a crucial decision that "never received the serious study and detached thought it deserved," a "hasty and ill-advised message" that constituted a green light to those who wanted Diem's downfall, and a "serious blunder which launched a period of deep political confusion in Saigon that lasted almost two years."[19]

DCI John McCone reported that he was told by Secretaries Rusk and McNamara on 4 September that they were unhappy with the manner in which the 24 August cable had been handled,[20] McNamara adding that the cable "did not represent the views of the President."[21] McCone, the administration's principal liaison to Dwight Eisenhower, briefed the former President about the cable a few days later. McCone circulated to Lodge (the former Republican Vice Presidential candidate) and others Eisenhower's advice that bringing off a coup would be no small task and would require great care and deliberation. The former President added that even if a coup were successful, the aftermath would have its own special problems.[22] Despite these and other cautions, neither the White House nor the State Department ever rescinded or substantially amended the cabled instructions to Lodge.

Ambassador Frederick Nolting, displaced in Saigon by Lodge and denigrated in Washington by Hilsman because of his pro-Diem arguments (but whose counsel the President sought in August 1963 to balance that of his detractors), later wrote that in 22 years of public service he had never seen anything "resembling the confusion, vacillation and lack of coordination in the U.S. Government" at that time. Although Nolting had

[16]Krulak, Memorandum for the Record, "Vietnam," 24 August 1963. *FRUS, 1961-1963,* Vol. III, pp. 630-631.
[17]JCS cable 3368-63, 28 August 1963. *FRUS,* as above, pp. 630-631.
[18]Maxwell Taylor, *Swords and Ploughshares* (New York: Norton, 1972), pp. 60, 61.
[19]Lyndon Johnson, *The Vantage Point* (New York: Holt, Rinehart & Winston, 1971), p. 292.
[20]McCone, Memorandum for the Record of Lunch with Rusk (at McCone's home), 3 September 1963, (S/Eyes Only). CIA/DCI files, Job No. 80B01285A, DCI/McCone, Box 2, Folder 2: "DCI (McCone) Memos for the Record, 23 July - 26 November 1963."
[21]McCone, Memorandum for the Record, 5 September 1963 (S). CIA/DCI files as above.
[22]In McCone, letter to Ambassador Henry Cabot Lodge, Jr., 19 September 1963 (S). CIA/DCI files, Job No. 80B1285A, Box 8.

sympathy for President Kennedy, he deplored "his failure to take control" and concluded that "the Harriman-Lodge axis seemed too strong for him."[23]

Harriman and Hilsman later sought to spread responsibility for the cable's dispatch, and the late Michael Forrestal is reported as having stated that President Kennedy was the key player all along and covertly supported those who pushed for a coup.[24] Although Kennedy cleared the cable, in the view of this author he did not hatch and manage the coup plotting but let it proceed despite some misgivings. This was the view, as well, of former DCI William Colby.[25] The published record and available documents show that the President repeatedly criticized the way the 24 August cable had been handled and gave lukewarm responses to contingency planning for a coup.[26]

At CIA Headquarters on that fateful weekend of 24 August the Deputy Director for Plans, Richard Helms, was simply briefed on the cable, not consulted. With DCI McCone in California at the time and Acting DCI Marshall S. Carter unavailable, Hilsman telephoned Helms to advise that new instructions to Lodge had been cleared by President Kennedy. Helms then discussed Hilsman's initiative with Far East Division chief Colby and Acting Director Carter; they decided to take no immediate action but to wait for a reaction from Ambassador Lodge.[27] The next day, 25 August, Colby notified Saigon Station that the Agency had not yet seen the text of the Hilsman cable and had not been consulted on it. His cable nevertheless advised that "In circumstance believe CIA must fully accept directives of policy makers and seek ways accomplish objectives they seek," although State's action "appears be throwing away bird in hand before we have adequately identified birds in bush, or songs they may sing."[28]

In later comments on his 24 August initiative, Roger Hilsman maintained that he had cleared his cable with President Kennedy and other Washington principals. Virtually all those officers have contested that

---

[23] Nolting, *From Trust to Tragedy*, p. 132.

[24] Remarks made to Professor Francis X. Winters of Georgetown University. Winters, to author, 6 May 1993.

[25] Colby, to author, 22 December 1993. Mike Forrestal was very close to John and Robert Kennedy, but it is possible that his statement to Professor Winters was prompted by the fact that Forrestal, who had been one of the most enthusiastic supporters of the coup idea, sought after the fact to distance himself from what had turned out to be a disaster.

[26] This author's findings accord with those of two colleagues who have plumbed Mr. McCone's record in detail: Walt Elder, previously McCone's Special Assistant; and Dr. Mary McAuliffe, formerly of CIA's History Staff.

[27] McAuliffe, *John A. McCone as Director of Central Intelligence, 1962-1965 (S),* June 1992, pp. 209-211. In CIA History Staff files.

[28] DIR 63855, reproduced in CIA/IG report, p. 5.

account, insisting that they had been hustled, not consulted. CIA's Marshall Carter in a 1967 memorandum took angry exception to an assertion Hilsman had recently published that he, Carter, had gone over the draft of the 24 August 1963 cable and had decided to approve it without disturbing DCI McCone's vacation. Carter asserted that Hilsman's statement was "totally false . . . at no time was the draft message ever discussed with me, shown to me, or concurred in by me." Carter added that he had been "totally unaware" of the intent of the cable until after it had been sent, that to the best of his knowledge no CIA officer had been consulted, and that the Hilsman cable was "ill-conceived, ill-timed, and inadequately coordinated."[29]

Sometime after that weekend, when he finally got to read the Hilsman cable, Carter as Acting Director asked Vietnam specialist George Carver for an evaluation of the Saigon scene for him. Carver, then an eloquent O/NE analyst who had been a junior case officer in Saigon and would later become the DCI's Special Assistant for Vietnam Affairs (SAVA), responded that the best hope for preserving US interests and attaining US objectives lay in the possibility of "an early coup d'etat, with sufficient military support to obviate a prolonged civil war."[30] Asked then by General Carter to discuss possible alternative leaders in Vietnam, Carver prepared a revised study on 28 August which included the judgment that the risks of not attempting the overthrow of Diem "are even greater than those involved in trying it," because "with the Ngo family regime in power, there is virtually no chance of achieving the objectives of our presence in South Vietnam."[31] Foreshadowing the influence George Carver's views were later to gain in policy circles, Acting

[29] CIA/IG files, Job No 74B779, Inspector General, Box 1, "Special Studies, 1964-1972," Folder: "Chronology on Vietnam, November 1964." These files include notes indicating that in l971 President Nixon requested that DCI Helms send the White House its files on the overthrow of President Diem, and that Presidential assistant John Ehrlichman "was fascinated by the account of CIA's noninvolvement in the assassination of Diem, which runs contrary to the impression he has held." From Kenneth E. Greer, Memorandum for the Record of 17 November 1971 (S). CIA/IG files as above.

[30] Carver, O/NE Staff Memorandum No. 60-63, "Present Prospects for South Vietnam." (S) CIA/DDI files, Job No. 80R1720R, O/D/NFAC, Box 3, "GAC Files," Folder 1, "Vietnam Historical File." O/NE's Sherman Kent allowed Carver's policy-laden memo to go forward only as Carver's personal views, not those of O/NE.

[31] Carver, Memorandum for the Acting Director of Central Intelligence, "Alternatives to the Ngo Family Regime in South Vietnam," 28 August l963. (S) CIA/DDI files, Job No. 79R00904A, O/D/NFAC, Box 10, Folder 1: "Memos for Directors - 1963." Gen. Bruce Palmer contrasts this initiative of Carver's with the manner in which Carver's parent office, O/NE had "scrupulously stayed out of the policy realm." Palmer, "US Intelligence and Vietnam," *Studies in Intelligence*, Vol. 28, No. 5 (Special Issue l984), p. l6.

Director Carter gave a copy of this personal memo to McGeorge Bundy. Carver's boss, O/NE deputy chief Abbot E. Smith, believed that Bundy then gave a copy of the memo to the President.[32]

On 3 September, O/NE sent forward its own formal views on these questions. Titled "South Vietnam's Leaders," that memorandum backed off from Carver's policy recommendations, but nonetheless held (1) that it was doubtful that the Ngo family could provide the necessary unified leadership in Vietnam, and (2) that although no one could guarantee a new regime would be more successful than Diem's, "it is possible, though far from certain" that new and more satisfactory leaders could be found.[33]

DCI McCone Opposes a Coup

DCI McCone, although he was not averse to eliciting policy analyses from his intelligence analysts, in no way shared these—or other— expressions of pro-coup sentiment. From the despatching of Hilsman's 24 August cable to the overthrow and murder of the Ngo brothers in November 1963, McCone repeatedly questioned both the assumptions behind the Hilsman-Harriman-Lodge course and the confused manner in which it was being pursued. During those weeks McCone stressed that the pro-coup decision had not been laid on properly, that the intelligence behind the decision was shaky, that by undertaking this course the United States was becoming too caught up in Vietnamese politics, that a coup would simply breed subsequent coups, and that it was consequently better to go along with what we had in Saigon than to place our bets on a new, unknown, and divided junta.

On 3 September, having returned from California, McCone met with Secretary Rusk, who "agreed with me that we should go slowly, that there was no apparent acceptable successor to Diem."[34] On 10 September, at a

---

[32] Abbot Smith, handwritten note on Carver's 28 August study.

[33] R. Jack Smith, the Acting DDI at the time, took exception to the views in this O/NE memorandum, arguing that one could "not rule out the possibility of winning the war under a Ngo administration." Smith told the Director that "it should be remembered that it took the British nine years of intensive effort to beat down the Communist rebellion in Malaya, where the problems were less than those of Vietnam." Smith, Memorandum for the Director of Central Intelligence, "ONE Memorandum on South Vietnam's Leaders," 4 September 1963 (S/NF). CIA/DDI files, Job No. 79R00904A, O/D/NFAC, Box 10, Folder 1, "Memos for Directors - 1963."

[34] Recorded by McCone, Memorandum for the Record, "Discussion with Secretary Rusk at Lunch at DCI Residence This Date," 3 September 1963. (S/Eyes Only) CIA/DCI files, Job No. 80B01285A, DCI/McCone, Box 2, Folder 8, "DCI (McCone) Memos for the Record, 23 July - 26 November 63." In this memorandum, Mr. McCone recorded that Rusk was "most complimentary of the reporting and judgment of Carter, Helms, and Colby in the meetings of last week." He noted also that Rusk had asked him to explore "the possibilities of an independent, unified Vietnam which would be neutral but free of Chi Com influence . . . this apparently is a French idea and if it could be accomplished would be a very stabilizing influence on all of Southeast Asia."

Presidential conference on Vietnam, McCone reminded the group that following "the National Estimate in May, which indicated that we could win," the Intelligence Community had produced an SNIE in July which held that the situation in Vietnam was deteriorating at such a rate that "victory is doubtful if not impossible."[35] At a second conference with the President the next day, McCone repeated his pessimistic prognosis, telling the group that within three months the situation in Vietnam "may become serious." And at that meeting, McCone agreed with Secretaries Rusk and McNamara that with respect to a possible change of government, "We should proceed cautiously."[36] Two weeks later, McCone repeated his concern regarding a possible change of government in Saigon, telling the CIA Subcommittee of the House Armed Services Committee that, because there did not appear to be any cohesive military group capable of ousting the Diem government, and because a new regime there would probably be no better, CIA was urging a cautious, slow approach to the problem.[37]

In Saigon, however, Ambassador Lodge had begun to criticize CIA Station Chief John Richardson sharply, and word of this development soon appeared in the press. McCone recorded in a memorandum for the record, dated 26 September, that because the Agency had been urging "care and deliberation" since Hilsman's 24 August cable, this caution had proved "highly exasperating to those who wished to move precipitously," and explained why those enthusiasts were now moving swiftly, "without coordination and without intelligence support, and why they were carrying on a campaign against the CIA and the Station."[38] On that same day, 26 September, James Reston of *The New York Times* told McCone that the press attacks on the CIA had been "obviously planted . . . probably a good deal of it from Harriman," and

---

[35] As recorded by Bill Colby, a participant in this Presidential conference. IG Report, p. 17. Mr. McCone here misspoke himself on two accounts: the NIE in question had been produced in April—there was no NIE on Vietnam in May; and the April NIE (53-63) did not say that "we would win." That was Mr. McCone's interpretation of what his remanded NIE had said, from which judgments he was now (September 1963) retreating. CIA/IG files.

[36] As recorded by Bromley Smith, White House assistant, in his Memorandum of a Conference with the President, White House, Washington, September 11, 1963, 7 p.m., "Vietnam." *FRUS, Vietnam, 1961-1963, Vol. IV*, p. 191. Word of this DCI caution found its way to the press; journalist David Halberstam wrote—inaccurately—that "almost all" the members of McCone's staff differed with him on this score. *The New York Times*, 15 September 1963.

[37] Joseph G. O'Neill, Jr., CIA Assistant Legislative Counsel, Memorandum for Assistant to the DCI, "DCI Congressional Briefings on Vietnam," 23 September 1963. (S) CIA/DCI files, Job No. 80B01285A, Box 3, DCI/McCone, Folder 14, "DCI (McCone) Vietnam, 01 Sept - 30 Sept 64." (Hereafter cited as O'Neill memorandum.)

[38] CIA/IG Report, p. 21.

that because the CIA had been taking a reserved position since late August, this might be causing "pain to some of those who wished to rush ahead."[39]

McCone continued to urge caution on these scores throughout October, the last month before Saigon's dissident generals finally carried out their coup. According to later testimony, in a meeting with the President on 5 October 1963 McCone told Kennedy that "if I was manager of a baseball team, [and] I had one pitcher, I'd keep him in the box whether he was a good pitcher or not'; McCone explained to the Senate's Church Committee in 1975 that by this he had meant that if Diem were removed, there would be not one coup but a succession of coups and political disorder in Vietnam.[40]

On 10 October 1963 the DCI told the Senate Foreign Relations Committee, "We have not seen a successor government in the wings that we could say positively would be an improvement over Diem"; therefore "we must proceed cautiously, otherwise a situation might flare up which might result in something of a civil war, and the Communists would come out the victor merely by sitting on the sidelines."[41] McCone repeated that caution on 16 October, telling a White House Special Group meeting that "an explosion" was imminent in Vietnam. The recorder of that meeting, Joseph W. Neubert, Special Assistant in State's Bureau of Far East Affairs, characterized the DCI's position as out of step with policy: "I believe we can expect McCone now to argue that the consequences of our present course are going to be unhelpful in the extreme and that we should, therefore, edge quite rapidly back toward what might be described as our policy toward Vietnam before last August."[42]

Until the coup on 1 November, McCone consistently voiced candid and, as events turned out, prescient criticisms of the Administration's pro-coup course. On 17 October, at a meeting of the Special Group, the DCI characterized US policy since August as being based on "a complete lack of intelligence" on the South Vietnamese political scene, as "exceedingly dangerous," and as likely to spell "absolute disaster for the

[39] McCone, Memorandum for the Record, "Luncheon Meeting with Mr. Reston of *The New York Times*-DCI Residence-26 September 1963." (S/Eyes Only). CIA/DCI files, Job No. 80B01285A, DCI McCone, Box 2, Folder 8, "DCI (McCone) Memos for the Record, 23 July–26 November '63."

[40] As quoted in *Alleged Assassination Plots Involving Foreign Leaders*, an Interim Report of the Select Committee to Study Governmental Operations with Respect to Intelligence Activities, U.S. Senate, 94th Congress, 1st Session, 1975, p. 221.

[41] CIA files, O'Neill memorandum.

[42] Neubert memorandum of 18 October 1963. *FRUS, 1961-1963*, Vol. IV, pp. 406, 407. Neubert added: "As I see it, it is quite clear that the first serious problem confronting us here in Washington as we attempt to pursue a policy that really satisfies no one is going to arise with CIA."

United States."[43] On 21 October, McCone repeated these same concerns privately to President Kennedy.[44] On the 24th he said at another meeting of the Special Group that US officials in Saigon were becoming too involved in conversations between the CIA's Lou Conein and the dissidents' Gen. Tran Van Don.[45] On the 25th, asked by President Kennedy why he was out of step with US policy, the DCI responded that the United States should be working with Diem and Nhu rather than taking aggressive steps to remove them, a policy which McCone held was certain to result in political confusion. At that White House meeting, the DCI told President Kennedy that Washington was handling a delicate situation in a nonprofessional manner, that the dissident Saigon generals could not provide strong leadership, and that their coup would be simply the first of others that would follow.[46] On 29 October, the DCI again opposed the coup course, telling the President that a coup might be followed by a second or third coup.[47]

The last occasion, prior to the coup, on which the DCI criticized the Administration's course, was just two days before the coup took place, when McCone told Averell Harriman at a luncheon on 30 October that it was difficult to understand why the 24 August cable had been sent out so precipitately, and why CIA's views had not been sought. According to the

[43]McCone, Memorandum for the Record, "Special Group 5412 Meeting—17 October 1963," 18 October 1963. (S) CIA/DCI files, Job No. 80B01258A, DCI/Executive Registry, Box 1, Folder 5. Mr. McCone told the Special Group that Ambassador Lodge's policies had "foreclosed intelligence sources" and consequently were undermining the American effort in Vietnam. At this meeting, the DCI also proposed that Bill Colby should be sent to Saigon as Acting COS, where he could reconstitute CIA's intelligence capabilities. White House adviser McGeorge Bundy responded that Mr. McCone was exceeding his authority as DCI and vetoed the proposal on the grounds that Colby's once-close relations with Diem and Nhu would send the wrong signals and confuse Lodge's negotiating tactics.

[44]McCone, Memorandum for the Record, "Discussion with the President—October 21" (S). CIA History Staff files.

[45]Paul Eckel, Memorandum for the Record, "Minutes of Meeting of the Special Group, 24 October 1963," 24 October 1963. CIA/IG files, Job No. 80B01285A, DCI/McCone, Box 2, Folder 8, "DCI (McCone) Memos for the Record, 23 July–26 November '63."

[46]CIA/IG Report, p. 32. See also McCone, Memorandum for the Record, "Meeting with the President," 25 October 1963. (S) McCone papers, as above, Box 6, Folder 5. Present also at this meeting were Attorney General Robert Kennedy, Secretary of Defense McNamara, and McGeorge Bundy.

[47]William E. Colby, Memorandum for the Record, as reproduced in CIA/IG Report, p. 34. See also Bromley Smith, Memorandum of a Conference With the President, White House, Washington, October 29, 1963, 4:20 p.m., Subject, "Vietnam." *FRUS, 1961-1963, Vol. IV*, pp. 468-471. At that meeting Robert Kennedy and Maxwell Taylor joined DCI McCone in criticizing the pro-coup course. And according to the meeting's recorder, Bromley Smith, President Kennedy held that if, as it appeared, the pro- and anti-Diem forces were about equal, then any attempt to engineer a coup would be "silly." *FRUS*, p. 471.

DCI's memo of this conversation, Harriman accepted no responsibility for the cable, claiming that he had been told it had been coordinated with CIA. McCone: "I corrected this impression."[48]

Right up to the eve of the coup there was considerable uncertainty in CIA—at Headquarters and in the field—about whether a coup would be attempted and how it might turn out. On 30 October, the DDI's special South Vietnam Task Force—not having been cut in on the "Ambassador Only" Hilsman cable of 24 August or on CIA operational developments in Saigon—responded to a McCone query with the judgment that Diem's government "probably has a slightly better than even chance of being able to outmaneuver disaffected military elements and survive for the moment," but only if the United States "discourages present coup sentiments or maintains an ambiguous posture which creates uncertainty in the minds of the regime's opponents as well as its leaders." In response to another question, the memorandum added that US objectives "(i.e., the reduction of the VC threat to a point where US forces may be withdrawn)" probably could be achieved "only with a substantially increased US commitment over a considerable period of time (well beyond present US military schedules and domestic expectations)."[49] Also on 30 October, Colby's Far East Division asked Saigon Station to comment on the judgment that "available info here indicates that generals do not have clear preponderance of force in Saigon area, posing possibility of extended fighting."[50] Saigon Station replied that it had been given neither the coup group's plans nor data on its forces but that "the units in the field can be expected to have sufficient ammunition for the coup." The Station cable also contended that because the generals are "basically cautious" it was "unlikely they would move without expecting success." According to the Station, MACV commander Gen. Harkins cabled the following comment on that Station assessment: "MACV has no info from advisory rpt advisory personnel which could be interpreted as clear evidence of an impending coup." CIA files indicate that Harkins's cable was sent from Saigon some 40 minutes before the shooting started.[51]

[48] McCone, Memorandum for the Record, "Discussion with Governor Averell Harriman at Lunch, October 30th," 31 October 1963. (S/Eyes Only) CIA/DCI files, Job No. 80B01285A, DCI/McCone, Box 2, Folder 8, "DCI (McCone) Memos for the Record, 23 July-26 November '63."

[49] Chester L. Cooper, Memorandum for the Director, "Viability of the GVN," 30 October 1963 (S). CIA/DDI files, Job No. 80R01720R, O/D/NFAC, Box 5, "GAC Files (SAVA-NIO)," Folder 1, "GAC Chrono-June 63-May 65." This task force included O/NE officers Harold P. Ford and George A. Carver, as well as several DDI officers.

[50] DIR 79126 (to SAIG/S/FLASH). CIA/GAC files, as above.

[51] SAIG Cable (IN 51983).(TS/Immediate) CIA/GAC files, as above. General Harkins was not alone in his untimely prediction. According to journalist Peter Arnett, Keyes Beech of the *Chicago Daily News* filed a story on the eve of the coup in which he stated that "Americans aren't any good at overthrowing governments, and the latest government we haven't bounced is the family concern in South Vietnam." Arnett, *Live From the Battlefield*, pp. 120-121.

And so ended the episode of the Agency's 1963 input into Vietnam policy. As we have seen, early in the year CIA's estimators had correctly gauged the shaky Vietnamese scene, but had then buckled under pressures exerted by the DCI and policymakers to give NIE 53-63 a markedly more optimistic cast. The authority given these intelligence judgments buttressed the decisionmakers' unfounded optimism; it also contributed to their swing to overpessimism within a few weeks' time, when the anti-Diem riots spread through most of South Vietnam and Buddhist priests began to immolate themselves. Thereafter, Director McCone consistently criticized the wisdom of Washington's coup course, as well as the manner in which Hilsman's 24 August cable had set it in motion. Yet the DCI's warnings made no more impact on policymaking than had the alarms the drafters of the initial NIE 53-63 had tried to sound early in the year.

The coup's consequences spelled disaster: America was tagged with part of the blame for Diem's murder; the Agency was tagged with having had a hand in engineering the coup, even though its DCI had not supported it; the coup indeed turned out to be just the first of others that followed;[52] and Saigon's subsequent rulers proved even less able than Diem and Nhu. Washington's policy managers now had to find some other expedient that might keep our Saigon ally from collapsing. The answer to which they stumbled, months later, was to take over the management of the war with direct and greatly expanded US air and ground force participation.

CIA and the Johnson Administration's Prescription for Saving the South

> While the military and political costs of a big US investment in helping SVN may be high, I cannot think of a better place for our forces to be employed to give so much future national security benefits to the United States. Thus my conclusion is that we . . . must go all out on all three tracks: counterinsurgency, covert countermeasures, and military pressures by US forces.

> DDI Ray S. Cline (Deputy Director/Intelligence), 8 September 1964[53]

---

[52] Later characterized by a senior DO officer as "the banana republic tradition of military coups became part of the thinking of every ambitious troop commander. . . ." (S). CIA/DDO files, Job No. 88-00067R, Folder 137-603-007.

[53] Cline, Memorandum for the Director, "Coping with the Chronic Crisis in South Vietnam," 8 September 1964 (S/Eyes Only). CIA files, Job No. 80B01285A, Box 3, DCI/McCone, Folder 14, "DCI (McCone) Vietnam 01 Sept–30 Sept 1964."

I think what we are doing in starting on a track which involves ground force operations . . . [will mean] an ever-increasing commitment of U.S. personnel without materially improving the chances of victory. . . . In effect, we will find ourselves mired down in combat in the jungle in a military effort that we cannot win, and from which we will have extreme difficulty in extracting ourselves.

DCI John McCone, 2 April 1965[54]

The assassinations of Diem on 1 November and of President Kennedy three weeks later, wrought profound political changes in Saigon and Washington. In South Vietnam the initial rejoicing over the coup[55] evaporated as the new regime quickly proved inept and divided, and the Viet Cong capitalized on the postcoup confusion by expanding the range, intensity, and frequency of their armed attacks.[56] In Washington, an untried President who lacked John Kennedy's charisma and foreign affairs experience had to avert a major policy failure in Vietnam without incurring risks and costs that could scare off voters in the presidential election campaign facing him some months hence. As we will see, President Johnson solved his dilemma by moving the United States, if haltingly, toward military escalation. From the outset of his administration, backstage discussions of policy options focused not on whether to raise the US military commitment, but on how to do so.[57] For public consumption, however, Johnson portrayed his Republican presidential opponent, Senator Barry Goldwater, as the war candidate.[58]

In moving slowly toward direct engagement in Vietnam, President Johnson displayed a policymaking style markedly different from that of his predecessor. Whereas Kennedy had sought the views of a wide spectrum of foreign policy lieutenants, Johnson listened principally to those who

[54] McCone, Memorandum for Secretary Rusk, Secretary McNamara, Saigon Ambassador Maxwell Taylor, and McGeorge Bundy. (TS). CIA/DDI files, Job No. 80T01629R, Box 3, O/D/NFAC, "SA-VA Policy Files," Folder 2, "Vietnam Committee." Mr. McCone hand-carried a copy of this 2 April memorandum to President Johnson on 29 April l965.

[55] From an Eyes Only cable from Ambassador Lodge to President Johnson, 6 November: "There is no doubt that the coup was a Vietnamese and a popular affair, which we could neither manage nor stop after it got started and which we could only have influenced with great difficulty. But it is equally certain that the ground in which the coup seed grew into a robust plant was prepared by us and that the coup would not have happened with [when] it did without our preparation." FRUS, 1961-1963, Vol. IV, p. 577.

[56] At a Honolulu conference on Vietnam questions, 20 November l963, MACV chief Harkins reported that immediately following the coup, Viet Cong incidents had "shot up 300-400% of what they were before." FRUS, as above, p. 6l2.

[57] Leslie H. Gelb and Richard K. Betts, The Irony of Vietnam: The System Worked (Washington, D.C.: Brookings Institution, l979), pp. l97-l98. In the Vietnam interagency working groups in which the author of this CIA History Staff study participated, l964-65, the focus of concern was solely on how best to escalate.

[58] At a small l966 dinner party in Taiwan for Mr. Goldwater, at which the author was present, the Senator repeatedly berated "that [expletive deleted] Lyndon Johnson" on this score.

agreed with him. As later characterized by NSC staffer Chester L. Cooper, Johnson "seemed to have a blind mind-set which made him pay attention to people who said that (a) he was right, (b) there was a way out, and (c) there were no other alternatives to what he wanted to do."[59] This change of style quickly froze out Vice President Hubert Humphrey, as well as Messrs. Harriman, Forrestal, Hilsman, and a number of State Department officials who previously had influential roles in Vietnam policymaking. Johnson now turned principally to Pentagon advisers, especially Secretary McNamara, as well as to ex-President Eisenhower.[60]

As for DCI McCone, President Johnson had periodically sought his personal advice on a wide range of issues, many of them involving sensitive policy and personnel matters far beyond strictly intelligence questions. A typical reflection of this closeness was a December 1963 McCone-Johnson discussion at the President's Texas ranch: Johnson told McCone that he wanted to change the DCI's cloak-and-dagger image to that of a presidential adviser on world issues. Among such activities the President wished him to take in the immediate future, the DCI recorded, was "to return to California to meet with President Eisenhower—to discuss with him certain aspects of the world situation and also the particular actions which President Johnson had taken in the interests of government economy."[61]

The DCI's Presidential advisory role did not extend to Vietnam; with rarely occasional exceptions, President Johnson never included John McCone among his innermost Vietnam advisers. Nonetheless, as we will see, until Johnson and McCone began to part company in late 1964 on issues concerning the war, the DCI and senior CIA officers participated actively in a number of policy-related endeavors.

---

[59] Cooper, letter of 5 December 1986, to William C. Gibbons of the Congressional Research Service, Library of Congress. A copy of Cooper's letter is on file in CIA's History Staff. Cooper also describes LBJ's style as one marked by "a certain ad hocing; there was a certain stretching for the gimmick; there was a certain business of piling extravaganza upon extravaganza . . ." Interview of Cooper, 7 August 1969, by Paige E. Mulhollan, for the University of Texas Oral History Project, Tape No. 2. A copy of that interview is on file in CIA's History Staff.

[60] Cooper testimonies, as above. For similar descriptons of Mr. Johnson's Vietnam policymaking style see Gelb and Betts, pp. 97-98; Marvin Kalb and Elie Abel, *Roots of Involvement*, pp. 167-169; Robert L. Gallucci, *Neither Peace Nor Honor: The Politics of American Military Policy in Vietnam* (Baltimore: Johns Hopkins University Press, 1975), pp. 32-34; Roger Hilsman, *To Move a Nation: The Politics of Foreign Policy in the Administration of John F. Kennedy* (New York: Doubleday & Co., 1964), p. 535; and David Halberstam, *The Best and the Brightest* (New York: Random House, 1969), p. 144.

[61] McCone, Memorandum for the Record, of 29 December 1963, of conversation with President Johnson, 27 December 1963 (S). CIA/DCI files, Job No. 80B1285A, Box 2, Folder 9, "DCI (McCone) Memos for the Record, 27 November-31 December 1963." In this folder, see also McCone memos for the record of similar meetings with President Johnson, 13 December and 21 December 1963 (S).

Gen. Paul Harkins

In these, McCone was consistently more pessimistic about likely developments than were virtually all of Washington's other senior officers, and certainly much more pessimistic than he had himself been, early in 1963, when he had decried the gloomy outlook of NIE 53-63 and demanded its revision. Soon after the Vietnamese generals' coup on 1 November, the DCI had registered his concern at a 20 November Honolulu policy conference, where he found MACV General Harkins's assessment of the Vietnam situation too rosy and returned to CIA "more discouraged about South Vietnam than ever in the past."[62] McCone was still troubled four days later when he told President Johnson that he did not agree with Ambassador Lodge's postcoup enthusiasms: "I concluded by stating that we could not at this point or time give a particularly optimistic appraisal of the future."[63]

The DCI also gave the intelligence subcommittee of the House Appropriations Committee a somber assessment on 6 December, testifying that he was "extremely worried" about Vietnam, even though he did not consider the situation desperate or in danger of "going down the drain." He did not hesitate to advise the committee that the United States should not get into the Vietnam conflict with its own combat forces, and that the going policy of training the South Vietnamese to do their own fighting was "sound."[64]

On 7 December, McCone named Peer DeSilva to be John Richardson's successor as COS in Saigon. On that same day, helping Director McCone pave the way for DeSilva, President Johnson sent Ambassador Lodge instructions that henceforth there "must be complete understanding and cooperation" between him and the CIA station chief, and no more inspired "mutterings in the press." LBJ told Lodge, "I cannot overemphasize the importance which I personally attach to correcting

[62] As described by memorandum for the record of the Honolulu conference, prepared by Enno H. Knoche. CIA/IG Report, p. 38.

[63] McCone, Memorandum for the Record of a Meeting, Executive Office Building, Washington, November 24, 1963, 3 p.m. *FRUS, 1961-1963, Vol IV*, pp. 635, 636. In his memoirs Lyndon Johnson gives a similar account of this, his first Vietnam policy conference: "Lodge was optimistic. . . . I turned to John McCone and asked what his reports from Saigon in recent days indicated. The CIA Director replied that his estimate was much less encouraging. . . . McCone concluded that he could see no basis for an optimistic forecast of the future." Johnson, *The Vantage Point* p. 43.

[64] CIA/IG Report, p. 39. As we will see, months later Mr. McCone reversed his position on this issue, holding in late 1964 that US bombing of the North would have little effect on Hanoi's willingness to continue the war unless the United States also committed ground troops to combat in the South.

the situation which has existed in Saigon in the past, and which I saw myself when I was out there."[65] Paralleling the President's admonishment, McCone cabled Lodge the same day that "acting on direction of higher authority," he would be arriving in Saigon on 18 December, accompanied by Marine General Krulak, Bill Colby, and Peer DeSilva, and that Secretary McNamara would be joining them the next day.[66]

In Saigon on 21 December the DCI met first with General Harkins, who told him that a disastrous situation that had just erupted in Long An Province, just south of Saigon, would be reduced to a "police action" by the "middle of 1964," a view the DCI viewed as overoptimistic.[67] That same day, after introducing DeSilva to Lodge, the DCI privately told the Ambassador that there was no excuse for the "totally erroneous" reporting on Long An, and that that intelligence failure must be corrected.[68] Later that day, in summing up the visiting party's discussions, the DCI registered his deep concern about South Vietnam, an estimate now far different from that he had held early in the year. He wrote:

> There is no organized government in South Vietnam at this time. . . . It is abundantly clear that statistics received over the past year or more from the GVN officials and reported by the US military on which we gauged the trend of the war were grossly in error. . . . The military government may be an improvement over the Diem-Nhu regime, but this is not as yet established and the future of the war remains in doubt. In my judgment, there are more reasons to doubt the future of the effort under present programs and moderate extensions to existing programs than there are reasons to be optimistic about the future of our cause in South Vietnam.[69]

Secretary McNamara returned from Saigon with similar views. On 21 December (Washington time) he gave President Johnson a dark assessment of the outlook in Vietnam. McNamara told the President that the situation in Vietnam was "very disturbing," and that unless current trends were reversed in the next two to three months, developments would move toward "neutralization at best and more likely to a Communist-controlled state." In his report, the Secretary said that the new government in Saigon was "the greatest source of concern," that the US

---

[65] CAP 636333 to Saigon. CIA/IG Report, p. 39.
[66] DIR 87711. CIA/IG Report, p. 40. Other members of the party were McGeorge Bundy and State's William Sullivan.
[67] McCone, Memorandum for the Record of conversation with Harkins, 21 December 1963. CIA/IG Report, p. 42.
[68] McCone, Memorandum for the Record of conversation with Lodge, 21 December 1963. McCone records that Lodge agreed with his criticisms of reporting. CIA/IG Report, p. 42.
[69] McCone, Memorandum, 21 December 1963. CIA/IG Report, p. 43.

Embassy's country team was "the second major weakness," and that the situation had "in fact been deteriorating in the countryside since July to a far greater extent than we realized because of our undue dependence on distorted Vietnamese reporting." McNamara assured the President that he and DCI McCone had discussed these reporting problems and were acting vigorously to improve CIA and Defense intelligence.[70]

CIA's Expanding Role

McNamara and McCone met with the President later the same day to report their conclusions in person. There McCone seconded McNamara's concerns about poor reporting and the uncertain outlook in Vietnam, although he added that he was perhaps not quite as pessimistic as the Defense Secretary. McCone emphasized that improvement did not lie in committing additional US strength; rather, the Vietnamese themselves must carry the main burden. The DCI concluded that subsequent coups in Saigon were likely.[71] Two days later, McCone reminded the President of concerns he had expressed on the 21st and reported that he was sending out a number of CIA's "old Vietnamese hands" to help expand covert capabilities to report on the effectiveness of the new ruling junta and the Vietnamese public's acceptance of it. The DCI acknowledged that while this had not been CIA's role in the past, it was now justified because the situation in Vietnam had become "so critical."[72]

McCone immediately began to implement this initiative, justifying it to Secretary Rusk on 7 January with the observation that MACV and Embassy reporting had proved "incorrect" because of their reliance on Vietnamese province and district chiefs who felt obliged to "create statistics" that would please their Saigon superiors.[73] McCone's scheme to

---

[70] McNamara, Memorandum for the President, 21 December 1963. *FRUS, 1961-1963, Vol. IV*, pp. 732, 733. Also recorded in CIA/IG Report, pp. 42-43. CIA/IG files indicate that despite the pessimistic judgments he had given the President privately, a week later Secretary McNamara told a House Armed Services subcommittee that the United States still hoped to carry out its earlier plans to withdraw most of its troops from Vietnam before the end of 1965. CIA/IG Report, p. 45. In January 1964, after listening to McNamara on the occasion of another of his trips to Saigon, COS DeSilva felt that the Secretary "simply had no comprehension of how the war should be handled. . . ." DeSilva, *Sub Rosa: The CIA and the Uses of Intelligence* (New York: Times Books, 1978), p. 230.

[71] William E. Colby, Memorandum for the Record. CIA/IG Report, p. 44.

[72] McCone letter to the President, 23 December 1963. CIA/IG Report, p. 45. On that same day, 23 December, McCone told his colleagues on the United States Intelligence Board that he had serious doubts about the Saigon government's ability to overcome the Viet Cong, and that he saw more reason to doubt the outcome than to be optimistic. Minutes of the Meeting, USIB-M-303, 23 December 1963 (S).

[73] McCone, letter to Rusk, 7 January 1964. *FRUS, 1964-1968, Vietnam*, Vol. I, p. 5.

report covertly on the GVN, however, encountered mixed reviews. On the one hand, NSC staffer Michael Forrestal thought it a good idea and recommended to his boss, McGeorge Bundy, that McCone should be encouraged.[74] But in his memo Forrestal recognized that McCone's idea would not go down well with Secretary McNamara, who would doubtless "have difficulty in accepting the thought that CIA should take on a separate reporting function" and would view McCone's scheme as "an implied criticism of the Saigon command and its uniformed counterpart in Washington." Forrestal's concern proved well-founded. Indeed, McNamara insisted that the group of experts sent out be broadened to a CIA-Defense-State team. And when that joint team's CIA members filed their evaluation of field reporting on 18 February, MACV commander Gen. Paul Harkins found some of its judgments overly pessimistic; he objected that the CIA group might be exceeding its terms of reference by reporting unilaterally and so "misleading the national decision process by forwarding information not coordinated and cleared with other elements of the U.S. reporting mechanism in Vietnam."[75]

Administration Ponders Escalation

In early 1964, while DCI McCone and virtually all officers and entities of the Agency nursed doubts about the field's reporting and the outlook in Vietnam, the Johnson administration's policy planners began a high-priority search for new avenues to victory over the Communists in South Vietnam. The planners' basic assumption was that punishing North Vietnam would "convince the North Vietnamese that it was in their economic self-interest to desist from aggression in South Vietnam."[76] The planned punishment took two forms: an initial battery of more aggressive covert operations against and within the DRV [Democratic Republic of Vietnam, or North Vietnam], and a quietly constructed contingency plan for an improved war effort in the south, strengthened by US military operations against North Vietnam. From the outset, CIA intelligence played an active part in both these new endeavors.

---

[74]Forrestal, Memorandum to Bundy, 8 January 1964. *FRUS*, as above, pp. 7-8. In this memo Forrestal held that the problem was that the field had been using an "excessively mechanical system of statistical reporting which had been devised in Washington and applied in Saigon [and] was giving us a grotesquely inaccurate picture. Once again it is the old problem of having people who are responsible for operations also responsible for evaluating the results." These views indicate how far Forrestal had travelled from early 1963, when he had been one of those officials most certain that available reporting did not support the skepticism of the draft NIE 53-63.

[75]*Pentagon Papers* (Gravel ed.), Vol. III, pp. 32-34.

[76]As described in footnote to McGeorge Bundy, Memorandum to the President, 7 January 1964. *FRUS, 1964-1968,* Vol. I, p. 4.

The first of these was a Defense Department covert action project titled Operations Plan (OPLAN) 34A-64, which had a proposed launch date of 1 February. Initial operations would include expanding intelligence collection by U-2 aircraft and electronic methods; expanding psychological operations via leaflet drops, phantom covert operations, and expanded black and white radiobroadcasts; and beginning a sustained program of airborne and maritime sabotage operations against such targets as bridges, railways, storage dumps, and small islands within North Vietnam.[77]

CIA's participation in OPLAN 34-A began with a response to a request from USMC Gen. Victor "Brute" Krulak (Special Assistant to the JCS for Counterinsurgency Operations) that O/NE comment on the probable Communist and international reactions to thirteen of the draft OPLAN's Phase I operational proposals. On 2 January O/NE concluded that the thirteen operations under review, "taken by themselves, and even if all were successful, would not 'convince the DRV leadership that their continued direction and support of insurgent activities in the RVN (South Vietnam) and Laos should cease'—this, according to the Op-Plan, being their stated goal."[78]

McCone was similarly skeptical. On 7 January he judged that "the operation, being a very modest extension" of previous covert operations, "will not seriously affect the DRV or cause them to change their policies"; therefore, he concluded, a "more dynamic, aggressive plan" should be substituted.[79] On that same day, he voiced similar doubts to McGeorge Bundy, telling him that he had no objection to the proposed covert operations, but that "the President should be informed that this is not the greatest thing

---

[77] *Pentagon Papers*, (Gravel ed.). Vol. III, pp. 150-151; Gibbons, Part II, pp. 210, 212-214. As 1964 wore on, OPLAN 34-A operations expanded beyond these measures. In August, prior covert raids by South Vietnamese gunboats on DRV islets figured prominently in the Tonkin Gulf incidents and Congress's passage of the Tonkin Gulf resolution.

[78] O/NE, Revised Memorandum for the Director, "Probable Reactions to Various Courses of Action with Respect to North Vietnam," 2 January 1964. (TS/Sensitive). CIA/DDI files, Job No. 79R00904A, O/D/NFAC, Box 10, Folder 3: "Memos for Directors, 1963-64." O/NE had long held that modest covert efforts planned against North Vietnam would be ineffectual in achieving US objectives, writing Director McCone in September 1962, for instance, that "we do not believe that even the most successful such operations would cause the DRV to cease completely its military-subversive efforts against South Vietnam." Sherman Kent, Memorandum for the Director, "Comment on DD/P Proposal to Special Group Concerning Operations in North Vietnam," 24 September 1962. CIA/DDO files, Job No. 72-233R, Box 1, Folder 6: "Switchback, Main Folder."

[79] McCone, "Memorandum Concerning Proposed Covert Operations Against North Vietnam," 7 January 1964. (TS). CIA/DCI files, Job No. 80B1285A, DCI/McCone, Box , Folder 10: "DCI (McCone) Memos for the Record, 1 Jan – 5 Apr '64."

since peanut butter."[80] Despite his want of enthusiasm, McCone nevertheless joined Bundy, Secretary Rusk, and Secretary McNamara in recommending that President Johnson approve OPLAN 34-A.[81]

CIA officials also participated in the administration's simultaneous policy search—one of far larger consequence—for the best ways, means, and timing to save South Vietnam. Here the prime movers urging President Johnson to expand the war were the Joint Chiefs of Staff, who argued tirelessly that active US combat intervention was mandatory to keep our Saigon ally from collapsing, and a number of civilian and military strategists who assured the President that bombing North Vietnam would bring Hanoi to the negotiating table and cause it to reduce its support of the Viet Cong.

In pushing for military intervention, the Joint Chiefs of Staff were reversing a position their predecessors had taken in 1954 when the Eisenhower administration had faced the problem of whether to commit US combat forces in Indochina. At that time the JCS had held that Indochina "is devoid of decisive military objectives and the allocation of more than token US armed forces to that area would be a serious diversion of limited US capabilities."[82] By 1961, different circumstances and new chiefs had begun to change that assessment. On 9 May of that year, JCS Chairman Lyman L. Lemnitzer urged that Diem should be encouraged to request that the United States fulfill its collective security obligation by sending "appropriate" forces to Vietnam.[83] Vice President Johnson had disagreed at that time, telling President Kennedy that "American combat troop involvement is not only not required, it is not desirable."[84] By early 1964, however, now President Johnson faced not only a sharply deteriorating situation in Vietnam, but a presidential campaign in which he did not wish to be seen as being "soft" on Communism.

---

[80] As described by participant William E. Colby, Memorandum for the Record, "Meeting on North Vietnam-January 1964." 9 January 1964 (S). CIA/DCI files, as above. In his account of this policy meeting, Colby noted that "Secretary Rusk believed that the President should also be informed that . . . 98% of the problem is in South Vietnam."

[81] Bundy, Memorandum for the President, 7 January. Johnson Library, National Security File, Memos to the President, Vol. I, McGeorge Bundy. *FRUS, 1964-1968*, Vol I, p. 4.

[82] Arthur Radford, Chairman, Joint Chiefs of Staff, Memorandum to the Secretary of Defense, "U.S. Military Participation in Indochina," 20 May 1954. *FRUS, 1952-1954*, Vol. XIII, *Indochina, Part 2*, p. 1592.

[83] Johnson Library, Vice Presidential Security File, as reproduced in Gibbons, Vol. II, p. 39. It is of note that General Lemnitzer subscribed wholeheartedly to the domino thesis. In January 1962 he told Secretary of Defense McNamara that the fall of South Vietnam would imperil the US strategic position from India to Japan, as part of the Communist Bloc's "timetable for world domination." Lemnitzer, Memorandum for SecDef, "The Strategic Importance of the Southeast Asia Mainland," *Pentagon Papers* (DoD ed.), Book 12, V-B-4, "US Involvement in the War, Internal Documents, The Kennedy Administration: January 1961–November 1963," Book 11, pp. 448-450.

[84] *Pentagon Papers* (DoD ed.), Book 11, as reproduced in Gibbons, Part II, p. 45.

A Leading Hawk

In 1963-64 the administration's primary civilian advocate of escalation was Walt W. Rostow, at the time Director of the Department of State's Policy Planning Staff, and later (1966) the NSC's Special Assistant to the President for National Security Affairs. A widely read economic theorist, Rostow had long proclaimed that the world was locked in a Communist-capitalist struggle whose outcome would be decided in the Third World; subsequently, he deemed South Vietnam to be the keystone of that anti-Communist arch. In 1961 he had told an Army audience that the Communists, in concentrating their pressures on the weaker nations, were the "scavengers of the modernization process," that communism is best understood as a "disease of the transition to modernization," and that "we are determined to help destroy this international disease."[85] From his vantage point at State, he had been arguing for some time that it would take US escalation of the war, especially bombing North Vietnam, to save South Vietnam from collapse.[86]

Now, in late 1963, moved especially by Secretary McNamara's concern that the situation had become so critical that South Vietnam might go Communist, Rostow ordered his Policy Planning Staff to prepare a preliminary examination of his thesis that the United States should construct an integrated plan for imposing sanctions "on an ascending scale" against North Vietnam. The aims of those measures, according to Rostow, were to cause North Vietnam to cease its infiltration of men and arms into South Vietnam and Laos, to cease its direction of Communist hostilities inside both countries, and to withdraw its own troops from South Vietnam and Laos. Rostow reasoned that the threat, or the actual implementation, of US bombing would "work" for essentially two reasons: the DRV now had an industrial base its leaders would not wish destroyed, and they would fear being driven by US attacks into a position of "virtual vassalage" to Communist China. In addition, he thought the USSR and China, fearing escalation of the war, might also prefer to damp it down.[87]

---

[85] From a speech to the US Army Special Warfare School, Fort Bragg, North Carolina, 28 June 1961, as cited in Lawrence E. Grinter, "How They Lost: Doctrines, Strategies and Outcomes of the Vietnam War," *Asian Survey*, XV, No. 12 (December 1975), p. 1124. Grinter holds that this "Rostow Doctrine" became "the principal rationale for U.S. intervention and conduct in Vietnam." Grinter, p. 1123. It is the view of the author of this History Staff study, who had considerable contact with Rostow on these scores in 1964, that Grinter's characterization is a bit sweeping, even though Rostow did play a significant role in the US decision to go big in Vietnam.

[86] Robert H. Johnson, as of 1963-64 one of Rostow's Policy Planning staff officers, who was tasked in early 1964 with closely examining Rostow's escalation theses, later wrote that he and Rostow had been arguing the latter's escalation idea "since 1961." Johnson, "Escalation Then and Now," *Foreign Policy*, No. 60 (Fall 1985), p. 131.

[87] State Department, Policy Planning Staff, "Outline of Issues Involved in Planning for the Imposition of Measured Sanctions against North Vietnam." 11 February 1964. (S/Noforn/Limited Distribution)." Attachment to William E. Colby, Memorandum for the Director, "Planning Paper for Southeast Asia," 19 February 1964. (S) CIA/DDO files, Box 78-597, DDO/ISS, Box 1, Folder 7, "State & Defense Papers on Vietnam, 1964."

This preliminary study was translated into a formal interdepartmental examination, as one response to an NSC directive of 14 February 1964 that established a special Vietnam Task Force under the direction of State Department officer William H. Sullivan.[88] The day following the promulgation of this NSAM, Secretary Rusk told an initial Sullivan Task Force meeting that their endeavors had "the highest priority," that developments in the Vietnam war might force them to "face some extremely dangerous decisions in the coming months," but that no planning was to be done on the subject of withdrawal from Vietnam.[89] According to CIA files, President Johnson told DCI McCone and other senior officers on 20 February that contingency planning for putting pressure on North Vietnam should be "speeded up," and that particular attention should be given to creating pressures that would "produce the maximum credible deterrent effect on Hanoi."[90]

Doubts About Attacking the North

Even before its formal constitution, the Sullivan Task Force on 9 February had put a subcommittee to work on a detailed examination of Rostow's thesis. Headed by State's Robert H. Johnson, its members were directed to return their findings by early March, in time for Secretary McNamara's next scheduled visit to South Vietnam. Bob Johnson's inter-agency team consisted of 12 members drawn from State, Defense, the Joint Staff, USIA, and CIA.[91]

Working days, nights, and weekends, this team produced a searching study that examined virtually all the military and political questions that might obtain, should the United States activate the Rostow plan. The group finished its examination on 1 March. The basic question was whether the proposed US attacks on the DRV would work: would those

---

[88] National Security Action Memorandum No. 280, attachment to John A. McCone, Memorandum for the President, "National Security Action Memorandum No. 280," 24 February 1964, (S), nominating FE Division Chief William E. Colby as CIA's representative to the Sullivan Task Force. CIA/DDO files, Job No. 78-597, DDO/ISS, Box 2, Folder: "Sullivan Committeee Meetings, Feb 1964-April 1964."

[89] William E. Colby, Memorandum for the Record, "Inter-agency Vietnam Working Group, 15 February 1964," 15 February 1964. (S) CIA/DDO/ISS files, as above.

[90] Michael V. Forrestal, Memorandum for the Record, "South Vietnam," 20 February 1964. (S) CIA files, Box 78-597, DDO/ISS, Box 1, Folder 8: "Meetings on Vietnam: 1963-Oct. 1964."

[91] Harold P. Ford, Memorandum for the Record, "Initial Meeting of Planning Sub-Committee of Vietnam Task Force, 19 February 1964," 19 February 1964. (S/Sensitive). CIA/DDO files, Box No. 78-597, DDO/IIS, Box 1, Folder 8: "Meetings on Vietnam, 1963-Oct. 1964." The author was at that time Chief of O/NE's Far East Staff and a CIA representative on this interagency team.

attacks cause the DRV to order the Viet Cong to cease its activities, and would the DRV cease its support of the Viet Cong? The group's answer was no, the scheme would not work:

> It is not likely that North Vietnam would (if it could) call off the war in the South even though U.S. actions would in time have serious economic and political impact. Overt action against North Vietnam would be unlikely to produce reduction in Viet Cong activity sufficiently to make victory on the ground possible in South Vietnam unless accompanied by new U.S. bolstering actions in South Vietnam and considerable improvement in the government there. The most to be expected would be reduction of North Vietnamese support of the Viet Cong for a while and, thus, the gaining of some time and opportunity by the government of South Vietnam to improve itself.[92]

On 2 March, CIA's senior representative on the subcommittee paraphrased this key judgment for DCI McCone: "The assessment's principal conclusions are . . . that we are not sanguine that the posited US actions would in fact cause Hanoi to call off the war in the South"; and that even if Hanoi did cease or reduce its support of the Viet Cong, "considerable political-military improvement would be necessary in SVN if the GVN were to have a chance of permanently reducing the VC threat."[93] This basic judgment, agreed upon by an interagency panel, closely paralleled positions CIA's Office of National Estimates had been taking since at least 1961, and foreshadowed judgments CIA representatives would continue to put forward in interagency forums throughout 1964.[94]

Robert Johnson's interagency intelligence officers did not confine themselves to questioning the efficacy of bombing the North; they raised broad political questions as well. Here again their judgments were somber.

---

[92] As quoted in *Pentagon Papers* (Gravel ed.), Vol III, p. 156. See also Policy Planning Staff, Department of State, "Alternatives for Imposition of Measured Pressures Against North Vietnam," 1 March 1964. (Originally TS, declassified 4 October 1983). A copy of this report is on file in CIA's History Staff.

[93] Harold P. Ford, Memorandum for the Director, "Completion of Interim Report by (North) Vietnam Planning Sub-Committee of Sullivan Task Force," 2 March 1964 (S). CIA/DDI files, Job No. 79R00904A, O/D/NFAC, Box 10, Folder 3, "Memos for Directors, 1963-64."

[94] "The gist of the SNIE [of 5 November 1961] was that the North Vietnamese would respond to an increased U.S. commitment with an offsetting increase in infiltrated support for the Viet Cong. . . On the prospects for bombing the North, the SNIE implies that threats to bomb would not cause Hanoi to stop its support for the Viet Cong . . ." *Pentagon Papers* (Gravel ed.), Vol. II, pp. 107-108. The Johnson group's judgment was also shared by William Colby, at the time Chief of CIA's Far East Division and CIA's representative to the Johnson group's parent body, the Sullivan Task Force. On 19 February 1964 Colby told McCone: "As you know I have some rather strong doubts as to the desirability or effectiveness of this overall course of action." Colby, Memorandum for the Director, "Planning Paper for Southeast Asia," 19 February 1964. (S). CIA/DDO files, Box 78-597, DDO/IIS, Box 1, Folder 7, "State and Defense Papers on Vietnam, 1964."

Their report suggested that the United States might get caught up in a situation in which the South Vietnamese or the Laotian Government might crumble in the midst of US escalation, thereby destroying the political base for the US actions. They also warned that if the US bombings of the North did not work, "the costs of failure might be greater than the cost of failure under a counter-insurgency strategy because of the deeper U.S. commitment and the broader world implications."[95]

The intelligence group's warnings had little if any effect on the policy decisions that were subsequently made—the fate of virtually all such intelligence inputs into the administration's 1964-65 contingency planning for expanding its role in Vietnam. In fact, even before the Johnson group had completed its deliberations, Walt Rostow met with his boss, Secretary Rusk, "to report to you the results of our individual review of the attached report on Southeast Asia prepared by the Policy Planning Council." Rostow told Rusk the concept of that report was that military and other sanctions against North Vietnam "could cause it to call off the war principally because of its fear that it would otherwise risk loss of its politically important industrial development; because of its fear of being driven into the arms of Communist China; and because of Moscow's, Peiping's and Hanoi's concern about escalation."[96]

There is no indication in available files that Rostow ever told the Secretary of State that Rusk's own study group had failed to support Rostow's assurance to the Secretary that bombing the North might save the South. Nor is there any indication that the group's judgments became known to or had any effect on top policymakers. Later in 1964, nonetheless, the Robert Johnson exercise did materially influence the administration's most outspoken senior skeptic, Under Secretary of

[95] George Ball, *Atlantic Monthly*, p. 4l; Policy Planning Staff, Department of State, "Alternatives" study, *passim*; and Robert Johnson, "Escalation Then and Now," *passim*. Among the authors who gave the Robert Johnson exercise high marks was David Halberstam: "It was an important study because it not only predicted that the bombing would not work, and predicted Hanoi's reaction to the pressure, which was to apply counterpressure, but it forecast that the bombing would affect (and imprison) the American government. That was particularly prophetic because America did eventually bomb with a view to bringing the North to the conference table. It would find that it was, instead of changing the North, sticking itself to a tar baby . . ." Halberstam, *The Best and the Brightest*, p. 357.

[96] Rostow, Memorandum to the Secretary of State, "Contingency Planning for Southeast Asia," l4 February l964. *FRUS, 1964-1968*, Vol. I, pp. 75, 76. The day before, Rostow had told Rusk that there was "a fair chance" that US bombing of the DRV would work because, among other things, "Ho [Chi Minh] has an industrial complex to protect: he is no longer a guerrilla fighter with nothing to lose." Rostow, Memo to Rusk, "Southeast Asia," 13 February l964. *FRUS*, as above, pp. 73, 74. In that memo of the 13th, Rostow placed this repeat of his preexisting position in the broader context of a needed Congressional resolution backing stronger US actions against the DRV. As we will see, the administration's policymakers had such a resolution ready, six months later, when the Tonkin Gulf incidents provided President Johnson an opportunity to ask the Congress for its formal support.

State George Ball. In October he prepared a long, scathing criticism of President Johnson's entire Vietnam course. His critique specifically cited the judgment by Robert Johnson's interagency group that probably the most that could be expected "in the best of circumstances" from US bombings of the North would be that North Vietnam would ultimately slacken and ostensibly cease its support of the VC, but that "We can, of course, have no assurance that such 'best of circumstances' would obtain, even if considerable damage had been done the DRV."[97]

While the Robert Johnson group toiled and the initial covert pressures conceived in OPLAN 34-A were being applied against North Vietnam, a second coup occurred in Saigon: on 30 January 1964, Maj. Gen. Nguyen Khanh overthrew the junta that had murdered President Diem. In succeeding weeks, CIA officers showered policymakers with assessments detailing the GVN's political and military malaise.[98]

CIA Realism

DCI McCone told Secretary Rusk on 6 February that there was evidence of increased Viet Cong activities and victories.[99] On 9 February, CIA sent Secretary McNamara a Saigon Station appraisal that the South Vietnamese population at large "appears apathetic, without enthusiasm either for the GVN or VC sides but responsive to the latter because it fears the VC."[100] On 10, 11, 14, and 18 February, a special CIA mission to Saigon sent policymakers assessments which "instead of finding

---

[97] Ball, letter to Rusk, McNamara, and McGeorge Bundy, 5 October 1964, (TS), as later reproduced in Ball, "A Light That Failed," *The Atlantic*, December 1972, p. 39. See also Halberstam, *The Best and the Brightest*, pp. 491-500; Stanley Karnow, (The Vietnam Years, Part I)," *The New Yorker*, 6 May 1991, p. 58. According to Robert Johnson, when his group completed its report in March 1964, Allen S. Whiting, then a State Department officer working for Ball, asked for and was given a copy of the group's report. Johnson, to author, 30 April 1993. Also, Mr. Ball's basic critique, that "once on the tiger's back we cannot be sure of picking the place to dismount," paralleled the Johnson group's earlier (March) judgment that the costs of failure might be greater if the US had escalated the war, thereby increasing its commitment, but still had not caused the DRV and the Viet Cong to slacken their pressures against the GVN.

[98] A measure of the JCS's appreciation of the deteriorating situation at this time: According to CIA files, on 17 February 1964 the JCS sought the views of CINCPAC and MACV on the proposition that "the wartime DOD-CIA command relationships for Vietnam" be activated. This state-of-war provision would have placed CIA's operations there under MACV. C/FE Colby, learning of this, recommended to DCI McCone that he "be prepared for such a suggestion and, if it comes, that you decline it." Colby, Memorandum for the DCI, "Military Command of CIA Station, Vietnam," 19 February 1964. (S). CIA/DDO files, Box 78-597, DDO/IIS, Box 1, Folder 8, "Meetings on Vietnam, 1963-Oct. 1964." Fortunately for CIA, its Saigon Station was not subordinated to MACV.

[99] McCone, Memorandum for the Record, "Discussion with Secretary Rusk at Luncheon, 6 February, 12:45 - 2:30" (S/Eyes Only). CIA/DCI files, Job No. 80B1285A, DCI/McCone, Box 2, Folder 10. "DCI (McCone) Memos for the Record, 1 Jan-5 April 1964."

[100] *Pentagon Papers* (Gravel ed.), Vol. III, p. 41

progress . . . reported a serious and steadily deteriorating situation."[101] On 12 February, the DCI and the Intelligence Community issued SNIE 50-64, "Short-Term Prospects in Southeast Asia," which held that the question at hand was whether the situations in South Vietnam and Laos "may be on the verge of collapse," and which judged that the South Vietnamese "have at best an even chance of withstanding the insurgency threat during the next few weeks or months."[102] On 18 February, Richard Helms, CIA's Deputy Director for Plans, wrote Secretary Rusk that the tide of insurgency in all four corps areas in Vietnam "appears to be going against GVN."[103] On 20 February, CIA Far East chief Bill Colby's briefing for the White House began, "The Viet Cong have taken advantage of the power vacuum . . . in Saigon to score both military and psychological gains in the countryside'; the belief appeared widespread among the Vietnamese that "the tide is running against the government in all areas of the country."[104] And on 29 February, McCone told Secretary McNamara that the outlook in Vietnam was "very bad, and that unless the Khanh government demonstrated an ability for leadership of the nation, we could expect further and perhaps fatal deterioration."[105]

Thanks in part to these CIA assessments, the growing appreciation in Washington of the fragile Vietnam situation led in mid-March 1964 to a landmark White House decision to begin contingency planning, backstage, for selective attacks against the DRV by US air and naval forces. The progression of steps in this direction were the President's decision to

---

[101] According to *Pentagon Papers* (DoD ed.), Book 3, Section IV-B-4, "Phased Withdrawal," p.33. On 10 February, CIA's Executive Director-Comptroller, Lyman B. Kirkpatrick, reported from Saigon his dismay at the unwillingness of South Vietnam's rural population to defend itself against the VC or to support the ARVN's actions against the VC. He also reported that he was "shocked by the number of our (CIA) people and of the military, even those whose job is always to say we are winning, who feel that the tide is against us." He held that "a major factor" in VC successes was "their superior intelligence based on nationwide penetrations and intimidation at all levels." Kirkpatrick report, l0 February 1964. *FRUS, 1964-1968,* Vol. I, pp. 65, 66.
[102] As reproduced in *FRUS,* as above, p. 7l.
[103] As reproduced in *FRUS,* p. 84.
[104] Colby, "DDP/FE Briefing for White House," 20 February l964 (TS/Compartmented). CIA/DDO files, Box 78 - 597, DDO/IIS, Box 1, Folder 8: "Meetings on Vietnam, 1963-Oct. 1964."
[105] McCone, Memorandum, "Discussion with Secretary McNamara and General Taylor this morning concerning our trip to South Vietnam," 29 February l964. (S/Eyes Only). CIA files, as above. McCone recorded that Secretary McNamara asked him for a very careful estimate of the situation in South Vietnam: "What McNamara was saying was that he was looking to us for the basic judgment of probable success or failure of the U.S. effort . . . From what he said I assume that he would use this judgment in formulating his recommendations concerning the future courses of U.S. action, such as staying as is, increasing the effort in South Vietnam along present lines, commit U.S. forces to combat, extending operations to North Vietnam, etc." Mr. McCone's assumption, however, proved unfounded. The logic of Secretary McNamara's subsequent policy recommendations during l964–early l965, the months in which the Johnson administration decided to deepen America's involvement in Vietnam, did not follow from the intelligence judgments given him by the DCI and CIA.

dispatch Secretary McNamara and General Taylor to assess the situation on the ground in Saigon; the President's acceptance on 4 March of the need to make Hanoi accountable for its actions in South Vietnam;[106] the return of McNamara and Taylor from their four-day trip to Saigon; and, based largely on their report of the grim situation there, a formal NSC action on 17 March which raised America's military commitment in Vietnam another notch. McCone was a member of the McNamara-Taylor party, and his pessimism about the Vietnam situation clearly contributed to the draining of the Pentagon leaders' remaining optimism about South Vietnamese conduct of the war.

On 3 March, in preparation for his Vietnam trip, McCone had drafted a gloomy personal appraisal of the situation. He held that many areas in the countryside were being lost to the Viet Cong, with the result that "there is a growing feeling that the VC may be the wave of the future." He complained that intelligence from the field had been spotty: "there has been submersion of bad news and an overstatement of good news"; for the past year, "we have been misinformed about conditions in Vietnam." Then the DCI directly challenged the concept that going North would save the South. In his view, carrying the action to North Vietnam would not guarantee victory in the absence of a strengthened GVN. And if present disruptive trends in South Vietnamese politics continued, bombing the North "would not win the war in South Vietnam and would cause the United States such serious problems in every corner of the world that we should not sanction such an effort."[107] On that same day Major General Krulak, who with McCone had criticized the NIE 53-63 estimators for not being sufficiently upbeat 12 months earlier, now registered a change of heart similar to that of the DCI. On 3 March, in the briefing book he was preparing for McNamara's Saigon trip, Krulak told the Secretary that South Vietnam now faced "the most critical situation in

---

[106]"The President accepted the need for punishing Hanoi without debate, but pointed to some other practical difficulties, particularly the political ones with which he was faced. It is quite apparent that he does not want to lose South Vietnam before next November nor does he want to get the country into war." Maxwell Taylor, Memorandum of a Conversation Between the Joint Chiefs of Staff and the President, Washington, March 4, 1964. *FRUS, 1964-1968*, Vol. I, p.129. At this time, in addition to Walt Rostow, two of the principal champions of the concept of hitting the North were Ambassador Lodge in Saigon, who on 20 February cabled that "various pressures can and should be applied to North Vietnam to cause them to cease and desist from their murderous intrusion into South Vietnam;" and the Joint Chiefs of Staff, who in a formal action on 2 March recommended direct strikes against North Vietnam. Respectively, CIA/IG Report, p. 50; and *Pentagon Papers* (Gravel ed.), Vol. III, p. 120.

[107]McCone, "Memorandum on Vietnam," 3 March 1964. *FRUS*, as above, pp. 122, 124, 125, 126. *FRUS*, n. 120, states that this memo had no designated recipient, but that Assistant Secretary of State William Bundy, for one, had initialed it. Portions of Mr. McCone's memo are also quoted in CIA/IG Report, p. 52.

its nearly 10 years of existence," and that all available evidence pointed to "a steady improvement in the VC's military posture, both quantitatively and qualitatively, throughout 1963 and the first two months of 1964."[108]

In Saigon, McCone received briefings from Station officers which detailed South Vietnam's numerous political and military weaknesses. He did not contest their assessments. He concluded that the United States should stick with General Khanh; that consideration should be given to moving "two or possibly three" of Taiwan's Chinese Nationalist divisions into the southern tip of South Vietnam's delta; that the measures Washington's policymakers were proposing would prove to be "too little too late"; and that in any event, hitting the North would prove unavailing unless accompanied by considerable political improvement in the South.[109] Another champion of using combat forces from Taiwan at the time was DDI Ray Cline, who had recently returned from talks with President Chiang Kai-shek in Taipei and who in early March recommended that Chinese Nationalist armed forces, including an air commando unit, be used in Vietnam.[110] McCone and Cline, however, received no significant backing on this score from senior decisionmakers, who saw numerous drawbacks to the idea.[111]

On 16 March, upon his return from Vietnam, McNamara gave President Johnson a detailed acounting of the fragile scene in Vietnam and offered a number of recommendations for improving the situation. Most of these concerned strengthening the GVN's political and military effectiveness. The Secretary concluded that direct US attacks on the North were premature, but that preparations should go forward that would permit the United States "to be in a position on 30 days' notice to initiate a program of 'Graduated Overt Military Pressure' against North Vietnam."[112] On 17 March the NSC issued National Security Action

---

[108] As quoted in *Pentagon Papers* (Gravel ed.), Vol. III, pp. 46, 47.

[109] CIA/IG Report, pp. 53, 54. See also McCone, Memorandum for McNamara, 14 March 1964, (S), CIA files, Job No. 80B1285A, DCI/McCone, Box 2, Folder 10, "DCI (McCone) Memos for the Record, 1 Jan-5 April 1964," and McCone's comments on McNamara memorandum for the President, 16 March 1964, in Gareth Porter (ed), *Vietnam: The Definitive Documentation of Human Decisions,* Vol II, p. 258.

[110] C/FE memorandum, "Possible GRC Aid to South Vietnam: The Effect of Such Action on the GRC and Chinese Morale," 4 March 1964. (S). CIA files, Box 78-597, DDO/IIS, Box 1, Folder 14: "Vietnam—CIA Papers Prepared by FE Division, 1958-1964."

[111] With policymakers' approval, Chinese Nationalist personnel did serve in Vietnam in certain capacities relating, among others, to covert air supply. The author's personal experience.

[112] The text of Secretary McNamara's report to the President may be found in Porter, Vol II, pp. 249-258; *Pentagon Papers* (Gravel ed.), Vol. III, pp. 499-6510; and *FRUS, 1964-1968*, Vol. I, pp. 153-168. In his report, Secretary McNamara nonetheless held that "Substantial reductions in the number of US military training personnel should be possible before the end of 1965 . . . ." CIA/IG Report, p. 55.

Memorandum 288, in which President Johnson accepted McNamara's recommendations and directed that the creating of a standby capability to bomb the North should "proceed energetically."[113]

Domino Thesis Questioned

"US Objectives in South Vietnam" were listed under that title on 17 March in National Security Action Memorandum 288, in which, inter alia, the National Security Council made the domino thesis an integral part of formal US policy. Unless South Vietnam could be changed into a viable, independent non-Communist state, NSAM 288 asserted, all of Southeast Asia would probably fall under Communist dominance or accommodate to Communist influence. "Even the Philippines would become shaky, and the threat to India on the West, Australia and New Zealand to the South, and Taiwan, Korea, and Japan to the North and East would be greatly increased."[114] The Johnson administration did not bother to ask for a CIA intelligence evaluation of these assumptions until some weeks later—and then ignored the response.

It was the Board of National Estimates, CIA's permanent panel of "wise men," that the White House at length asked to pronounce the analytic judgment on the domino thesis. The loss of Vietnam would of course be a shock, replied the Board on 9 June, but with the possible exception of Cambodia, the rest of East Asia would probably not fall rapidly to Communist control, and there would be much the United States could do to shore up the area.[115] It is noteworthy (1) that the Board called into question one of the primary theses on which US policy and military planning were being based and, by June, briskly executed; (2) that CIA had not been asked for its view of the domino thesis until 10 weeks *after* the NSC had already inscribed it as formal US policy; and (3) that the Board's conclusions had no apparent impact on existing or subsequent policy.

March 1964 closed with new doubts being expressed by the NSC Staff's Michael Forrestal, one of those officials who had rejected the NIE 53-63 draft a year before for being too pessimistic. On 30 March 1964

[113] *Pentagon Papers* (*The New York Times* ed.), pp. 243, 283-285; and *Pentagon Papers* (Gravel ed.), Vol. III, pp. 50-56.

[114] *Pentagon Papers* (*The New York Times* ed.), p. 284.

[115] *Pentagon Papers* (*The New York Times* ed.), p. 254. DDI Ray Cline did not share O/NE's view, having told the DCI in March that "I think the loss of virtually all U.S. prestige and influence in Southeast Asia is likely if a favorable trend does not set in South Vietnam soon." Cline, Memorandum for the Director, "Recommended Actions for South Vietnam," 14 March 1964. (S). *FRUS, 1964-1968*, Vol. I, pp. 146-147. Also, in this memo, written 12 months before the US did commit combat troops in Vietnam, Cline recommended that "a U.S. combat unit (perhaps a battalion landing team)" be committed to insure the security of US personnel "and—implicitly—the Khanh regime's control of the Saigon area."

he wrote his boss, McGeorge Bundy, that "warning indicators" were now flashing, and that "Chet Cooper is completely right. This is a Greek tragedy, and the curtain is slowly descending."[116]

War Gaming Heightens Doubts

The thesis that bombing the North would save the South was examined again in April, this time by a JCS military-political war game titled SIGMA-I-64. CIA and Intelligence Community officers were well represented in all three of the game's teams, Blue, Red, and Control, staffed mostly by lieutenant colonels through brigadier generals and their civilian equivalents. Although the Blue Team fielded some true believers in victory through airpower, the game's posited US escalation did not work: the DRV did not knuckle under to the heightened pressures but counterescalated by pouring more troops into the South. As the game progressed, the military-political situation played out in South Vietnam went from bad to worse, and the United States ended up in a no-win situation, its policy options essentially narrowed to two unpromising alternatives. On the one hand, it could try to seek a military decision by greatly expanding hostilities against the DRV—which SIGMA-I's players judged might risk repeating the Korean experience of massive Chinese intervention. Or, Washington could begin deescalating—which the players held could cost it a marked loss of US credibility and prestige.[117] The thesis of escalated punishment of North Vietnam had again been tested by interagency experts and found wanting.

Two of the CIA officers who participated in the war game, the author and the Deputy Chief of DDP's Far East Division, were so upset by some of SIGMA-I's assumptions and outcomes that they sent DCI McCone a critique that went beyond mere intelligence questions. In their view, the concept that hitting the North would save the South was "highly dubious" because "the principal sources of VC strength and support are indigenous, and even if present DRV direction and support of the VC could be cut off, these would not assure victory in the South." Attacking the North should be considered a supplementary course of action, not a cure-all, and such action could be effective "only if considerable GVN political-military improvement also takes place." Further, they observed,

---

[116]Forrestal, memo to McGeorge Bundy, "South Vietnam," 30 March 1964. (S). *FRUS*, as above, pp. 199, 201.

[117]Robert Johnson, "Escalation Then and Now," pp. 136-137; and Harold P. Ford, "The US Decision to Go Big in Vietnam," *Studies in Intelligence* Vol. 29, No. 1 (Spring 1985), pp. 6-7. (Initially Secret, declassified 27 August 1986). CIA players included the author, O/NE officer Chester L. Cooper, and two DDO officers. One of the senior officers who critiqued SIGMA-I on its last day, Gen. Curtis LeMay, then Air Force Chief of Staff, furiously charged (in the author's presence) that the game had been rigged.

the war game seriously underestimated the impact and influence of adverse public, Congressional, and world opinion: "There would be widespread concern that the U.S. was risking major war, in behalf of a society that did not seem anxious to save itself, and by means not at all certain to effect their desired ends in the South." These officers concluded that "the United States should not move against the DRV blithely, but know beforehand what we may be getting into, military and politically;" unless there is enough military-political potential in the South to make the whole Vietnam effort worthwhile, they concluded, "the U.S. would only be exercising its great, but irrelevant, armed strength."[118]

The war game's failure to validate the thesis that punishing the DRV would save the South failed to derail or even slow the administration's deliberate pace toward a Northern solution. According to available files, the only significant high-level attention to SIGMA-I's negative outcome was given by Under Secretary of State George Ball a few weeks later when he asked Secretary Rusk why the United States was contemplating air action against the North "in the face of a recently played war game that demonstrated the ineffectiveness of such a tactic."[119] Ball's question apparently went unanswered.

Planning for the Northern Option

In April-June, the tempo of the Johnson administration's Vietnam planning rose several more notches with a top-level conclusion that the military situation in the South had deteriorated to the point that the Pentagon's role had to be significantly expanded. Many officials who had been confident of South Vietnamese progress now expressed dismay at the worsening situation. Most significantly, Secretary McNamara now reversed earlier strategic policy by at last canceling plans made under President Kennedy to begin withdrawing US military personnel from Vietnam, and announced that more might have to be sent there. CINC-PAC and the JCS began quietly drawing up folders of bombing targets in North Vietnam. Senior White House, State, and Defense officials held conference after conference, with McCone and Colby present on virtually every occasion, to discuss means of carrying the war to North Vietnam—with never a reference to the conclusions of the earlier Robert Johnson interagency study group and the Sigma-I war game that bombing the North would not work. Other officials began making ready a draft

---

[118]"Comment on the Vietnam War Games, SIGMA-I-64, 6-9 April 1964," 16 April 1964. As cited in Ford, *Studies in Intelligence*, pp. 7-8.
[119]Ball, Letter to Rusk, 31 May 1964. *FRUS, 1964-1968*, Vol. I, p. 404. The files of DCI McCone contain no indication of his reaction to the SIGMA-I wargame nor any record of the critique sent him by two of his officers.

enabling resolution against the day when Congressional approval might be sought. When at this time French President de Gaulle proposed that Vietnam be neutralized, the White House sought to counter de Gaulle by asking Canada to tell Ho Chi Minh that the Johnson administration was prepared to carry the war to the North if it did not markedly cut back its support to the Viet Cong.

One of the clearest examples of policymakers' dismay at this time was Secretary McNamara's private admission, contrary to his continuing public assurances that things would ultimately be well in Vietnam, that the situation there was in fact shaky. As recorded by William Colby, at a meeting with President Johnson and Director McCone on 14 May, McNamara termed the Saigon Country Team "a mess," criticized Ambassador Lodge for keeping COS DeSilva at arm's length, and described Country Team morale as "extremely low" because no direction was being given the counterinsurgency program. He observed that Ambassador Lodge was becoming despondent and had recently stated that, if General Khanh's government should fall, the US should establish a base at Cam Ranh Bay and "run the country." At this 14 May White House meeting, President Johnson confided that his principal concern was American public opinion, given what he considered to be a widening belief that the United States was losing the war and that the administration was pursuing a no-win policy. Johnson told McNamara that the administration must do more but, as recorded by Colby, "he does not know what. . . . He said he does not want to get into a war but he is willing to take some risks if necessary. The overall posture must be improved beyond 'more of the same.'"[120]

Four days later, DCI McCone joined Secretary McNamara and State's William Bundy[121] in telling President Johnson that the situation in Vietnam had become so precarious that the chances were now "at least 50-50" that in the absence of action against North Vietnam, both Vietnam and Laos would "deteriorate by the latter part of this year to a point where they would be very difficult to save." According to a CIA file copy of Bundy's record of this agreement, "a select group" had been working since early March on a "possible sequence of actions to be followed if a

[120]Colby, Memorandum for the Record, "Report by Secretary McNamara-14 May 1964." 14 May 1964. (S). CIA Files, Job No. 80B01258A, DCI/Executive Registry, Box 6, Folder 8. Colby's memo does not indicate what positions, if any, Director McCone took at this Presidential meeting. In any event, the next day, the DCI sent the President a DDI assessment that held that the overall situation in South Vietnam was "extremely fragile," and that if the tide of deterioration were not arrested by the end of 1964, the anti-Communist position in South Vietnam would probably become "untenable." DDI Memorandum, 15 May 1964. *FRUS*, as above, p. 336.

[121]William Bundy, former O/NE and Defense Department officer, and McGeorge Bundy's brother, had replaced Hilsman, with the title of Assistant Secretary of State for East Asia and the Pacific.

decision were taken to hit the North."[122] CIA files do not record whether Bundy told the President that in March that group's intelligence subcommittee had concluded that the Rostow bombing thesis would not work.

During May and June specific clues began to appear as to what the scope of expanded US participation in the war might involve. According to CIA files, a scenario prepared by the State Department dated 23 May recommended that US and South Vietnamese aircraft bomb DRV communication lines, harbors, and industries, and suggested that the use of nuclear weapons be considered in the event Communist China entered the war in force.[123] On 25 May, according to DCI McCone's notes, Secretary McNamara told President Johnson that "any action against North Vietnam must anticipate the commitment of at least seven divisions in Southeast Asia."[124] At a policy conference in Honolulu on 1 and 2 June, according to McCone's account, Secretaries Rusk and McNamara agreed that "we must prepare for extreme contingencies even though we consider them improbable."[125] On 2 June, the Joint Chiefs of Staff recommended that the United States should take "positive, prompt, and meaningful military action" to "accomplish destruction of the North Vietnamese will and capabilities" to support the Communist insurgencies in South Vietnam and Laos.[126] And on 5 June, Ambassador Lodge in Saigon recommended heightened US actions against the DRV: "Not only would screams from the North have a very tonic effect and strengthen morale here; it is also vital to frighten Ho."[127]

All the while DCI McCone was persistently warning policymakers that South Vietnam was in deep trouble. In early May he had told House and Senate intelligence subcommittees that the situation was bleak. On 12 May, he cabled Bill Colby, then in Saigon, that he was "deeply concerned that the situation in South Vietnam may be deteriorating to a greater extent than we realize," and commissioned Colby to check on whether intelligence reporting "is providing proper appreciation of the

---

[122] William P. Bundy, Memorandum for the President, "Possible Action Against North Vietnam." 18 May 1964. As reproduced in CIA/IG Report, p. 60.

[123] W. P. Bundy, Draft Memorandum for the President, "Scenario for Strikes on North Vietnam," 23 May 1964. (TS). CIA files, Job No. 78-597, DDO/ISS, Box 1, Folder 6: "Executive Committee Meetings on Southeast Asia, Sunday, 24 May 1964."

[124] According to McCone's Memorandum for the Record of that Presidential meeting. CIA/IG Report, p. 65.

[125] According to McCone's Memorandum for the Record of that conference. CIA/IG Report, p. 69.

[126] JCS Memorandum to the Secretary of Defense, "Objectives and Courses of Action—Southeast Asia," *FRUS, 1964-1968, Vol. I*, pp. 437-438.

[127] EmbTel 2414. Literally "eyes only" for Rusk and McNamara). *FRUS*, p. 456.

actual situation . . .".[128] McCone reported that at the Honolulu conference of 1-2 June he took exception to certain of the optimistic assessments of the situation in South Vietnam advanced by the new MACV commander, Gen. William Westmoreland, averring instead that there was an "erosion of the will of the people to resist" and that "the downward spiral would continue."[129]

By now McCone shared the belief that the war must be taken to the North, though he differed with some of the military particulars being suggested. As we have seen, on 18 May he had agreed that the South might be lost unless the United States took military action against the North. The following week, at a meeting of the NSC's Executive Committee, 24 May, he had urged that "if we go into North Vietnam we should go in hard and not limit our action to pinpricks."[130] And at the June conference in Honolulu he agreed with Secretaries Rusk and McNamara that the United States must prepare for extreme contingencies.[131]

McCone felt strongly at this time, however, that US airstrikes against the North would suffice to contain and deter the enemy and that US ground forces should not be committed in the South. After a meeting with the President and the Secretary of Defense on 25 May, he wrote that he had differed sharply with McNamara's assessment that any US action against the DRV should anticipate the commitment of at least seven divisions in Southeast Asia. "I took issue with this point," wrote McCone, because he felt that air attacks would be more decisive and possibly conclusive. He argued that "we had better forget" the idea of sending US troops to Vietnam because "the American people and Congress would not support such an action under any conditions."[132] Contrary to McCone's expectation, as we will see, the President did receive widespread public support, at least for some months, when in early 1965 he at last made his decision to dispatch combat troops to Vietnam.

[128] DIR 20682 to Saigon, as reproduced in CIA/IG Report, p.58. In responding, Colby felt that what needed special improvement was "frequent and objective" appraisals of the data being collected. He criticized US policy for being swamped in details at the expense of overall vision: "I am concerned primarily at the tendency toward chasing wills-of-the-wisp rather than cleaving firmly to a fundamental strategy for this war." Colby, SAIG 6316, 13 May 1964, as reproduced in CIA/IG Report, p. 59.

[129] According to McCone's Memorandum for the Record of this conference. CIA/IG Report, p.69. Also in "Summary Record of Meetings, Honolulu, June 2, 1964, 8:30-11:50 a.m. and 2:15-4 p.m." *FRUS*, as above, p. 429.

[130] Bromley Smith, Summary Record of that meeting. *FRUS*, p. 370.

[131] According to McCone's notes of that conference. CIA/IG Report, p. 69.

[132] According to McCone's notes of that meeting. CIA/IG Report, p. 65. It should be noted that available documents indicate that during these weeks there were differences of emphasis among the policymakers as well. While agreeing with the general concept of punishing the North, Dean Rusk, Maxwell Taylor, George Ball, and McGeorge Bundy took more moderate positions on the details than did some of their colleagues.

Although McCone had long since come around to the more pessimistic views of Vietnam held by his staff, the months of May through July 1964 saw some distinct gaps open up between these officers and the Director over how to save the situation. Whereas he now felt that this could best be accomplished by carrying the war to the North, most of his Vietnam specialists—in the DDP, DDI, O/NE, and elsewhere—continued to insist, as they had for some time, that the war had to be won in the South through substantially improved GVN political-military performance.

On 21 May, just three days after DCI McCone had joined McNamara and Bill Bundy in telling the President that South Vietnam might be lost unless the United States went North, CIA officers Bill Colby and Chet Cooper championed an alternative course, one they termed "massive counterinsurgency" in the South.[133] Meanwhile, on 27 May O/NE prepared a draft memorandum for the United States Intelligence Board (USIB) addressing McNamara's recommended deployment of seven US divisions to Southeast Asia. This, it was argued, would "tend to convey precisely what it was not supposed to, that the US was resolved to transform the struggle over South Vietnam into a war against North Vietnam in which the survival of the DRV regime would be at stake." Furthermore, according to O/NE, the expanded US commitment "would provoke a generally more adverse world reaction" than previous NIEs had indicated; meanwhile, the enemy would not cease and desist.[134]

The Johnson administration received additional unwelcome views from CIA when on 8 June, O/NE Board member Willard Matthias ventured to surmise that the situation in South Vietnam had so deteriorated that "some kind of negotiated settlement based upon neutralization" might develop in the world. (This senior CIA officer's judgment would precipitate a flap in August when his heresy was leaked to the press.)[135] On the same day the CIA General Counsel (1) advised the DCI that there

---

[133] Memorandum by William E. Colby and Chester L. Cooper, "A Program for Laos and South Vietnam." CIA/IG Report, p. 62.

[134] O/NE, Draft Memorandum for the USIB, "New Estimative Questions Concerning US Courses of Action re Vietnam," 27 May 1964 (S) . CIA files, Job No. 78-597, DDO/ISS, Box 1, Folder 6: "Executive Committee Meetings on Southeast Asia, Sunday, 24 May 1964." Also, CIA/IG Report, p. 67. The views expressed in that memo were not O/NE's alone: a Note on the first page of the study explained that it had been prepared "with the assistance of a special panel of USIB representatives (Senior Members of DIA and INR)."

[135] CIA/IG Report, p. 70; *The New York Times*, 23 August 1964; and Matthias, to author, 12 February and 20 April 1990. Matthias's point about possible neutralization was part of an NIE study he had been commissioned to draft on the world situation. According to Matthias, at McCone's request O/NE declassified this draft so that the Director could take it up to Gettysburg and show it to ex-President Eisenhower. Even though CIA subsequently classified the draft "US Government Only," someone leaked it to the press, the *Chicago Tribune* in the first instance. Matthias, to author, 12 February 1990.

was "a serious domestic problem in [the administration's] taking increasingly militant steps without any specific congressional approval," and (2) seconded the DCI's earlier expressed view that the President would not be able to obtain a meaningful joint resolution from the Congress.[136] And it was on the next day that O/NE questioned the embrace the NSC had given the domino thesis in March.[137]

In July, developments in South Vietnam seemed to strengthen the case for hitting the Vietnamese Communists harder and more directly. On 24 July, McCone cautioned President Johnson that the Viet Cong were growing stronger and the situation increasingly critical.[138] Confirming McCone's analysis, Saigon Station Chief Peer DeSilva reported two days later that a crisis appeared at hand, "possibly involving the will of the present leadership to continue the war." General Khanh now purported to believe that war weariness in the South had reached such an acute state that "heroic new measures, beyond the borders of South Vietnam" were now necessary to bring any prospect of victory.[139] In a parallel cable, the new Ambassador in Saigon, Gen. Maxwell Taylor, reported that Khanh had apparently come to believe the Viet Cong could not be defeated by counterinsurgency means alone, and therefore he had launched a deliberate campaign to get the United States to "march North." Taylor added that if Khanh and his colleagues were not successful in this effort, strong pressures might develop within the GVN to seek a negotiated settlement: "there are signs that this possibility cannot be excluded . . ."[140] The Ambassador requested that he be authorized to tell

---

[136] Memorandum for the DCI, "Legal Aspects of the Southeast Asia Situation," 8 June 1964. CIA/IG Report, p. 71.

[137] The NSC and CIA positions are contrasted on p. 56 above; see citations from O/NE's dissent on p. 215-216 below. The full text of O/NE's dissent on the domino thesis is given in *FRUS, 1964-1968*, Vol. I, pp. 484-487. Also, CIA/IG Report, p. 71. O/NE had long questioned the validity of the domino thesis and continued so to do. On 12 September 1967, for example, DCI Richard Helms sent President Johnson a sharp critique of that concept, written by O/NE Board member (and future BNE Chairman) John Huizenga (S). CIA Files, Job No. 80B01285A, Box 11, DCI/Helms, Folder 4: "1 Aug-31 Dec '67."

[138] McCone, Memorandum for the Record, "Meeting with the President—11:15 a.m., 24 July 1964," 24 July 1964. (S/Eyes Only). CIA files, Job No. 80B01258A, DCI/Executive Registry, Box 6, Folder 9. On that occasion McCone asked President Johnson for greater opportunity to "sit down with him occasionally to exchange views on matters of importance to him" because through the written word, the President was not getting the full benefit of the views and judgments of what McCone told him were "the most competent intelligence experts and analysts that existed anywhere in the world . . . in my experience in many departments in government and in industry I had never encountered as high a level of competence or intellectual capability as I found in the CIA."

[139] SAIG 7680, 25 July 1964. CIA/IG Report, p. 74.

[140] EmbTel 213 (Flash precedence), 25 July 1964. *FRUS, 1964-1968, Vol. I*, pp. 563, 566. Also, CIA/IG Report, p. 74.

Khanh that although the idea of expanding hostilities beyond South Vietnam "has not been seriously discussed up to now . . . the time has come for giving the matter a thorough [joint] analysis."[141]

Washington's answer was a cautious OK. Following Presidential conferences on 25 July, attended by DDCI Carter and C/FE Colby, Ambassador Taylor was instructed that joint planning should go forward focused primarily on improving counterinsurgency efforts in the South, but stopping short for the moment of measures involving overt US military action against the North.[142] At the same time, the White House gave CIA the high-priority task of estimating Communist reactions to various new courses of action which might include "selected air missions using non-US unmarked aircraft against prime military targets" in the DRV.[143] Thus, just three months before the November Presidential election, the Johnson administration was preparing contingency plans for expanding US participation in the war but was keeping both the plans and the act of planning quiet.

Within a week's time, events in the Gulf of Tonkin changed the situation. In early August, in response to what were perceived as attacks by DRV patrol boats on the USS Maddox and the USS Turner Joy, US Navy planes bombed military targets along 100 miles of North Vietnam's coastline, and President Johnson had whiffed his long-prepared Joint Resolution through the Congress.[144]

August-October 1964 saw more heated backstage policy debate on whether to "go North," principally between the Joint Chiefs of Staff and the Secretary of Defense. The JCS maintained that only airstrikes against the North could save the South; others who held similar views included MACV General Westmoreland, Secretary of State Rusk, McGeorge Bundy, and Walt Rostow. By contrast, McNamara insisted that the prime requirement remained stability in the South, and that bombing the North would not ensure that result; weighing in with similar arguments were Ambassador Maxwell Taylor and his Saigon country team, the Pentagon's International Security Affairs bureau, and State's William Bundy. These conflicting arguments were aired during a September-October interagency policy examination led by DoD/ISA, which specifically

[141] EmbTel 214 (Flash) 25 July 1964. *FRUS*, as above, pp. 566-568. Also, CIA/IG Report, p. 75.
[142] DepTel 253 (Flash), State-Defense message, 25 July 1964, and DepTel 254, Joint State—AID message, 25 July 1965. *FRUS*, as above, pp. 569-571, 571-573. Also, CIA/IG Report, p. 76.
[143] Memorandum, McCone to the President, "Probable Communist Reactions to Certain US or US-Sponsored Courses of Action in Vietnam and Laos," 28 July 1964. *FRUS*, as above, pp. 585-587. Also, Sherman Kent memorandum to the DCI, same subject, 26 July 1964. CIA/IG Report, p. 77.
[144] In requesting the Joint Resolution, which won overwhelming Congressional support, Johnson administration officers did not reveal that shortly before the attacks on our destroyers, covertly operated South Vietnamese gunboats had raided North Vietnamese islands in the general vicinity.

revisited Walt Rostow's thesis that bombing the North would save the South.[145] The President and his senior advisers, who might have entered or refereed the debate, were besieged at this time by more pressing developments external to Vietnam, chief among them the fall of Soviet Premier Khrushchev, Communist China's detonation of a nuclear device, crises in Africa, and—not least—President Johnson's race against what he termed "the war candidate," Senator Barry Goldwater.

Although they were not major participants in the Vietnam strategy debates, DCI McCone and his officers did not hesitate to offer numerous judgments concerning related events and policy issues. On 4 August, at the height of the argument over how to respond to the Tonkin Gulf attacks, McCone told the President and the NSC that those attacks had been a defensive reaction by the North Vietnamese to prior covert gunboat raids (part of OPLAN 34A) on North Vietnamese islands: "They are responding out of pride and on the basis of defense considerations." In the DCI's view, the North Vietnamese attacks did not "represent a deliberate decision to provoke or accept a major escalation of the Vietnamese war," but were a signal to the United States that Hanoi was determined to continue the war and was "raising the ante."[146] On 9 September, McCone told Ambassador Taylor that the Intelligence Community now considered the situation in the South so fragile that it was doubtful national unity could be established there. The DCI in addition judged that the DRV would match any introduction of US ground forces in the South: "The Communists would pin our units down by matching them with equal or superior force."[147] Also on 9 September, McCone participated in a Presidential conference on Vietnam, where he remarked that CIA was "very gravely concerned" about the situation in the South. Then, contrary to views his Board of National Estimates had been maintaining for some time, McCone held that the loss of Vietnam would lead, dominolike, to the loss of Southeast Asia.[148] Later in September, DDCI Carter told Secretaries Rusk and McNamara that the situation in Vietnam was deteriorating "quite rapidly," and that there was some doubt that the GVN could hold on in the face of internal disintegration and increasing Viet Cong pressures.[149]

---

[145] *Pentagon Papers* (Gravel ed.), Vol. III, pp. 200-206.

[146] Bromley Smith, Summary Notes of the 538th Meeting of the National Security Council, Washington, August 4, 1964, 6:15-6:40 p.m, (For the President Only). *FRUS, 1964-1968*, Vol I, p. 6ll.

[147] Talking paper on South Vietnam, 9 September 1964. (S/Eyes Only); and attached Memorandum for the Record by William E. Colby, "Meeting with Ambassador Taylor, 9 September 1964," 10 September 1964. (S/Eyes Only). CIA files, Job No. 78-597, DDO/ISS, Box 1, Folder 8.

[148] McGeorge Bundy, "Memorandum of a Meeting, White House, Washington, September 9, 1964, ll a.m." *FRUS, 1964-1968, Vol. I*, pp. 750, 752-753; and Lyndon Johnson, *The Vantage Point*, p. 120.

[149] Carter, "Summary," 25 September 1964, (S); and attached Memorandum for the Record by Robert J. Myers, "Meeting on Possible Action to Support South Vietnam, 25 September 1964," 25 September 1964, (S). CIA files, Job No. 78-597, DDO/ISS, Box 1, Folder 8.

During the busy weeks of August-October, the Intelligence Community estimators were fed a series of Vietnam strategy options to ponder, and they responded with some new judgments that strengthened the logic that extraordinary new policy measures were necessary. On 1 October, SNIE 53-2-64 held that the outlook among the South Vietnamese was one of "increasing defeatism, paralysis of leadership, friction with Americans, exploration of possible lines of political accommodation with the other side, and a general petering out of the war effort."[150] SNIE 10-3-64 of 9 October, written specifically to address the Rostow thesis, muted previous CIA skepticism and judged that the North Vietnamese, if subjected to a program of gradually increasing US air attacks, would probably suspend military attacks in the South temporarily but would renew the insurgency there at a later date. The State Department's Bureau of Intelligence and Research dissented from this conclusion, contending that it was more likely Hanoi's reaction would be to raise the tempo of Communist attacks in South Vietnam. As events would prove before October was over, and as Gen. Bruce Palmer later wrote, "the SNIE was dead wrong while INR was right on the money."[151]

C/FE Colby, participating in many policy forums during these weeks, was also very pessimistic about the South's situation. On 14 October, for example, he told the White House's Mike Forrestal that the Viet Cong's regular forces had "grown considerably," that GVN political fragmentation was evident not only in Saigon but also in the countryside, and that local GVN authorities lacked the force to deal with Viet Cong attacks.[152] In making these judgments, however, Colby did not offer his own policy recommendations.

Not so O/NE officer George A. Carver. Shortly after the Gulf of Tonkin attacks, for example, he gave DCI McCone a sharp critique of the modest reprisals then being proposed by Assistant Secretary of State William Bundy.[153] Carver argued that the proposed measures were not likely to have much effect on the situation, North or South. Later he sent Bundy a similar critique, noting for the record that it had not been seen or approved by any member of the Board of National Estimates and that "Bundy understands it is for his personal use only."[154]

[150]*FRUS*, as above, p. 806. *The Pentagon Papers* state that that SNIE caused the policy debate picture to become "even gloomier." (Gravel ed.), Vol. III, p. 206.

[151] Bruce Palmer, "US Intelligence and Vietnam," pp. 33-34.

[152] Colby, Memorandum for the Record, "Forrestal Committee Meeting, 14 October 1964." (S). CIA files, Job No. 78-597, Box 2, Folder: "Sullivan Meetings II, May 1964-Dec 1964."

[153] Carver and Edward A. Hauck, Memorandum for the Director, "Comment on Assistant Secretary William P. Bundy's 13 August 1964 Memorandum, 'Next Course of Action in Southeast Asia,'" 14 August 1964. (TS). CIA Files, Job No. 80R1720R, O/D/NFAC, Box 5, "GAC Files (SAVA-NIO)," Folder 1.

[154] Carver memorandum, 31 August 1964. Same CIA file as above.

More War-Gaming, More Skepticism

In September 1964, Johnson administration officers tested the Rostow thesis once more in a second JCS political-military war game, SIGMA II. Here the players for the most part were not working-level officers, but JCS Chief Earle Wheeler, Gen. Curtis LeMay, Deputy Secretary of Defense Cyrus Vance, McGeorge Bundy, and other principals. But, like its predecessor war game, SIGMA II ended up a stalemate, US bombing of the North not having brought victory nearer. Robert J. Myers, one of CIA's participants in SIGMA II, thereafter made a sharp critique of US policy, holding that the war game had illustrated that bombing the North would have only limited effect, and that the deployment of up to five US divisions in Southeast Asia "would not materially change the situation." Given the results of SIGMA II, Myers drew a searing conclusion: if bombing the North would not work, he wrote, and if the United States was reluctant to use nuclear weapons in Vietnam, then "there is a grave question of how the US is supposed to win the type of war being fought on the ground by large numbers of combat forces of the enemy deployed in small units and spurred by a very able political and propaganda program."[155]

Like the SIGMA I war game played earlier in 1964, however, SIGMA II and its depressing outcome had no apparent dampening effect on senior decisionmakers' certainty that the way to save South Vietnam was to bomb the North and employ US combat forces in the South. Strategists continued their contingency planning toward those ends as if the outcome of SIGMA II (plus SIGMA I and Robert Johnson's earlier NSC working group study) had not occurred. The realism of SIGMA II would, however, get an early confirmation: the officer playing the role of the President committed a US Marine expeditionary force to South Vietnam's defense on 26 February 1965 of the game's calendar. President Johnson did send just such a Marine force on the actual date of 8 March 1965, only 10 days later than in the war game.[156] According to Walt Elder, McCone's former Special Assistant, the DCI participated in only one session of Sigma II because he "hated all war games"; on this one occasion he went out of "innate snobbery, when he learned that the other seniors would be there."[157]

[155] Myers, Memorandum for the Record, "Comments on SIGMA II - South Vietnam War Game, 2-17 September 1964," 1 October 1964. (S). CIA files, Job No. 78-3041/DDO/ISS/IPG, Box 1, Folder 9.

[156] Sigma II is discussed by several authors, among them Thomas B. Allen, "Twilight Zone at the Pentagon," *MHQ: The Quarterly Journal of Military History*, Vol. II No. 2 (Winter 1990), p.52; Halberstam, *The Best and the Brightest*, p.463; and Stanley Karnow—who characterizes SIGMA II's outcome as "depressing: no amount of American pressure could stop the Communists. . ." *Vietnam: A History*, pp. 399-400.

[157] Elder, to author, 25 June 1990.

In the meantime, the slide toward escalation was again being tilted by dramatic events in the field: in their most devastating raid to date, on 1 November the Viet Cong destroyed five B-57 bombers at the Bien Hoa airfield near Saigon and damaged eight more; four Americans were killed and many others wounded. The Joint Chiefs of Staff immediately recommended "a prompt and strong response," including US air strikes on the DRV.[158] Instead of accepting these recommendations for reprisal on the eve of the US presidential election, President Johnson commissioned a special NSC Working Group, headed by Assistant Secretary of State Bill Bundy, to draw up and evaluate various political and military options for direct action against North Vietnam.[159] Their milestone mandate was not to determine whether the United States should expand its participation in the war, but to recommend how to do it.

Shortly following President Johnson's landslide election victory, the Bundy group offered up three theoretical options for US air action against the DRV: (1) reprisal strikes; (2) a "fast squeeze" program of sudden, severe, intensive bombing; and (3) a "slow squeeze" option of graduated airstrikes. The "slow squeeze" option was essentially the course the United States employed when it began systematically to bomb the DRV some weeks later.

The NSC-commissioned Bundy exercise provides a relevant gauge of the influence—or the lack thereof—that intelligence had on Vietnam policymaking. Basing their views on existing National Estimates, the panel of intelligence officers within the Bundy group judged that bombing the North would probably not work; it would not impel Hanoi to lessen its direction and support of the Viet Cong's war effort.[160]

---

[158] *Pentagon Papers* (*The New York Times* ed.), pp. 308, 320-321. Ambassador Taylor, viewing the VC attack as "a deliberate act of escalation and a change of the [war's] ground rules," also recommended a reprisal attack on a DRV target. EmbTel 1357 (Flash), 1 November 1964. *FRUS, 1964-1968*, Vol. I, p. 873.

[159] On 1 November, in a State cable "Literally eyes only Ambassador from Secretary," Rusk explained that in weighing Taylor's arguments for immediate retaliation, "we are inevitably affected by election timing. Quick retaliation could easily be attacked as election device here . . ." DepTel 979 (Immediate). *FRUS*, as above, p. 878.

[160] The author was CIA's representative to this NSC Working Group (and the chairman of its intelligence panel). The Bundy exercise is treated by numerous authors, among them *FRUS, 1964-1968*, pp. 882-883, 914-929; *Pentagon Papers* (Gravel ed.), Vol. III, pp. 210-215, 645-655; Halberstam, *The Best and the Brightest*, pp. 501-502; Karnow, *Vietnam, A History*, pp. 403-404; Larry E. Cable, *Conflict of Myths: The Development of American Counter-insurgency Doctrine and the Vietnam War* (New York: New York University Press, 1986), pp. 237-238; Robert L. Gallucci, *Neither Peace Nor Honor: The Politics of American Military Policy in Vietnam* (Baltimore: Johns Hopkins University Press, 1975, pp. 41-45; Col. Dave R. Palmer, *Summons of the Trumpet: U.S.-Vietnam in Perspective* (San Francisco: Presidio Press, 1978), pp. 75-77; R. B. Smith, *An International History of the Vietnam War: The Kennedy Strategy* (New York: St. Martin's Press, 1985), Vol. II, pp. 329-332; and Harold P. Ford, Memorandum for the Director, "Comment on the (Bundy) Vietnam Working Group Papers," 21 November 1964. (TS/Sensitive). CIA files, Job No. 80B01285A, Box 3, DCI/McCone, Folder 15.

Several considerations produced this skepticism. First, these officers argued that Hanoi's leaders, in launching and maintaining their war effort, had made a fundamental estimate that the difficulties facing the United States were "so great that US will and ability to maintain resistance in that area can be gradually eroded—without running high risks that the US would wreak heavy destruction on the DRV or Communist China."

Second, although the intelligence panel recognized that North Vietnam's leaders were "acutely and nervously aware" that their transportation system and industrial plant were vulnerable to attack, the DRV's economy was "overwhelmingly agricultural and to a large extent decentralized in a myriad of more or less economically self-sufficient villages." Hence, even though US bombing was expected to cripple North Vietnamese industry, seriously restrict its military capabilities, and to a lesser extent degrade Hanoi's capabilities to support guerrilla war in South Vietnam and Laos, it would probably not have a "crucial effect on the daily lives of the overwhelming majority of the North Vietnam population." Nor would the posited US bombing be likely to create unmanageable control problems or cause Hanoi's leaders to shrink from suffering some damage in the course of a test of wills with the United States.

Third, the intelligence panel concluded that Hanoi "probably believes that considerable international pressure" would develop against a US policy of expanding the war to the North, and that negative world opinion "might impel the US to relax its attacks and bring the US to an international conference on Vietnam."[161]

According to CIA files, one of the issues raised in the course of the NSC Working Group's study was whether under certain circumstances the United States should use nuclear weapons. By personal memo Chairman William Bundy quietly asked two of his group members to consult with their principals on whether, in the event there were extreme Communist reactions to a new course of punishing the DRV, the United States might be compelled "to choose between sharp territorial losses or even defeat on the ground, or the use of at least tactical nuclear weapons." Bundy himself held that such US action would have "catastrophic"

---

[161] The text of the Bundy group's intelligence panel is given in full in *Pentagon Papers* (Gravel ed.), Vol. III, pp. 651-656. As characterized by Stanley Karnow, "The Bundy group's intelligence expert [pointed out that the Viet Cong] would carry on the insurgency even if North Vietnam were 'severely damaged' by U.S. bombing. He saw no early end to the war." Karnow, *Vietnam: A History*, p. 403. In his *In Retrospect*, Robert McNamara discusses part of this dissent by the Bundy group's interagency intelligence panel, but misrepresents its source. He states that the dissent was a "CIA" view only, and cites as his source the *Pentagon Papers* (Gravel ed.), Vol. III, p. 651, whereas that Gravel edition citation in fact reads "*NSC Working Group on Vietnam . . .*" McNamara, *In Retrospect*, pp. 162, 367.

consequences, and the Working Group, per se, did not pursue the question or report on it.[162] That this extreme issue was raised nonetheless attests to both the quandary US policy faced at the time and the depth of Bundy's probing.

Intelligence Panel Disregarded

In the end, the views of the Bundy group's intelligence panel failed to carry any weight when the final policy decisions were made. For one thing, not all the NSC Working Group's members, especially the representatives of the JCS, shared the intelligence panel's skeptical view of the efficacy of going North. And when President Johnson met with his principal advisers on 19 November for a progress report on the Bundy group's efforts, Rusk, McNamara, and Bundy himself refrained from mentioning the doubts the group's intelligence officers had raised. Two days later, moreover, when the NSC Working Group's final report was passed upwards, it bore no indication that its intelligence officers had dissented. Once again, senior policy advisers had brushed aside intelligence judgments they found uncongenial or unlikely to sell.[163]

The NSC Working Group's examination of the Rostow thesis proved to be Washington's last testing of the premise that drastically expanding US participation in the war would turn the tide, although debate continued among the President and his senior advisers through the waning weeks of 1964.

On 16 November, for example, Walt Rostow stressed that the central purpose of bombing the DRV should be the sending of a signal to Hanoi that the US is "ready and able to meet any level of escalation" the North Vietnamese might mount in response.[164] The Joint Chiefs of Staff were concerned especially with the domino consequences of South Vietnam's fall: in a memo dated 23 November they warned McNamara that its loss

---

[162] Bundy, Memorandum for John McNaughton (DoD/ISA) and Harold Ford (CIA), "Attached Additional Point Under Section VI," 13 November 1964. (TS/Eyes Only). CIA files, Job No. 80T01629R, O/NFAC, Box 3, "SAVA Policy Files," Folder 4: "Sullivan/Bundy Working Group on VN - Nov 1964." In his cover note Bundy explained that "I am sending this page only to you two, for your exclusive use with your principals. It is the sort of question that should come up only in the very smallest top-level groups, but I do think we should face it and see whether we agree with the viewpoint I have tried to express."

[163] James Thomson, Memorandum for the Record of a Meeting, White House, Washington, November 19, 1964, 12:30 p.m., "Vietnam Item, Meeting with the President." *FRUS, 1964-1968, Vol I*, pp. 914-916; and William Bundy and John McNaughton, Paper Presented by the National Security Council Working Group, "Courses of Action in Southeast Asia," 21 November 1964. *FRUS*, pp. 916-929. Thomson's account of the Presidential meeting on 19 November lists John McCone as being one of the participants. *FRUS*, p. 914.

[164] Rostow, Memorandum for Secretary of Defense McNamara, "Military Dispositions and Political Signals." (Personal). *FRUS*, pp. 906-907.

would weaken India, isolate Australia and New Zealand, undermine US prestige and influence throughout the world, and encourage the Communists to extend their "wars of national liberation" into new areas.[165] In late November, Gen. Maxwell Taylor made a flying visit from his post as Ambassador to Saigon to warn that "we are playing a losing game in South Viet-Nam," that it was "high time" we changed course, and that the United States should launch "immediate and automatic reprisals" against the DRV in the event of further enemy atrocities—but only after prior steps had been taken to shore up the security position of Americans in South Vietnam.[166] In December, McGeorge Bundy struck a fairly cautious note in holding that "No matter which course is taken, it seems likely to us that we face years of involvement in South Vietnam. . . . We do not want a big war out there," but neither do "we intend to back out of a l0-year-long commitment."[167]

Enemy saboteurs came close to provoking major US reprisals against the DRV when they bombed an American officers' billet (the Brinks Hotel) in Saigon on Christmas eve. President Johnson made a temporizing response to the many recommendations from the US military and the Saigon Embassy that the United States retaliate strongly. He spelled out his concerns in a 30 December cable to Ambassador Taylor. Emphasizing that he was especially concerned about protecting Americans in Vietnam from a concentrated VC attack against them, a threat the Intelligence Community had told him was the most likely enemy reaction to a US reprisal against DRV targets, Johnson explained: "Every time I get a military recommendation it seems to me that it calls for large-scale bombing. I have never felt that this war will be won from the air." In his view, what was needed was a larger and stronger US force on the ground: "We have been building our strength to fight this kind of war ever since l961, and I myself am ready to substantially increase the number of Americans in Vietnam if it is necessary to provide this kind of fighting force against the Viet Cong."[168]

[165]"A Strategic Evaluation," Appendix A to Memorandum, Earle G. Wheeler, "Courses of Action in Southeast Asia." (TS/Sensitive). CIA files, Job No. 80B01285A, Box 3, Folder 15: "DCI (McCone) Vietnam, 01 Nov–30 Nov 1964."

[166]Taylor, Memorandum (which he hand-carried to Washington), "The Current Situation in South Viet-Nam—November 1964." (TS). CIA files and folder, as above; and *FRUS*, as above, pp. 948-953.

[167]Bundy, Memorandum to the President, l6 December l964. Enclosure to letter from President Johnson to Senator Mike Mansfield, l7 December, in which LBJ states that he had asked Bundy to comment on a letter the Senator had sent to the President criticizing the US drift toward escalation. *FRUS*, pp. l0l0-l0ll.

[168]CAP 64375, Telegram from the President to the Ambassador in Vietnam. *FRUS*, pp. l057-l059.

This policy debate about whether to expand the war and, if so, how, was again rudely interrupted—and at last decided—by a shattering Viet Cong attack on US installations at Pleiku in central South Vietnam, 7 February 1965. That attack killed eight Americans, wounded l09, and damaged numerous aircraft. A significant influence upon the policy debate that ensued was the fact that President Johnson's Special Assistant for National Security Affairs, McGeorge Bundy, happened just then to be visiting South Vietnam—his first visit, incidentally, to East Asia—at the same time as by coincidence Soviet Premier Aleksei Kosygin was visiting Hanoi. Four days prior to that attack, DCI McCone had told President Johnson that Kosygin would shortly be visiting the DRV and that this signalled a more active Soviet policy in Southeast Asia. According to Johnson's later account, McCone told him on this occasion, 3 February, that the Soviet leaders "may have concluded" that Hanoi was about to win the war in Vietnam and had accordingly decided to move in to share credit for the DRV's anticipated victory. Therefore, McCone held, Moscow would probably give Hanoi greatly increased economic and military aid, including antiaircraft missiles, and would encourage Hanoi to step up its subversion of the South.[169]

In Saigon, McGeorge Bundy immediately telephoned Washington that the Viet Cong, in collusion with Soviet Premier Kosygin, had "thrown down the gauntlet," and recommended that the United States retaliate at once against the DRV. Bundy was not "losing his cool," according to Chester Cooper, an NSC staff officer and former senior O/NE official who at the time was accompanying Bundy. On the day before the Pleiku attacks Cooper and Bundy, assisted by the Pentagon's John McNaughton and State's Alexis Johnson, had drafted a recommendation that US forces retaliate against North Vietnam. As Cooper later characterized that draft, "You just couldn't start bombing North Vietnam *de novo*," what was required was a Communist act "so atrocious" that it would justify the new US course; in the meantime, "We would take our lumps until something very dramatic and very obscene happened."[170] Bundy and his colleagues had had to wait only one day.[171]

[169] Lyndon Johnson, *The Vantage Point*, pp. 123-124.
[170] Cooper, statement to University of Texas oral history program, August 1969. Copy on file in History Staff.
[171] Their pre-Pleiku draft, emphasizing the "grim" prospect in Vietnam and the "astonishing" energy and persistence of the Viet Cong, recommended that the United States adopt a policy of "sustained reprisal" that would allow it to "speak in Vietnam on many topics and in many ways, with growing force and effectiveness." Porter, Vol. II, pp.349-357. See also Gibbons, Part III, pp. 60-62; Karnow, *Vietnam: A History*, pp. 4ll-4l3; Halberstam, *The Best and the Brightest*, pp. 520-52l; and Chester Cooper, *The Lost Crusade: America in Vietnam*, pp.256-259. In these pages, Cooper states that in Saigon he and Bundy learned at the time that the Viet Cong "held the initiative throughout much of the Vietnamese countryside. . . and were roaming at will around the outskirts of the capital. . ."

In recommending that US forces strike North Vietnam, McGeorge Bundy may not have lost his cool, but his assumption that Pleiku was a carefully timed and orchestrated Communist provocation has remained open to doubt. Among the doubters is George Allen, at the time a senior CIA analyst in the Saigon Station: "I never met anyone who shared Bundy's view that the Pleiku incident was deliberately arranged to coincide with his visit and with that of Kosygin to Hanoi." Allen bases his skepticism in part on the testimony of a VC sapper taken prisoner at Pleiku, who disclosed that he and his party had been rehearsing the attack for 100 days before they struck. Allen noted, "Not even Bundy knew at that time that he would be visiting Saigon in February."[172]

Bombing of North Begins

By a month's time following the Pleiku attack and a subsequent VC attack on a US base at Qui Nhon on 10 February, the die had been cast. By 9 March, US and South Vietnamese planes were bombing targets in North Vietnam, 3,500 Marines had landed at Danang "to protect its perimeter," many more US troops were in process of being committed to combat operations, and the policy debate had narrowed largely to ways and means of winning what had now become essentially a US war. We had at last gone big in Vietnam.

Skepticism at CIA

In the months just prior to and immediately following this escalation, CIA provided decisionmakers a steady flow of intelligence data, while O/NE analysts calculated the probable reactions of North Vietnamese, Chinese Communist, Soviet, and Free World governments tailored to this and that theoretical US course of action; for this latter purpose, policy planners served up a series of graduated or alternative strategies to O/NE. While this exercise proceeded, and perhaps inspired by it, certain CIA officers also submitted unsolicited opinions on whether or not to expand the war and, if so, how to do it. Their skeptical offerings, which went beyond intelligence matters, were by now heretical. Though differing in focus and emphasis, these officers' views revealed a common, widely held doubt within the Agency that bombing the North would, by itself, do much to improve the US-GVN situation.

For example, on 5 November 1964, C/FE Bill Colby sent State's Bill Bundy and the White House's Mike Forrestal a private think piece on a possible negotiated solution in Vietnam. Citing as a model the successful modus vivendi that had recently been reached with the Communists in

---

[172] Allen, "The Indochina Wars," pp. 232-233.

Laos, Colby suggested that Washington consider a somewhat similar solution to the stalemated situation in Vietnam. He proposed that Laotian Prince Souvanna Phouma and Cambodian Prince Sihanouk lead a conference in which Saigon's General Khanh and Hanoi's Ho Chi Minh would seek to end hostilities in Vietnam and so avoid an expanded war that might draw their people into a major US-Chinese Communist confrontation.[173]

In late November, DDI Ray Cline raised his own doubts about the efficacy of bombing the North. Offering DCI McCone certain propositions discerned "out of the fog of medieval scholasticism" in which the Vietnam policy debate was being conducted, Cline judged that US bombing would at best buy time for the GVN, but "would not in and of itself" ensure the creation of a stable and effective South Vietnam. Cline did consider the chances "better than even" that Hanoi would "intensify its efforts to negotiate on the best terms available," but only in the event the United States had taken "extreme" military actions against the DRV.[174]

The chief of FE Division's Vietnam-Cambodia Branch minced no words in also criticizing the momentum toward bombing the North. In his view, volunteered on 19 November, military action of this kind would be a "bankrupt" move, an admission of unwillingness to "engage ourselves other than in a military fashion in a struggle to establish the proper condition of man in the modern world." Victory could not be gained in Vietnam or in other troubled areas of the world by "rockets and bombs and napalm."[175] Saigon COS DeSilva also doubted the wisdom of bombing the North: according to journalist David Halberstam, in late 1964 DeSilva "accurately forecast that the bombing would have virtually no effect other than provoke Hanoi into sending more troops down the trails."[176] By early January 1965, CIA's Chet Cooper, by then a principal NSC staff officer, had also come to the view that bombing the DRV

[173] Colby, "Indo-China," 5 November 1964. (S). CIA files, Job No. 78-597, DDO/ISS, Box 1, Folder 14: "Vietnam-CIA Papers Prepared by FE Division, 1958-1964."

[174] Cline, Memorandum for the Director, "Vietnam," 25 November 1964. (TS). CIA files, Job No. 80B01285A, Box 3, DCI/McCone, Folder 15; also *FRUS*, 1964-1968, Vol. I, pp. 962-964. In judging that the DRV would seek to negotiate if faced with "extreme" US action, Cline added the proviso that such US action involved stopping short of the "occupation of NVN territory by substantial numbers of U.S. ground forces." This was in fact a contingency far from any US course of action being considered at the time.

[175] Smith, Memorandum for Chief, Far East Division,"Recommended CIA Position on the Continuation of the Struggle in Indo-China," 19 November 1964. (S). CIA files, Job No. 78-597, DDO/ISS, Box 1, Folder 14: "Vietnam—CIA Papers Prepared by FE Division, 1958-1964." This officer, a veteran of years of experience in and concerning Vietnam, had been a consistent critic of greater US military participation in the war since late 1961, when the Kennedy administration had decided to up the US ante in South Vietnam.

[176] Halberstam, *The Best and the Brightest*, p. 485.

would not cause it to stop its support of the Viet Cong or become more amenable to negotiations. "There were many among my colleagues who shared this doubt and conviction."[177]

One of the last of these unsolicited judgments, chronologically, that CIA officers offered up concerning the wisdom of US policy came in early April 1965, following the landing of the Marines and the beginnings of sustained US bombing programs against the DRV. The author of the present study, who had represented CIA in interagency working groups on Vietnam, gave DCI McCone a sharp, across-the-board criticism of these new US military departures. He was unaware at the time that Vice President Humphrey, Under Secretary of State Ball, and several senior members of Congress already had privately voiced similar doubts when he based his critique on "a deep concern that we are becoming progressively divorced from reality in Vietnam . . . and are proceeding with far more courage than wisdom."

The critique judged that the United States did not have the capability to achieve the goals it had set for itself in Vietnam, "yet we think and act as if we do." There was no certainty that bombing the North would "work," and the most likely outcome of committing a few US combat divisions in the South would be "a long, drawn-out war, retention of the principal cities, and constant enemy attrition of the US and allied forces." Nor would the new US military measures necessarily prevent the collapse of the Army and the Government of South Vietnam: "We [must not] forget the sobering fact that—despite the rising DRV ingredient—the VC insurrection remains essentially an indigenous phenomenon, the product of GVN fecklessness, VC power, and peasant hopelessness." After observing that there seemed to be a congenital American disposition to underestimate Asian enemies—"We are doing so now. We cannot afford so precious a luxury."—the thinkpiece restated what had come out of several NSC working groups, National Intelligence Estimates, and war games: bombing will not in itself cause the DRV and the Viet Cong to cease and desist. "The enemy is brave, resourceful, skilled, and patient. He can shoot down our fancy aircraft, and he can shoot up and invest our bases." We cannot expect the enemy to reason together with us; his thought patterns are far removed from ours: "Tough and hard-bitten, he has been at the job of subverting all of Indochina for over thirty years." Hanoi is patient, prepared to go the distance, and now smells victory in the air. Hence US military pressures will not cause Ho Chi Minh to negotiate meaningfully with us. In sum, "the

[177] Cooper, *The Lost Crusade*, pp. 258-259.

chances are considerably better than even that the US will in the end have to disengage in Vietnam, and do so considerably short of our present objectives."[178]

DCI McCone's Evolving Views

The most weighty CIA opinions were of course those the President's chief intelligence adviser, John McCone, carried to the White House during the key months of Vietnam policy formulation in late 1964 and early 1965—but even the DCI's counsel made little apparent impact on the President's policy decisions. McCone did share the Johnson administration's basic view that a much greater US military input was mandatory to keep South Vietnam from collapsing. He nonetheless differed with the President's choice of specific ways and means of implementing the policy. During these weeks the DCI also changed his mind on several key aspects of how best to commit US force against the enemy. And, although he looked more favorably on the idea of bombing the North than did most of his CIA experts, he took issue with the President's military advisers on a number of points.

Many other world questions were demanding McCone's attention at the time, President Johnson was increasingly holding him at arm's length, and the DCI had already decided that he wanted to return to private life, but during the key months of the Vietnam escalation debate he persevered in pushing his views on the White House.[179] After the Viet Cong's devastating raid on Bien Hoa on 1 November, he recommended to Secretary McNamara that a program to punish the North should be instituted with a clear signal that such punishment could be stopped when Hanoi stopped its "illicit operations" in the South and in Laos. At that time, however, McCone advocated that the United States should punish the DRV deliberately and slowly, as contrasted with the Joint

[178] Harold P. Ford, Memorandum, "Into the Valley," 8 April 1965. (TS, subsequently declassified, 10 May 1993). Copy on file in CIA History Staff. No reply to these unsolicited views was received from the Director. In February 1965 Vice President Humphrey had privately given the President a stinging critique of his decision that South Vietnam could be saved by markedly expanding the war—a critique similar in some respects to the doubts certain CIA officers had had for some time about Vietnam. Humphrey told LBJ on 15 February 1965 that US public backing of the new course was mandatory but lacking: "American wars have to be politically understandable by the American public. There has to be a cogent, convincing case if we are to enjoy sustained public support. . . . People can't understand why we would run grave risks to support a country which is totally unable to put its own house in order. The chronic instability in Saigon directly undermines American political support for our policy. . . . We now risk creating the impression that we are the prisoner of events in Vietnam." Humphrey, *The Education of a Public Man: My Life and Politics* (Garden City, N.Y.: Doubleday & Co., 1976), pp. 322-323. Humphrey nonetheless continued outwardly to support administration Vietnam policy until late in his own presidential campaign in 1968.
[179] The interplay of these elements is discussed in an unfinished CIA History Staff study of McCone's directorship. CIA/History Staff files.

Chiefs' recommendation that 400 aircraft be sent en masse to bomb the North. That option, he held, was unwarranted, one that world opinion would construe as the act of a "frustrated giant."[180]

The DCI was one of the few Presidential advisers who warned at this time that the United States should expect enemy reprisals within South Vietnam for attacks on the North; for this reason he advised that each bombing raid against Hanoi should be specifically authorized in Washington. When the Viet Cong blew up the US officers' billet in Saigon at Christmastime in 1964, McCone cautioned against immediate punishment of the DRV, arguing that it would be difficult to document that Hanoi, and not just the Viet Cong, was responsible, and that a stronger government should be in place in the South before the United States launched major reprisals against the North.[181]

In early February 1965, McCone still favored a cautious program of bombing, proposing that the United States conduct one bombing raid a day against the North, starting in the southern part of the DRV and working steadily northward. His rationale was that such a strategy would carry less danger of provoking major Chinese Communist intervention in the war than would deep strikes into DRV territory, as the JCS preferred.[182] But by early April, McCone had reversed this position. Reflecting on the audacious, damaging Viet Cong attacks on Pleiku (6 February) and Qui Nhon (10 February), McCone on 2 April recommended that US air forces should strike hard and deep against the DRV.

He argued that intense bombing would be necessary to impel the North Vietnamese to seek a political settlement through negotiation and thus avoid the destruction of their economy. If the United States contin-

---

[180] McCone, Memorandum for the Record, "Discussion with Secretary McNamara on 16 November 1964," 19 November 1964. (S/Eyes Only); and "Meeting on 11/24/64." (TS). Both in CIA files, Job No. 80B01285A, DCI/Executive Registry, Box 2, Folder 14. (Hereafter cited as McCone memos). Reflecting how far his appreciation of the fragility of South Vietnam had come since early 1963, when he had remanded NIE 53-63 for having been too pessimistic about the GVN, is the assessment McCone appended to his 16 November 1964 document (above): "Finally, it must be realized that if the NVN actually stop infiltration and direction of the VC movement, there remains a very serious indigenous VC force in SVN far greater than the indigenous forces in either Malaya or the Philippines and it will quite possibly take years to overcome this force and bring order into South Vietnam."

[181] McCone, Memorandum for the Record, "Briefing of President Johnson at Johnson City, Texas, December 28, 1964," 4 January 1965. (S/Eyes Only). McCone memos, Box 6, Folder 10. McCone recorded that on this occasion he told the President "again and again that we were wrong in knocking over Diem, that I had told President Kennedy that if we moved in this direction it would result in political chaos, and this is what had happened. We went forward without being prepared to take the consequences of every possible result, and the possibility had happened and therefore we were in trouble."

[182] McCone, Memorandum, "Discussion with the President re South Vietnam," 3 February 1965. (S). McCone memos, Box 6, Folder 11.

ued to limit its bombing attacks to northern bridges, military installations, and lines of communication, wrote McCone, this would in effect signal to Hanoi that "our determination to win is significantly modified by our fear of widening the war." The Director argued that without effective punishment of the DRV, the United States would be starting down a track "which involves ground force operations [in the South] which, in all probability, will have limited effectiveness . . . [and will lead to] ever-increasing commitment of U.S. personnel without materially improving the chances of victory." In his view, US ground forces in the South would therefore become "mired down in combat in the jungle in a military effort that we cannot win, and from which we will have extreme difficulty in extricating ourselves." Instead, he recommended that the United States should shock the DRV by hitting it hard and all at once.[183]

The last occasion on which DCI McCone had an opportunity to tell President Johnson, face-to-face, of his many serious objections to the developing US military course in Vietnam was an NSC meeting on 20 April, to which McCone brought the new Director-designate, Adm. William F. Raborn, Jr. The discussion focused on Secretary McNamara's proposals to commit more US combat troops in the South and continue bombing secondary targets in the DRV. Air raids in the North would be targeted against lines of supply and infiltration in order to support and protect ground operations in the South; no longer would bombing targets be picked in expectation that their threatened destruction would cause Hanoi to seek a negotiated settlement. As McCone later recorded that meeting, McNamara's recommended course of action "troubled me greatly." McCone told those present that the proposed level of bombing would stiffen Hanoi's determination and lead to heightened Viet Cong activity in the South. This, said McCone, "would present our ground forces with an increasingly difficult problem requiring more and more troops." Thus the United States would "drift into a combat situation where victory would be dubious and from which we could not extricate ourselves." He concluded that he was not against bombing the North, but that the commitment of US combat forces in the South must be accompanied by a more dynamic program of airstrikes against "industrial targets, power plants, POL centers, and the taking out of the MIGs."[184]

The President and the NSC adopted McNamara's proposals, not McCone's, but on his last day as DCI, 28 April 1965, McCone repeated many of his cautions in a farewell note to President Johnson. The United States should "tighten the tourniquet" on North Vietnam, he argued: "In

---

[183] McCone, Memorandum for Secretaries Rusk and McNamara, Ambassador Taylor, and Mc-George Bundy, 2 April 1965, (TS). McCone memos, Box 6, Folder ll; *Pentagon Papers* (Gravel ed.), Vol. III, pp. l00-l0l; Lyndon Johnson *The Vantage Point*, p. 140; and Gibbons, Part III, pp. 200-201.
[184] McCone, Memorandum for the Record, "NSC Meeting—20 Apr 65," 21 April l965(S). CIA files, Job No. 80B0l285A, DCI/Executive Registry, Box 6, Folder 11.

my opinion we should strike their petroleum supplies, electric power installations, and air defense installations . . . . I do not think we have to fear taking on the MIGs, which after all the Chi Nats (Chinese Nationalists) defeated in 1958 with F-86s and Sidewinders . . ."[185]

The President's response to McCone's parting advice was to ask his successor, Admiral Raborn, to comment on it, and Raborn apparently left his swearing-in ceremony 28 April with McCone's memo of that date in hand. A week later he replied to the President in a letter that gave qualified support to the proposition of concentrated bombing attacks on Hanoi, closely coordinated with political efforts to get the North Vietnamese to the negotiating table. Raborn argued that, if the United States did not punish the DRV severely, then "we will in effect be pressing the conflict on the ground where our capabilities enjoy the least comparative advantage." The United States might then find itself "pinned down, with little choice left among possible subsequent courses of action: i.e., disengagement at very high cost, or broadening the conflict in quantum jumps." Raborn nonetheless placed more emphasis than had McCone on the centrality of winning the war in the South. In the Admiral's view, it would be the antiguerrilla effectiveness of US/GVN forces that would "almost certainly prove the key determinant of whether, over a period of some time, we can impel the enemy to meet our terms." Raborn cautioned that in its "preoccupation with military action," the United States must "not lose sight of the basically political aspect of the war. In the final analysis, it can only be won at the SVN hamlet level."[186]

The President also asked his close adviser Clark Clifford to critique McCone's parting counsel. Clifford later wrote that as he studied McCone's recommendations, "I reached a conclusion exactly opposite to his." According to Clifford, if McCone thought the only way to avoid defeat was by large-scale bombing, "then we should not escalate at all

---

[185] McCone letter to the President, 28 April 1975. (TS). CIA files, Job No. 80T01629R, O/NFAC, Box 3, "SAVA Policy Files," Folder 2: "Vietnam Committee." At the end of this letter McCone told Johnson that he was attaching "a copy of my memorandum of April 2nd, which may not have come to your attention, since it argues this case in a little more detail." Historians George Kahin and John Lewis assert that McCone's 2 April memorandum "was apparently withheld from the President, and that the CIA chief was obliged to hand-deliver a copy to him as his last official act before resigning." Kahin and Lewis, *The United States in Vietnam*, Rev. ed. (New York: Dial Press, 1967), p. 317. These authors offer no documentation to support their assertion. In any event, McCone had already given the President his candid criticisms of the new US course, face-to-face, in the NSC meeting of 20 April.

[186] Raborn, Memorandum of 6 May 1965. (TS/Sensitive). CIA files, as above. Attached to that memo in the files are a cover letter of 6 May, Raborn to Rusk and McNamara; and a note for the files, 11 May, by O/NE Director Sherman Kent. In his letter to the President (with copies to Secretaries Rusk and McNamara), Raborn used a number of views, verbatim, that O/NE had recently given the DCI's office. See author, O/NE Memorandum (Revised), "Comment on Mr. McCone's Views, Dated 28 April 1965," 5 May 1965. (TS/Sensitive). CIA files, as above.

[because the] level of bombing he advocated would shock and horrify the entire world, and even he admitted that there was no guarantee we would prevail."[187]

It will of course never be known whether hitting the DRV hard at the outset of a US bombing campaign would have shocked Hanoi into materially lessening its support of the Viet Cong, at least for awhile, as John McCone (and others) had argued. Certainly the middle course subsequently chosen by President Johnson and his aides, that of cautiously bombing the North, made no crucial impact on Hanoi's determination to continue the war. And later, when the United States did hit the North hard, there was less shock effect because in the meantime the DRV had become inured to bombing, and its improved defenses now degraded the bombers' accuracy and effectiveness—in the process confounding the Rostow thesis of victory through air power. At the same time, there is certainly no guarantee that even McCone's recommended level of bombing in the North in 1964 would have substantially improved the situation on the ground in South Vietnam, where CIA officers and many of their Intelligence Community colleagues had long insisted the war would be won or lost.

Retrospect

As I analyze the pros and cons of placing any considerable number of Marines in Danang area beyond those presently assigned, I develop grave reservations as to wisdom and necessity of so doing. . . . White-faced soldier armed, equipped and trained as he is not suitable guerrilla fighter for Asia forests and jungles. French tried to adapt their forces to this mission and failed. I doubt that US forces could do much better. . . . Finally, there would be ever present question of how foreign soldier could distinguish between a VC and friendly Vietnamese farmer. When I view this array of difficulties, I am convinced that we should adhere to our past policy of keeping our ground forces out of direct counterinsurgency role.

Gen. Maxwell Taylor, 22 February 1965[188]

Whether accurately or not, most CIA officers had for years given policymakers skeptical evaluations of the outlook in Vietnam, similar in some respects to those Ambassador Maxwell Taylor privately voiced in February 1965 as the United States prepared to commit combat troops in the South and begin bombing the North. As far back as March 1952, as

---

[187]Clifford, "Annals of Government," *The New Yorker*, 6 May 1991, p.48.
[188]Taylor, EmbTel (Saigon) 2699, as reproduced in Gibbons, Part III, p. 122.

we have seen, CIA and the Intelligence Community had estimated that enemy forces would grow stronger, and the French would eventually withdraw from Vietnam.[189] Thereafter, with one principal exception, most working-level CIA analysts fairly consistently held that Washington should not underestimate the strength and staying power of the enemy, nor overestimate that of our South Vietnamese ally.

As noted earlier, that primary exception occurred when DCI McCone remanded the analysts' draft of NIE 53-63 in February 1963 because it did not mirror the optimism held by most of the makers and executors of US policy in Vietnam at that time. Less than a month after McCone had disseminated a reworked, much more optimistic NIE, the situation in South Vietnam began suddenly and swiftly to unravel. Thereafter, during the months when the policymakers and their assistants were deciding whether, how, and when to "go big" against the Communist insurgency, McCone shared the gloomy perceptions of most of his analysts about the Government of Vietnam and its armed forces. They did not agree, however, on many other Vietnam questions. McCone, for example, accepted the domino thesis; his officers in O/NE had several times questioned the relevance of that analogy to the struggle for Indochina. McCone appeared more convinced than most of his officers that bombing the North would markedly help the South; they consistently held that the war was essentially a political struggle that had to be won on the ground in the South.

CIA's Lack of Impact

Whatever the differences of emphasis between McCone and his CIA officers, the record suggests that McCone's advice about Vietnam only occasionally influenced White House decisions betweeen 1963 and 1965, and that the collective and individual judgments of other Agency officers hardly registered at all. The fact that McCone agreed in early 1963 that things were going fairly well almost certainly fed the administration's confidence that the South Vietnam Government was making sufficient progress in the war effort that some US military advisers could begin to be withdrawn. Later, the DCI's endorsement of the domino thesis may have helped blunt the effect upon decisionmakers of O/NE's doubt (registered in June 1964) that the loss of Vietnam would necessarily have a sudden and catastrophic effect on the security position in the rest of East Asia.

With these exceptions, the views of McCone and his senior officers on events and prospects in Vietnam during the 1963-65 period made little apparent impact on strategy and policy decisions. The Kennedy

---

[189] NIE 35/1, "Probable Developments in Indochina Through Mid-1952," 3 March 1952. *FRUS, 1952-1954, Vol. XIII, Indochina, Part II*, p. 53-55.

administration turned against President Diem and facilitated his overthrow despite McCone's cautions. The Johnson administration ignored the repeated judgments of intelligence officers in CIA and other agencies that bombing the North probably would not work, and that brightening the light at the end of the tunnel depended primarily on improving the South Vietnamese Government's political and military performance. Finally, in early 1965, when the White House at last composed its policy of direct military engagement in Vietnam, President Johnson not only ignored McCone's urging that the DRV be bombed suddenly and severely, but froze the DCI out of the close relationship he had earlier enjoyed.

Why this lack of impact? Why did so many of CIA's professional judgments and analyses (and some informal views of CIA officers on policy ways and means) find so little resonance in the higher reaches of MACV, our Saigon Embassy, the Pentagon, State, and the White House? In a technical sense the US intelligence machinery had functioned well. Decisionmakers had repeatedly asked intelligence officers for their views, and, with only a few dissents and split opinions, the Intelligence Community had usually been able to respond with agreed judgments. From June 1964 to June 1965, O/NE and USIB had prepared a dozen National Estimates on Vietnam, eight of them on probable reactions to various possible US courses of action (which policymakers had supplied the Intelligence Community for the purpose of making its estimative judgments). Supplementing the estimates, many officers of the Agency and the Intelligence Community had prepared numerous additional assessments and had disseminated them to policymaking consumers.

Yet the impact of intelligence on the decisions to escalate America's role in the war was slight. Why? In essence, there was little impact because CIA's intelligence and policy-related inputs were not what these decisionmakers wanted to hear at the time. Prior to mid-1963, the cautions consistently voiced by CIA officers did not jibe with the images of progress that senior administration officials continued to hold, or at least continued to hold out to the American people. And by 1964, when the GVN's perilous situation had at last become apparent to the policy managers, CIA skepticism about the newfound cure-all, bombing the North, was an unwelcome guest at the advisory table.

As of 1964–early 1965, the resistance of CIA's senior consumers to its views on Vietnam was deeply rooted. The Agency's no-clothes vision clashed with their widely held views that:

- World Communism is essentially monolithic, and the Vietnam war is part of a world conspiracy run from Moscow and Beijing.

- The United States cannot let Soviet Premier Khrushchev push us around; to make America's world commitments credible we have to take a stand somewhere, and that place will be Vietnam (despite the fact that, as we have seen, the JCS had held a decade earlier that Indochina was devoid of decisive military objectives).

- The domino thesis: if Vietnam "went," so would America's strategic position in East Asia (a judgment O/NE's estimators did not share, but DCI McCone did).

Also, contrary to repeated CIA judgments that the struggle for dominance in Vietnam was essentially a political one that had to be won by improved South Vietnamese administrative and military performance, most decisionmakers overestimated what the United States could accomplish through military means against the Viet Cong and the DRV. And many of them were confident that Vietnam's enormous complexities could be reduced to made-in-America solutions and statistical measures of progress, epitomized by Secretary of Defense McNamara's assurance in 1962, that "every quantitative measure we have shows we're winning this war."[190]

Another primary cause of the Johnson administration's resistance to CIA's judgments was the fact that, as we have seen, senior policymakers had for years been misled by unwarranted accounts of progress in Vietnam. Down the lines of command, senior MACV and US Mission officers—those in charge of seeing that progress was made—had long put the best light on their own reporting and were disinclined to accept and to pass upward the generally much more candid assessments their working-level field officers gave them. Evaluations became more optimistic at each level of command, so that by the time they got to Washington, they generally were deficient in candor and overfull of alleged good news. Senior policy managers understandably welcomed such assurances of policy successes, and it was not until 1964 that the GVN's manifest political-military disarray pierced their distorted images of reality. Senior policymakers were also justified in their reluctance to accept the views of intelligence estimators who in September 1962 had proved wrong on the critical question of whether the USSR was implanting nuclear weapons in Cuba. Moreover, as we have seen, the estimators had sometimes been off the mark on Vietnam.

---

[190] As cited by Arthur Schlesinger, *A Thousand Days*, p. 549; and by Neil Sheehan, *A Bright Shining Lie*, p. 290.

But whether US intelligence was right or wrong or was or was not making a major impact on policymaking was hardly the most important aspect of the Johnson administration's decision to escalate the war. The decisionmakers did not enjoy the intelligence analyst's luxury of simply assessing a situation; they had to *act*. The basic, hardly disputable fact was that in 1964 the military-political situation was deteriorating badly: during the year there were seven successive governments in Saigon. This fact of life was appreciated widely, even by some of the most loyal supporters of the war effort. Gen. William E. DePuy, who had commanded the 1st Division in Vietnam, later recalled that in 1964-65 there had not been a Vietnamese government as such: "There was a military junta that ran the country. . . . [its officers were] politically inept. The various efforts at pacification required a cohesive, efficient governmental structure which simply did not exist. Furthermore, corruption was rampant. There was coup after coup, and militarily, defeat after defeat."[191]

Hence the United States had little policymaking leverage in this very soft situation in South Vietnam, and it is understandable that frustrated US planners considered whether that situation might be remedied by taking the war to the North and by committing US troops to combat in the South. As momentum in Washington grew, if unevenly, for a major escalation, the bounds of policy debate narrowed and articulate advocates continued to assure President Johnson that only if the US took the war to the enemy in a big way could South Vietnam be saved. Even those senior advisers who might have been impressed by CIA's negative arguments may have decided the circumstances required a gamble, even at worse than 50-50 odds. In the end, however, it was the shocking attacks the Viet Cong made on American men and equipment, coincident with the sweeping reelection of Lyndon Johnson, that capped this long process and at last precipitated the President's decision.

[191] DePuy, as quoted by Lt. Cols. Romie L. Brownlee and William J. Mullen III, *Changing An Army: An Oral History of General William E. DePuy, USA Retired* (Carlisle Barracks, PA ; U. S. Military History Institute, 1990), p. 123.

Episode 3, 1967-1968
CIA, the Order-of-Battle Controversy, and the Tet Offensive

If SD [Viet Cong Self-Defense forces] and SSD [VC Secret Self-Defense forces] are included in the overall enemy strength, the figure will total 420,000 to 431,000. . . . This is in sharp contrast to the current overall strength figure of about 299,000 given to the press here. . . . We have been projecting an image of success over the recent months. . . . Now, when we release the figure of 420,000-431,000, the newsmen will . . . [draw] an erroneous and gloomy conclusion as to the meaning of the increase. . . . In our view the strength figures for the SD and SSD should be omitted entirely from the enemy strength figures in the forthcoming NIE.

Gen. Creighton Abrams, Deputy Commander, MACV,
20 August 1967[1]

As we have seen, in the first decade of direct US involvement in Vietnam, dating from the French surrender at Dien Bien Phu in 1954, policymakers seeking good news had encouraged optimistic reporting and ignored or complained about intelligence analysis that failed to support their expectations. The bliss of ignorance had several times cost the US war effort dearly, but worse was in store at the end of January 1968, when a misreading of the enemy's intentions and a calculated understating of his strength left the nation and its political leaders wide open to the shock of the Communists' unprecedentedly massive spring military campaign, the "Tet (Spring) Offensive." This episode portrays the role CIA played in the related episodes of the MACV order-of-battle (O/B) controversy and the runup to the Tet offensive. We will see that CIA's estimates of the enemy's strength were considerably more accurate than those turned out elsewhere; that CIA's Saigon Station accurately warned that a Tet-like general offensive was coming; that CIA Headquarters did not share that warning; and that senior policymakers, in any event, both

---

[1] Abrams cable to Gen. Earle G. Wheeler (Chairman, Joint Chiefs of Staff). Attachment to letter, Congressman Paul N. McCloskey (R-CA) to DCI William Colby, 6 June 1975. CIA Files, Job No. 80R01720R, O/D/NFAC, Box 1, "GAC Files (SAVA-NIO)," Folder 9.

overrode CIA's insistence that MACV's estimates of the enemy's order of battle were much too low, and ignored Saigon Station's warning that an unprecedented enemy offensive was at hand.

The O/B Controversy

So far, our mission frustratingly unproductive since MACV stone-walling, obviously under orders. . . . [the] inescapable conclusion [is] that General Westmoreland (with [CORDS Chief] Komer's encouragement) has given instruction tantamount to direct order that VC total strength will not exceed 300,000 ceiling. Rationale seems to be that any higher figure would generate unacceptable level of criticism from the press. This order obviously makes it impossible for MACV to engage in serious or meaningful discussion of evidence.

George A. Carver (DCI's Special Assistant for Vietnam Affairs),
10 September 1967[2]

For years US military chiefs in Vietnam had estimated the enemy's military and guerrilla forces at much lower levels than CIA analysts in Saigon and Washington thought justified.[3] Ultimately, it would take the Communist Tet Offensive of 1968 to rip away the paper backdrop MACV's order-of-battle staff had erected behind the "command estimate" of enemy strength. The last of several attempts to resolve the disparity ended abruptly some four months before the Tet Offensive when emissaries of the Intelligence Community went head-to-head with General Westmoreland and his immediate MACV subordinates. Despite the Viet Cong's demonstrated persistence and strength, and in the face of evidence that Communist regulars and irregulars might total half a million, MACV insisted that enemy forces in South Vietnam could not be numbered at more than 300,000. The Intelligence Community, not without working-level protests, so reported to the President. MACV and the White House continued to use these lower figures in their public pronouncements.

---

[2]Carver cable (SAIG) 1826, IN 49006) to DCI Helms (only), attachment to Carver Memorandum for the DCI, "1967 Order of Battle Cables," 28 November 1975. (S). CIA files, Job No. and Folder as above.

[3]See, for example, John M. Newman, *JFK and Vietnam* (New York: Warner Books, 1992). Newman, making use of Kennedy Library materials, discusses at length the battles over O/B that preceded President Kennedy's decision in late 1961 to expand the level and nature of US military support in South Vietnam. See also James J. Wirtz, *The Tet Offensive: Intelligence Failure in War* (Cornell University Press, 1991), which draws on original cables and documents declassified for the *Westmoreland v. CBS* trial.

MACV stuck to its lower O/B estimates for several reasons. First, the MACV staff had been claiming for some time that the enemy was suffering great losses in Vietnam, and in mid-1967 predicted that a "crossover" would soon occur when losses would exceed the replacement capacity; an accounting correction in the O/B would muddy the arithmetic behind this claim. Second, as CIA files show, MACV based its O/B estimates heavily on South Vietnamese (GVN) sources.[4] Third, MACV used mainly Confidential-level documents and prisoner interrogation reports, and, in contrast with CIA's practice, did not generally use data derived from intercepted enemy radio signals, or SIGINT.[5] And MACV's position rested on an O/B estimation process whose flaws its own officers could (and, later and privately, did) point out.

But the most important regulator of the MACV O/B estimates was the fact that General Westmoreland and his immediate staff were under a strong obligation to keep demonstrating "progress" against the Communist forces in Vietnam. After years of escalating US investments of lives, equipment, and money, of monthly increases in MACV's tally of enemy casualties, and of vague but constant predictions of impending victory, it would be politically disastrous, they felt, suddenly to admit, even on the basis of new or better evidence, that the enemy's strength was in fact substantially greater than MACV's original or current estimates.

Working-level intelligence analysts were less affected by this MACV concern, and by early 1967 even some senior Pentagon officials, both military and civilian, had become uneasy with challenges about the accuracy of MACV's judgments on a number of questions, among them the enemy's O/B and the overall progress of the war. In January of that year Gen. Earle Wheeler, Chairman of the Joint Chiefs of Staff (JCS), registered his dissatisfaction with "the contradictory order of battle and infiltration statistics which are contained in numerous documents now being circulated."[6] Responsibility for solving the problem was thereupon given

[4]"MACV's present estimates on the strength of Viet Cong irregulars are derived from estimates provided by GVN province chiefs." *Report of the Honolulu Intelligence Conference to Standardize Methods for Developing and Presenting Statistics on Order of Battle, Infiltration Trends and Estimates—6-12 February 1967*, p. 10. (C). CIA files, Job No. 78T02095R, Box 1, O/DDI, Folder 2. Former CORDS chief Robert Komer's view is that as of 1967, "MACV's intelligence for the most part was terrible." Komer, to author, 21 May 1990. According to George Allen, MACV had lowered the number of estimated enemy irregulars in 1965, "although no one had really done much research in depth on the question." Allen, to author, 11 April 1990.
[5]Discussed in some detail in CIA, *Response to the Questions on Vietnam Posed in National Security Study Memorandum Number 1*, 7 February 1969. (S/Sensitive). CIA files, Job No. 78-906, DDO-ISS IP, Box 2, Folder: "Vietnam-National Security Council." A March 1968 MACV cable states that the only new element in the O/B picture at the time is "the correct assertion that MACV OB figures do not always reflect all-source intelligence." MACV 05301 (exact date illegible). (S/Eyes Only). CIA files, Job No. 78T02095R, O/DDI, Box 4, Folder 13.
[6]*Report of the Honolulu Intelligence Conference*, p.1.

to CINCPAC, the armed services' commander-in-chief in the Pacific theater, who convened representatives from his own headquarters in Honolulu and from MACV, the Defense Intelligence Agency (DIA), the National Security Agency (NSA), and CIA. The conferees were directed "to standardize and agree upon definitions, methodology and reporting procedures" on some 15 questions concerning the enemy's military strength, and in due course they agreed to adopt a number of positive new measures. In subsequent practice, however, MACV did not budge from its previous O/B estimates.

Meanwhile, the principal Pentagon skeptic about MACV's judgments had become none other than Secretary of Defense Robert McNamara. CIA's George Allen had received intimations of this as far back as 1964, when during a trip to Saigon, McNamara had confided to him that the situation in Vietnam was "far worse" than the Pentagon at large realized.[7] By 1966, following a year of US airstrikes against North Vietnam, McNamara's continued concern about MACV's claims of "progress" had impelled him to ask CIA's Directorate of Intelligence for a private assessment of the enemy's will and ability to continue the war. The study, delivered to McNamara on 26 August 1966 under the title "The Vietnamese Communists' Will to Persist," concluded that planned US measures were not likely to deter the North Vietnamese. According to historian Gen. Bruce Palmer, Jr., this CIA assessment made a deep impression on Secretary McNamara and "no doubt had much to do with changing his views about the war."[8] In any event, in April 1967, according to CIA files, McNamara took the extraordinary step of asking CIA, a nonmilitary agency, to provide him periodic, independent assessments of enemy O/B, as well as of the effectiveness of US air operations against the North and the progresss of pacification efforts in the South.[9] It was

[7] Allen, to author, 11 April 1990. As of 1964, Allen was a CIA/OCI (Office of Current Intelligence) officer stationed in Saigon. Earlier an officer of the Army's G-2 and DIA, Allen subsequently became deputy chief of SAVA.

[8] Palmer, "US Intelligence and Vietnam," p.47. At the time he wrote this study, General Palmer was a member of the DCI's Senior Review Panel. He had earlier been General Westmoreland's deputy in Vietnam, and then Army Vice Chief of Staff. General Palmer is also the author of a highly regarded unclassified history, *The 25-Year War: America's Military Role in Vietnam* (New York: Simon & Shuster, 1984).

[9] Richard Helms, Memorandum for Robert S. McNamara, "Servicing of Vietnam Assessment Requests," 27 April 1967, (S/Sensitive/Eyes Only). CIA files, Job No. 80B01285A, DCI, Box 11, "DCI Helms," Folder 3. According to Hans Heymann, who was one of the compilers of *The Pentagon Papers* and who had wide access to McNamara's private papers, by 1967 the Secretary had become so scornful of military reporting from Vietnam that he began scribbling "I don't believe it"–type marginalia on some of those reports, in one instance writing, "This is a lot of crap." Heymann, to author, 26 September 1991. Heymann had earlier been a RAND Corporation officer concerned with Vietnam questions, and in the early 1980s became the National Intelligence Council's National Intelligence Officer (NIO) for Economics.

two months later, in June 1967, that McNamara quietly directed a small group of staff officers (military and civilian) to compile the massive record of the US war effort that became known as *The Pentagon Papers.*

Until McNamara made his unusual request of the Agency, there had been no centralized or systemized CIA work on the Vietnamese Communist O/B, mostly because of a general appreciation within the Agency that this chore was the proper responsibility of MACV, not a civilian office. Prior to McNamara's tasking, certain officers in various offices of the Agency—SAVA, O/NE, OCI, and ORR (Office of Research and Reports)—had dug into the O/B problem informally from time to time. Though differing in approach and degree, they reached a common conclusion: MACV's estimates of enemy O/B were much too low.

For instance, when CIA analysts focused on the mostly civilian and irregular components of the O/B as a legitimate object of their analysis, they found many problems. As veteran military analyst George Allen later wrote, MACV's order-of-battle holdings had long been "misleadingly low. . . . They had done almost no real research on the guerrilla-militia forces; their estimate remained at the 'guesstimate' my [DIA] team had come up with in Saigon early in 1962."[10] Allen's boss at CIA, Special Assistant George Carver, told a White House military aide in September 1966 that MACV's estimate of 100,000 to 120,000 Viet Cong irregulars "may be extremely low."[11] In January 1967, O/NE observed that documentary evidence suggested that the enemy's irregular strength in South Vietnam had reached 250,000 to 300,000 by the end of 1965, whereas MACV was still sticking to its 100,000 to 120,000 estimate.[12] In May 1967, shortly after McNamara's tasking of CIA and at a time when MACV was carrying a *total* enemy O/B in South Vietnam of 292,000, CIA responded to an inquiry by Under Secretary of State Nicholas Katzenbach that the enemy's paramilitary and political organization in South Vietnam "is still probably far larger than official US order of battle statistics indicate," and thus that the total enemy O/B there "is probably in the 500,000 range and may even be higher."[13]

CIA's most diligent researcher into the O/B problem and Washington's boldest champion of a higher O/B figure was Sam Adams, a brilliant, energetic OCI and (later) SAVA officer. By December 1966, for

[10] Allen, "The Indochina Wars," p. 312.
[11] Carver, Memorandum for Lt. Col. Robert M. Montague, Military Assistant to Mr. Komer, "Calculation of Viet Cong Irregular Strength," 28 September 1966, (S). CIA files, Job No. 80B01721R, O/D/NFAC, "Substantive Policy Files, DDI Vietnam Files," Folder 7.
[12] Abbott Smith (Deputy Director, O/NE), Memorandum for Sherman Kent, "The War in Vietnam," 9 January 1967, p.9, (S). CIA Files, Job No. 78S02149R, Box 3, O/DDI, Folder 10.
[13] CIA Memorandum, "Input to the DCI Audit Project Chaired by Under Secretary of State Katzenbach," 23 May 1967, (S). CIA files, Job No. 85T00268R, DCI/O/DCI, Box 7.

example, after examining the situation firsthand in Vietnam and digesting stacks of raw reports at CIA Headquarters, Adams concluded that the total number of enemy forces in South Vietnam was 600,000.[14]

Contrary to his later claims, Adams was not a lone voice crying in the wilderness. Through mid-1967 at least, his boss, George Carver, and many officers elsewhere in CIA agreed with his general argument that the enemy O/B figures, especially those for VC irregular forces, should be much higher than what MACV was accepting. In January 1967, Carver advised the DDI that MACV's O/B total "should be raised, perhaps doubled."[15] In April, Carver took Adams's conclusions to NSC staffer Robert Komer—soon to be the President's deputy for civil operations and rural development support (CORDS) under General Westmoreland in Saigon. He told Komer that while O/B data on North Vietnamese and Viet Cong Main Force and Local Force units were fairly reliable, the accepted number of irregular forces was being substantially underestimated and might number "more than 300,000," making the total O/B "as high as 500,000."[16] In May, drawing on Adams's work, Carver drafted the report CIA gave Under Secretary of State Katzenbach, referred to above, which held that the total enemy O/B was about 500,000 and might be even higher. And in June, Carver cabled Komer in Saigon that "the fundamental problem at this time is to overcome the longstanding cultural

---

[14] Adams, "Vietnam Cover-up: Playing War with Numbers," *Harpers*, May 1975, *passim*. The author of this History Staff study knew Adams, subsequent to the events discussed in this study. Adams was a prodigious researcher whose findings were groundbreaking and generally more accurate than those prepared by other officers; he repeatedly hurt his case, however, by overstatement and self-defeating conduct. Numerous observers have discussed the Sam Adams phenomenon. See, for example, a rejoinder letter to the editor by James C. Graham (a former member of the Board of National Estimates), *Harpers*, June 1975, pp.15-16; Eleanor Randolph, *The Washington Post*, 8 November and 3 December 1984, 10 January, 30 January, 13 February, and 18 February 1985; Bob Brewin and Sydney Shaw, *Vietnam on Trial: Westmoreland vs. CBS* (New York: Atheneum, 1987); T. L. Cubbage II, *"Westmoreland vs. CBS: Was Intelligence Corrupted by Policy Demands?"*, *Intelligence and National Security*, July 1988, pp.118-180; Thomas Powers, *The Man Who Kept the Secrets: Richard Helms and the CIA* (New York: Knopf, 1987); Renata Adler, *Reckless Disregard: Westmoreland vs.CBS et al.*: (New York: Knopf, 1986); George Allen, "The Indochina Wars;" John Ranelagh, *The Agency: The Rise and Decline of the CIA* (New York: Simon & Shuster, 1986), pp.457-465; and Sam Adams, *War of Numbers*, (South Royalton, Vermont: Steerforth Press, 1994) *passim*.

[15] Carver, Memorandum for the DDI, "Revisiting the Viet Cong Order of Battle," 11 January 1967, (S). CIA files, Job No. 80B01721R, O/D/NFAC, Box 1, "Substantive Policy Files, DDI Vietnam Files," Folder 7.

[16] Carver, Memorandum for The Honorable Robert W. Komer, "Vietcong Desertions," 3 April 1967, (S). CIA files, Job No. 80R01580R, DCI/ER Subject Files, Box 15, Folder 8. The next month, May 1967, President Johnson sent Komer (a former O/NE officer) to Vietnam with ambassadorial rank to head the CORDS program there. As we will see, a few months after taking up his CORDS position, Komer played a central role in influencing the outcome of the Saigon O/B showdown between MACV and CIA.

lag in MACV's holdings which have never reflected the substantial growth in non-combat, non-main force strength which occurred between 1962 and 1966."[17]

CIA's formal estimators, the Office of National Estimates (O/NE), did not accept Adams's highest O/B estimates, but did give him several hearings and did agree that MACV was significantly underestimating enemy O/B. In January 1967, O/NE told DCI Helms that there "is now documentary evidence which strongly suggests that at the beginning of 1965, [VC] irregular strength was about 200,000," that is, twice the going estimate accepted by MACV, and that during 1966 the number of irregulars had probably grown to some 250,000 to 300,000.[18] Adams's strongest backer in CIA was George Allen, who had been studying the Vietnamese "people's war" in Indochina since the early 1950s. When, along with Adams, he expressed certainty that MACV was grossly underestimating the enemy's irregular forces, he was drawing not only on years of immersion in Vietnamese military affairs, service as both a US Army and a DIA analyst, and careful study of available intelligence, but also on his reading of Hanoi commander Vo Nguyen Giap's doctrine that the irregular troops, guerrillas, and militia constituted "core forces" which had an "extremely important strategic role" to play in the war effort.[19]

Coincident with these developments at CIA, a few military officers had begun to agonize about MACV's O/B totals. According to George Allen, Col. Gaines Hawkins (chief of MACV's O/B section) confided to him in July 1967 his belief that the proper O/B figure ought to be much higher, but said "our hands are tied; this is a command position; we have to stay within a total figure of 300,000; I personally share your 500,000 estimate, but we cannot accept it."[20] Field reports sent to the Pentagon by Hawkins's boss, Gen. Joseph A. McChristian (MACV J-2), had contributed to a growing belief among working-level officers of the Defense Intelligence Agency that General Westmoreland's official O/B estimates were too low.[21] Even though McChristian and Hawkins did not succeed in

[17] DIR 14655, 26 June 1967, (S). CIA files, Job No. 80B01721R, O/D/NFAC, Box 1, "Substantive Policy Files, DDI Vietnam Files," Folder 7.

[18] Abbot Smith (Deputy Chairman, Board of National Estimates), Memorandum for the Director, "The War in Vietnam," 9 January 1967, (S). Copy on file in CIA History Staff.

[19] Allen, Memorandum for William J. Jorden, Senior NSC Staff Member, "Comments on Giap's Speech on the Role of the Militia," 20 April 1967, (S). CIA files, Job No. 80R1720R, O/D/NFAC, Box 5, "GAC Files (SAVA-NIO), Folder 6.

[20] Allen, to author, 11 April 1990.

[21] According to George Fowler, DIA's representative to the coordination meetings on SNIE 14.3-67. Fowler, to author (in Taipei, Taiwan), September 1967. Fowler explained that his DIA office was caught in a no-win crossfire at that time between MACV (which was putting pressure on DIA not to budge from MACV's official O/B figures) and CIA (which was berating DIA for ignoring the research and analysis behind the Agency's higher O/B estimates).

getting General Westmoreland to revise his "commander's estimate" of enemy forces, their reports from the field, together with CIA's document-based O/B assessments, generated enough concern at the top of the Pentagon to cause JCS Chairman Wheeler to convoke the Honolulu conference and Secretary of Defense McNamara to commission regular independent O/B assessments from the CIA.

Responsibility for resolving the now-open dispute among the O/B analysts rested ultimately with the Chairman of the United States Intelligence Board, DCI Richard Helms. Helms was a reluctant adjudicator. As early as January 1967, he foresaw that what he termed "the Vietnam numbers game" would be played "with ever increasing heat and political overtones" during the year.[22] By May, at least, he had recognized the disruptive potential of the commission McNamara had given the CIA, a civilian office, to report to him regularly, without DIA or MACV coordination, on its O/B figures[23] So Helms told CIA and the military intelligence agencies to come up with an agreed figure, if at all possible, in a definitive Special National Intelligence Estimate (SNIE 14.3-67) in which the question of the enemy's O/B could not be ducked. When the military and civilian analysts deadlocked on their disparate bookkeeping of enemy strength figures, Helms personally called an interagency meeting on the draft SNIE late in June and told those present that the O/B question had become "the most important disagreement about the war," that "we've got to come to an agreement," and that the disputants should go back and work out an answer to the problem.[24]

The impasse nevertheless persisted, with DIA insisting on MACV's "official" figures, even though some of these had not been changed in several years of combat and seemed to lack evidentiary basis. Nor did it help that MACV sent some of its intelligence staffers to Washington to join the discussions; the problem, as Colonel Hawkins (above) revealed to George Allen, was that the MACV representatives were under orders not to yield on their "commander's estimate" of fewer than

[22] As recorded by Carver, Memorandum for the DDI et al., "CIA Vietnam Statistics," 12 January 1967, (S). CIA files, Job No. 80R01580R, DCI/ER Subject Files, Box 15, Folder 8.
[23] "Input to the DCI Audit Project Chaired by Under Secretary of State Katzenbach," 23 May 1967, (S). CIA files, Job No. 85T00268R, DCI/O/DCI, Box 7, "NSC Papers," Folder 7. Former DDI chief R. Jack Smith later emphasized the emotional nature of this unique commission: "Never before had a civilian intelligence organization challenged an army in the field about its orders of battle. . . . But here were a bunch of civilians telling not only the Pentagon but also the forces in the field that the number they were facing was higher. That created a very difficult position: it was their war. They were the ones getting killed. There was a lot of emotion involved in that." Smith, to interviewer John Ranelagh, as cited in the latter's *CIA: A History* (London: BBC Books, 1992), p. 127.   ·
[24] According to Thomas Powers, *The Man Who Kept the Secrets*, pp. 186-187. Also, on a memo Carver sent Helms on 1 May 1967, "Order of Battle Note" (S), Helms wrote: "Good—But let's try to simplify these suggestions, tighten up the language, and move to get agreement from the military." CIA files, Job No. 80T01719R, O/D/NFAC, Box 3, Folder 7.

300,000 men. Helms, as USIB Chairman, then commissioned his Special Assistant for Vietnam, Carver, to take a team of Intelligence Community analysts to Saigon and grind out directly with MACV an agreement on the estimated strengths of the enemy's several armed components.

Intelligence Team Stonewalled in Saigon

The Saigon conference ensued, Carver heading a Washington team that included Sam Adams; William Hyland, chief of O/NE's Far East staff; the chief of the North Vietnam branch in CIA's Office of Current Intelligence; and George Fowler, DIA's senior civilian analyst on Vietnam. In Saigon Carver ran into a MACV brick wall. Although he and his experts poked gaping holes in the evidentiary basis for MACV's O/B estimates, Carver could not budge Col. Daniel O. Graham and his MACV O/B estimates team. Cabling Helms on 10 September, Carver characterized his mission as "frustratingly unproductive since MACV stonewalling, obviously under orders." MACV's officers will not accept any O/B total larger than 298,000, said Carver, and "the inescapable conclusion" must be drawn that Westmoreland "with Komer's encouragement has given instructions tantamount to direct order that VC strength total will not exceed 300,000 ceiling." Carver added that he hoped to see Westmoreland and Komer the next day and would "endeavor to loosen this straitjacket. Unless I can, we are wasting our time."[25]

According to Carver, he and his Washington colleagues found some of the top Saigon officers not only adamant but also personally insulting. Reporting to Helms on the 12th, Carver described his meeting the previous day with Komer and Maj. Gen. Phillip Davidson (McChristian's successor as Westmoreland's J-2) in these terms: the meeting ended in an "impasse"; at one point "I was frequently and sometimes tendentiously interrupted by Davidson . . . [who] angrily accused me of impugning his integrity," and who stated that the figures MACV had tabled were its "final offer, not subject to discussion. We should take or leave it."[26]

---

[25] SAIG 1826, to Helms (only), (S). Attachment to Carver, Memorandum for the DCI, "1967 Order of Battle Cables," 26 November 1975, (S). CIA files, Job No. 80R01720R, O/D/NFAC, Box 1, "GAC Files (SAVA-NIO)," Folder 9.

[26] SAIG 1826, to Helms (only), as above. Many CIA officers found General Davidson more difficult to work with than they had McChristian. Even after the Saigon conference and apparent agreement had been reached on how the upcoming SNIE should present its O/B figures, Carver described what he termed "MACV J-2 childishness": CIA's files show that its Saigon Station officers were finding it necessary to get prior written permission from MACV Headquarters in order to visit working-level J-2 officers, "as if CIA officers were acting as agents of potentially hostile foreign power." (Carver drafted) DIR 49100 to Saigon, 3 November 1967, (S). CIA files, Job No. 80R01720R, O/D/NFAC, Box 5, "GAC Files (SAVA-NIO)," Folder 8. Former CORDS chief Komer, however, holds that Davidson was "a great improvement over McChristian—much more able, and much more willing to defend his views when questioned by Westmoreland." Komer, to author, 21 May 1990.

Carver found Komer similarly difficult. He reported that at their 11 September meeting, Komer "launched into an hour-long monologue, " stressing MACV's inability to convince the press and the US public of "the great progress being made" in the war effort and of "the paramount importance of saying nothing that would detract from the image of progress" being made in Vietnam. Komer criticized the SNIE draft under way in Washington, "faulting the quality of its prose and its analysis and calling it a sloppy, thin and altogether disappointing piece of work." Komer then derided the Agency's entire analytic effort on Vietnam: in his view, CIA had "only a small number of analysts working on Vietnam, none of whom know much about it," and CIA's analysis consequently "could not expect to compete in depth and quality to that of MACV." Komer concluded that there must not be any quantifying of the enemy's irregular forces, on the grounds that so doing "would produce a politically unacceptable total over 400,000."[27]

Carver had no better success in budging Westmoreland's officers from their insistence that no figure for enemy irregulars could or should be included in the total estimated O/B. The MACV officers based their insistence on several arguments: the difficulty of categorizing such an amorphous and differing body of part-time enemy forces; the paucity of hard intelligence on such forces; and the argument that, at least according to MACV, such irregulars were not very important to the enemy war effort anyway. At the forefront of MACV's adamant position was its J-2 estimates chief, Col. Daniel O. Graham. Having for some time predicted the imminent arrival of the "crossover point," in Saigon (according to George Allen), Graham now challenged Carver's presentation of Washington's O/B analysis, disparaging the irregular forces as having no military significance. Years later Graham admitted to George Allen that "of course" he had not believed MACV's 300,000 figure but had defended it because it was "the command position."[28]

[27] SAIG 1926, 12 September, (S). CIA file as SAIG 1826, above. The author of the present study has for years been a close friend and associate of both Bob Komer and CIA's Vietnam analysts of the period under review. In his 11 September 1967 meeting with Carver, Komer, characteristically given to brash overstatement, seriously understated the quality of CIA's analytic talent. Carver, George Allen, Bob Layton (O/NE), and other CIA officers had not only been following Vietnam affairs in depth for years, but also had racked up high batting averages in their assessments and estimates. By contrast, in addition to being pressured by their seniors not to admit the existence of more than 300,000 enemy forces, total, in South Vietnam, MACV's intelligence officers were in the main much less experienced and acute.

[28] Allen, "The Indochina Wars," pp. 317-318. According to Allen, Graham made this statement in 1984 at the time of the *Westmoreland v. CBS* trial. In late January 1968 Graham told the author of this study, then visiting Saigon, that things were fairly quiet there. The next day the enemy launched its Tet Offensive. Graham eventually became a Lieutenant General, the Director of DIA, and, in retirement, the founder of "High Frontier," a foundation championing a US antiballistic missile defense system.

Carver's task in Saigon that September was further complicated by the fact that his own team was not of one mind. According to Bob Layton, an analyst then serving at Saigon Station, O/NE's William Hyland told Sam Adams that the particular O/B numbers didn't make much difference, while Adams raged against what he termed the "rug bazaar bargaining" by which MACV proposed to reach an agreed estimate.[29] And Carver's DIA team member, George Fowler, took positions midway between those of Carver and MACV.[30] Moreover, Saigon Station officers had for some time tended to defend MACV's O/B ceilings because of their own concern about the political embarrassment that might ensue if they were radically expanded.[31]

Carver Outgunned, Reverses Position

In any event, after three days of heated exchanges with MACV, George Carver suddenly changed course, agreeing (over Sam Adams's outraged protests[32]) to a major compromise which essentially accepted MACV's position. On 14 September, all parties—MACV, DIA, INR, and CIA (represented by Carver)—agreed (1) that the total enemy O/B figure should be 249,000; (2) that the total enemy political cadre O/B should be 85,000; and (3) that no quantified estimate should be given for "irregulars," that is, enemy self-defense forces, secret self-defense forces, assault youth, and so on. This agreement was reached, moreover, in an atmosphere entirely different (or ostensibly so) from that of the conference's stormy beginning. Upon returning to Washington, Carver now asked DCI Helms to express gratitude to General Davidson and "all of his able, most impressive staff, the thanks of the entire Washington delegation for their effective, comprehensive briefings and other invaluable contributions to the success of our joint endeavor."[33] Helms was able to report to

---

[29] Bob Layton (of CIA's Saigon Station, present on that occasion), to the author, 18 February 1992. Also Adams's highly personal later account, in which he quoted Hyland as saying that the "political climate" would not permit MACV to accept higher O/B figures and that he, Adams, was "living in a dream world." Adams, *War of Numbers* p.118.

[30] Fowler, to author, September 1967.

[31] SAIG 0826 (IN 35169), 19 August 1967, (S). CIA files, Job No. 80B01721R, O/D/NFAC, Box 1, "Substantive Policy Files, DDI Vietnam Files," Folder 6. Also, some analysts in CIA had been hesitant, at least initially, to accept the higher O/B figures championed by Carver, Allen, and Adams. In June 1966, for example, the North Vietnam Branch of OCI reported that its analysts "have concluded that current MACV estimates on infiltration into South Vietnam and on Communist order of battle in the South can be used with confidence. ORR analysts concur in this view." David Siegel, Memorandum for the Director of OCI, "The Accuracy of MACV's Reporting on Infiltration and Order of Battle," 27 June 1966, (S, compartmented). CIA files, Job No. 78T02095R, O/DDI, Box 4, Folder 17.

[32] Adams, p.118.

[33] Carver, Memorandum for DCI Helms, "Agreement on Viet Cong Strength Figures," 18 September 1967, (S). CIA files, Job No. 80R01720R, O/D/NFAC, Box 1, "GAC Files (SAVA-NIO)," Folder 7.

Under Secretary of State Katzenbach that agreement had been reached on the O/B figures, that Ambassador Bunker was consequently "most pleased," and that Bunker and General Westmoreland were "very complimentary about [the] Washington delegation mission."[34]

The key question, then and now, is what pressures prompted Carver suddenly to agree to a virtual 180-degree turnaround on figures and mood. The available documentary record is not clear and the recollections of participants differ. There appear to have been several reasons why Carver backed off from his initial anger at MACV officers' stonewalling and peremptory behavior. As we have seen, Carver's team was itself not of one mind, nor had all CIA's Washington analysts agreed with the initial Carver-Allen-Adams positions. And even though he initially argued in Saigon for much higher O/B figures, Carver's freedom of action was circumscribed by the general requirement DCI Helms had given him to reach an agreed figure with MACV.

Ultimately, however, Carver had to cave in because he was up against a hostile united front of superior officers who feared the adverse political consequences of a suddenly enlarged O/B total. Heading that opposition was not only MACV commander Westmoreland but also Ambassador Ellsworth Bunker. Even after the conference had ended to the Saigon establishment's complete satisfaction, Bunker the next month sent an Eyes Only cable to the White House warning that there would be a "devastating" result "if it should leak out . . . that despite all our successes in grinding down VC/VNA here," statistics showed that "they are really much stronger than ever."[35] Gen. Creighton Abrams, the MACV deputy to Westmoreland, had made the point explicit when he reminded JCS Chairman Wheeler in August 1967 that "We have been projecting an image of success" over recent months, and warned that, if a much higher O/B figure were released, newsmen would draw "an erroneous and gloomy conclusion as to the meaning of the increase."[36] National Security Assistant Walt Rostow repeated the argument in Washington, advising President Johnson that "the danger is press will latch on to previous underestimate [of O/B] and revive credibility gap talk."[37]

[34] Helms, Memorandum for The Honorable Nicholas deB. Katzenbach, 15 September 1967, (S). CIA files, Job No. 80B01285A, DCI, Box 11, Folder 11.

[35] According to documents released in connection with the later Westmoreland vs. CBS case, 1984, as reported in the The New York Times, 9 October 1984.

[36] Abrams, cable to Wheeler, 20 August 1967. Attachment to letter, Congressman Paul N. McCloskey (R-CA) to DCI Colby, 6 June 1975. CIA files, Job No. 80R01720R, O/D/NFAC, Box 1, "GAC Files (SAVA-NIO)," Folder 9.

[37] 21 November 1967. According to documents released in conjunction with the Westmoreland vs. CBS case. The New York Times, 9 October 1984.

Robert Komer

These were the arguments given Carver by the immediate point man for Saigon's defense of its numbers, Ambassador Robert Komer—who was not only chief of CORDS but a close aide of LBJ's, a friend of Carver's, and a very forceful personality known appropriately as Blowtorch Bob. In June 1967 Komer had cabled Carver from Saigon that any upward revision of O/B would make it appear that the United States had not been doing a good job of whittling down enemy strength.[38] When Carver visited Saigon the next month, Komer told him that the release of increased O/B figures would cause political problems for MACV because this would come at a time when General Westmoreland was asking for more US troops.[39] And after Carver returned to Washington in August, Komer cabled him that he could not see the case for including "low-grade part-time hamlet self-defense forces" in a new O/B; doing so would create a "ruckus" that would further widen the credibility gap at the very time "when in fact we are moving toward much more valid estimates."[40] Then, according to George Allen, during the September conference in Saigon, Komer told Carver over dinner that "You guys simply have to back off. Whatever the true O/B figure is, is beside the point." If a much larger figure should be published, said Komer, within hours "some dove in State will leak it to the press; that will create a public disaster and undo everything we've been trying to accomplish out here."[41]

[38] Carver, Memorandum for the Director, "Komer Correspondence," 27 June 1967, (S). CIA files, Job No. 80R01720R, O/D/NFAC, Box 5, "GAC Files (SAVA-NIO)," Folder 7.
[39] According to Cubbage, "Westmoreland vs. CBS," p. 129.
[40] Komer cable, attachment to letter from Representative McCloskey to DCI Colby, 6 June 1975. CIA files, Job No. 80R01720R, O/D/NFAC, Box 1, "GAC Files (SAVA-NIO)," Folder 9.
[41] Allen (who was present during that coversation), to author, 11 April 1990.

An important question raised about Carver's sudden cave-in to MACV is whether DCI Helms ordered it in a cable to Carver during the Saigon conference. Here the record is contradictory. A few participants in the O/B controversy maintain that Helms did send such an explicit cable. For example: Robert Komer: "Why did George Carver cave in and compromise with MACV on the O/B question? Because that's what Helms told him to do."[42] Thomas Powers: "The deadlock was finally broken on September 11, 1967, when the CIA station in Saigon received a cable for FUNARO (Carver's official CIA pseudonym) from KNIGHT (Helms's pseudo) which directly ordered Carver to reach agreement."[43] Sam Adams: "The Saigon conference was in its third day when we received a cable from Helms that, for all its euphemisms, gave us no choice but to accept the military's numbers."[44]

The testimony of other observers is less clear as to whether Helms directly ordered Carver to back down. Bob Layton: "I heard long ago that Helms sent such a cable but I have never seen it; my position in the Saigon Station at the time was one where I would have been unlikely to have been cut in on such a sensitive directive."[45] R. Jack Smith recalls that it was Carver who suggested the compromise and that Helms then "instructed Carver to proceed according to his own best judgment."[46] John Ranelagh: "At the end of the Saigon meeting on September 13 Carver cabled to Helms that he had made a major concession in not quantifying the irregular forces, because this had been MACV's major sticking point."[47] On 13 September 1967, Carver cabled Helms that he, Carver, had worked out an O/B compromise with Westmoreland, subject to Helms's concurrence.[48] Carver later recalled, "I saw Westy and suggested the deal . . . I then told Dick what we were going to do; he did not give me any orders."[49] Helms said in 1992: "I have no recollection of

[42] Komer, to author, 21 May 1990.
[43] Powers, *The Man Who Kept the Secrets*, p. 188. A sidelight to the O/B quarrel: In June 1967 Carver had told Helms that the White House Situation Room had recently been "somewhat shaken up looking around for a staffer named Funaro." Carver, Memorandum for the Director, "Komer Correspondence," 27 June 1967, (S). CIA files, Job No. 80R01720R, O/D/NFAC, Box 5, "GAC Files (SAVA-NIO)," Folder 7.
[44] Adams, "Vietnam Cover-Up," p. 75.
[45] Layton, to author, 18 February 1992.
[46] Smith manuscript, "Richard Helms and Intelligence Production," August 1983, (S), pp.8-9. On file in CIA History Staff. At the time of the Saigon conference, Smith was CIA's Deputy Director for Intelligence. His then staff aide, Richard Kovar, has the same recollection of the Carver-Helms cables. Kovar to author, 27 November 1995.
[47] Ranelagh, *The Agency*, p. 458.
[48] Carver, SAIG 1988 (IN 51159), (S). Attachment to Carver, Memorandum for the Director, "1967 Order of Battle Cables," 28 November 1975, (S). CIA files, Job No. 80R01720R, O/D/NFAC, Box 1, "GAC Files (SAVA-NIO)," Folder 9.
[49] Carver, to author, 11 May 1992.

having cabled George in Saigon, ordering him to strike a bargain. He already knew my basic views: that because of broader considerations we had to come up with agreed figures, that we had to get this O/B question off the board, and that it didn't mean a damn what particular figures were agreed to."[50]

DCI Richard Helms

Although the record is ambiguous, it is clear that Carver and the facts of intelligence were outgunned. Whatever the O/B evidence, the governing considerations were political, especially the need to protect a beleaguered administration against a new, crucially damaging embarrassment. Certainly there were broader considerations underlying Helms's decision to direct (or to accept) a major compromise with MACV. In the view of this author, the DCI may have believed that CIA's future analytic credibility, as well as his own continuing entree to policymakers, could be better served if he did not arbitrarily marry the Agency to particular O/B estimates that other officials considered extreme. In any case, Dick Helms had numerous equities in maintaining good relations with the military members of the Intelligence Community on other questions. He also was still in a sharp struggle with the military and the White House on a crucially important question: CIA's support of Secretary McNamara's view at the time that US bombing campaigns in Vietnam were not materially hampering the enemy's war effort. As biographer Thomas Powers has phrased it, that bitter bureaucratic struggle "made the OB fight look like a mild disagreement," and Helms gave in to MACV's O/B position "because he just did not want to fight about the OB along with everything else."[51]

[50]Helms, to author, 11 May 1992. Available CIA files do not contain any communication from Helms to Carver either directing him to compromise, or agreeing to a Carver proposal that he should back off from the O/B estimates he had previously championed so strongly.
[51]Powers, *The Man Who Kept the Secrets*, p. 189. Richard Lehman, at the time deputy chief of the Office of Current Intelligence, recalls that he was "of the impression" that DCI Helms had discussed this O/B question with President Johnson and that the President was aware that the official O/B estimate might be too low. Lehman, to author, 14 March 1995.

Whatever the reasons, reactions to Carver's Saigon concessions varied widely. George Allen recalls his fury upon learning of the suddenly struck bargain: "I had never been so angry in my life, and I toyed with the idea of resigning from CIA."[52] Similarly, at the Westmoreland vs. CBS trial in 1984, Allen termed "unprincipled" the O/B positions MACV had taken in 1967, a "prostitution of intelligence"; the CIA "had sacrificed its integrity on the altar of public relations and political expediency."[53] Understandably, Sam Adams was also dismayed: "I left the Saigon conference extremely angry," and when he was asked thereafter by a member of the Board of National Estimates whether CIA had "gone beyond the bounds of reasonable dishonesty," he replied that that had occurred even before the Saigon conference.[54] Adams told Carver that General Westmoreland's O/B figures had been "a monument of deceit," and that the Agency's retreat had been an "acquiescence to MACV half-truths, distortions, and sometimes outright falsehoods."[55] Even Saigon Station observed after the conference that MACV was still "officially carrying the ridiculous [O/B] figure of 112,760 irregulars, unchanged for over a year and a half."[56]

Not all CIA officers were critical of the compromise struck in Saigon. George Carver continued to defend the bargain he struck, holding that the enemy's later inability to follow up on its Tet Offensive showed that it did not have the requisite strength; consequently, in his view, the O/B figures that had been agreed to in Saigon proved "essentially in the right ball park."[57] R. Jack Smith, the DDI in 1967, who had to sign off on the SNIE draft, took a similar position: the agreement worked out by Carver was "a highly enlightened formulation," and it would have been "simplistic and intellectually dishonest" to have insisted on the higher CIA O/B figure, "based as it was on 'spongy' evidence and a complex methodology."[58]

Endorsements of the Saigon conference compromise were undercut by military officers' later admissions that they had known at the time that General Westmoreland's insistence on an O/B total of no more than 300,000 was an artificial position dictated by political considerations, and that the true number of enemy forces had almost certainly been much

[52] Allen, to author, 11 April 1990.
[53] As cited in Cubbage, "Westmoreland vs. CBS," p. 157.
[54] Adams, "Vietnam Cover-up," p. 65.
[55] As cited in Brewin and Shaw's study of the Westmoreland vs. CBS case, "Vietnam on Trial," p. 262.
[56] SAIG 4140 (IN 85887), 3 November 1967, (S). CIA files, Job No. 80R01580R, DCI/ER Subject Files, Box 15, Folder 7.
[57] Carver, to author, 11 May 1992.
[58] Smith, History Staff manuscript, "Richard Helms and Intelligence Production," p. 12.

higher. In addition to General Graham's admission, discussed above, former MACV J-2 officers General McChristian and Col. Gaines Hawkins so testified at the CBS trial.[59]

Controversial SNIE

Even so, having concluded the September 1967 Saigon bargain with MACV, when CIA's intelligence managers moved to coordinate the long-fought SNIE they found that their analysts still had to battle separate MACV estimates and characterizations of the enemy forces. The coordination process took two more months, during which time CIA and the military clashed repeatedly over markedly differing estimates of the enemy's irregular strength. Those differences surfaced almost immediately after the Saigon conference, according to Carver, when the military backed away sharply from the agreement struck with him there. In Washington, the Pentagon's Assistant Secretary for Public Affairs, Philip Goulding, circulated a draft press statement announcing that enemy irregular strength in Vietnam was now *down*. Carver protested angrily, telling Goulding that what he proposed did not jibe with the Saigon negotiations and, furthermore, that "evidence continues to come in showing that the VC make considerable use of these 'irregulars' and not infrequently assign them actual combat tasks."[60]

MACV, according to CIA files, also prepared a press statement on O/B that deserted the positions it had just hammered out with CIA. The MACV statement inflamed a senior Office of Economic Research (OER) officer who had been helping coordinate the SNIE (and whose office soon came to have primary responsibility within CIA for following enemy O/B). He alerted Carver that the statement implied a coincidence of views between MACV and CIA that did not exist; the draft even suggested that "we have *overestimated* guerrilla forces" and, in sum, constituted "one of the greatest snow jobs since Potemkin constructed his village."[61] Despite objections by CIA officers, MACV proceeded to announce that the total North Vietnamese/Viet Cong order of battle in South Vietnam had dropped from an estimated 285,000 to 242,000, a decline of 43,000.[62] CIA files show that MACV's classified estimate, produced by

---

[59] Cubbage, "Westmoreland vs. CBS," *passim.*

[60] Carver, Memorandum for The Honorable Philip Goulding, "Proposed MACV Press Briefing on Enemy Order of Battle," 13 October 1967, (S). CIA files, Job No. 80R01720R, O/D/NFAC, Box 3, "GAC Files," Folder 4.

[61] Walsh, Memorandum for Carver, "MACV Press Briefing on Enemy Order of Battle," 11 October 1967, (S/NF). (Emphasis in the original). CIA files, Job No. 80B01721R, O/D/NFAC, Box 1, "Substantive Policy Files, DDI Vietnam Files," Folder 6.

[62] *The New York Times*, 12 November 1967.

Col. Graham, was even more optimistic, holding that enemy strength in South Vietnam had dropped from an estimated 285,000 to 235,000, a decline of 50,000.[63]

As work on the SNIE ground forward into November, Saigon Station offered up an imaginative suggestion for a wholly new approach to quantifying VC irregular strength. The Station asserted that the VC had access to between 2 1/2 and 3 million people in territories they controlled, plus more in disputed and GVN-held territory. The VC considered all these people to be "resources" to be used in war, and "a large part of them are directly employed on a sporadic, part-time, or full-time basis in military and quasi-military activities. . . .What they do for the Viet Cong is largely done by uniformed full-time troops in allied forces, which makes comparison of numbers misleading."[64]

Such efforts to persuade the military analysts to rethink their artificially constructed tallies of irregular forces proved unavailing, and the finished SNIE,[65] published on 13 November 1967, represented a rout of CIA's yearlong efforts to show that the enemy in Vietnam was far more numerous than MACV had been estimating. The SNIE's Conclusions, outlined at the beginning of the Estimate, and a table accompanying the text, stated that enemy regular force strength there was 118,000 and its guerrilla strength 70,000 to 90,000, for a total of 208,000 at most. This was substantially less than Carver's team and MACV had agreed to in Saigon just two months previously. Even more remarkable, to those readers familiar with it, was the contrast with the previous year's National Intelligence Estimate of the enemy's O/B in South Vietnam, which in July 1966 had judged that the enemy had some 285,000 to 305,000 troops.[66] The new SNIE reduced that total by close to 100,000.

SNIE 14.3-67 did explain that its statistical categories differed from previous NIEs, and in its Discussion section it did admit that the enemy's total strength, counting his entire military and political organization, was "of course considerably greater than the figure given for the Military Force." Prose caveats buried deep in the SNIE, however, could not compete among senior readers with the impression created by the

[63] From MACV J-2's Monthly Order of Battle Summary for October 1967, as cited in SAIG 5297 (IN 04823), 3 December 1967, (S). CIA files, Job No. 80B01721R, O/D/NFAC, Box 2, "Substantive Policy Files, DDI Vietnam Files," Folder 5.

[64] SAIG 4140 (IN 85887), 3 November 1967, (S). Attachment to Carver Memorandum for the Director, "More Vietnam Numbers Problems," 3 November 1967, (S). CIA Files, Job No. 80R01720R, O/D/NFAC, Box 2, Folder 11.

[65] SNIE 14.3-67, "Capabilities of the Vietnamese Communists for Fighting in South Vietnam." (Originally TS; declassified 1 December 1975.)

[66] NIE 14.3-66, "The North Vietnamese Military Potential for Fighting in South Vietnam," (TS). CIA files, Job No. 80R01720R, O/D/NFAC, Box 5, "GAC Files (SAVA - NIO)," Folder 11.

tabulation of ostensibly hard numbers up front in the Conclusions section.[67] The SNIE, moreover, repeatedly stressed that the enemy's strength in South Vietnam was declining and his guerrillas had "suffered a substantial reduction." There was "a fairly good chance" that the overall strength and effectiveness of his military forces and political infrastructure would "continue to decline." Thus, said SNIE 14.3-67, the enemy has been reduced to carrying out a protracted war of attrition: he would still have the capability to continue "some forms of struggle—though at greatly reduced levels."

Of the many and various reactions in CIA that the SNIE evoked, the following three fairly represent the spectrum:

- On the eve of the SNIE's publication, Sam Adams sent DCI Helms some blistering comments on the draft. In Adams's view the Estimate was ill formed and incoherent, less than candid, and unwise: it did not come to grips with "the probability that the number of Viet Cong, as currently defined, is something over half a million. Thus it makes canyons of gaps, and encourages self delusion."[68]

- Sherman Kent's successor as head of O/NE, Abbot Smith, told Adams that the SNIE's managers and the Board of National Estimates "had had no choice: Helms had agreed to accept the military's figure, it was his paper ultimately, what could they do?"[69]

---

[67] The author's judgment that paragraphs of prose relegated to the back of a National Intelligence Estimate cannot compete with hard numbers and crisp Conclusions up front in the Estimate, especially in their impact upon senior policymaking readers, is based on decades of personal first-hand experience in writing, managing, and marketing National Estimates. Gen. Bruce Palmer is similarly critical of SNIE 14.3-67 on these scores: "Although, according to Carver's argument, the total North Vietnamese structure approaching the half million mark in strength is described in the text, the fact remains that the summary of the estimate (all that would probably be read by most busy senior policymakers) cited a total of 188,000-208,000." Palmer, "US Intelligence and Vietnam," p. 51. George Allen: "In the end Carver and the SNIE ended up with no figure at all for the irregulars and only a general prose statement that there might be lots of these guys; to the reader this could not help but look like a complete CIA back off, an admission that their much higher VC irregular force figure had been wrong all along." Allen, to author, 11 April 1990.

[68] Adams, Memorandum for the Record, "Comments on the Current Drafts of the Introductory Note and Text of National Intelligence Estimate 14.3-67," 7 November 1967, (S). CIA files, Job No. 80R01720R, O/D/NFAC, Box 1, "GAC Files (SAVA-NIO)," Folder 9.

[69] Quoted in Powers, *The Man Who Kept the Secrets*, p.189. The CIA retreat on O/B which the SNIE represented was almost certainly influenced in part by the fact that the Board of National Estimates was now headed by Abbot Smith. The author of this study was for years a colleague and close friend of the late Dr. Smith. He was a brilliant and perceptive officer, a man of great integrity. He was a scholar, however, not a bureaucratic scrapper. Moreover, his philosophy of estimating was that the most important service an NIE or SNIE could perform was to present the greatest degree of agreed judgments, not sharp alternative views.

- Helms, who recognized that the SNIE's disputed O/B figures could prove very sensitive politically, told President Johnson the day after the completed SNIE had been disseminated that he had considered not publishing it at all.[70]

In such manner the intelligence and policy communities entered the new year of 1968 with MACV, the CIA, and an authoritative SNIE backing up the perception that the enemy did not have the capability to launch major operations. Most important, the publishing of the Estimate coincided with a White House–orchestrated public relations campaign that emphasized the bright developments supposedly taking place in the war effort. Typical of such claims was General Westmoreland's speech to the National Press Club in Washington on 21 November 1967, just a week after the SNIE had been published, in which he said, "I am absolutely certain that whereas in 1965 the enemy was winning, today he is certainly losing. . . . It is significant that the enemy has not won a major battle in more than a year. . . . [He] has many problems: he is losing control of the scattered population under his influence. . . . He sees the strength of his forces steadily declining."[71]

And so, as the 1968 Tet holiday approached in Vietnam, optimism was about to be revealed as self-delusion.

The Coming of the Tet Offensive

These same [enemy] documents call for all-out, coordinated attacks throughout South Vietnam utilizing both military and political means to achieve "ultimate victory" in the near future. . . . VC/NVA strategy toward the war appears to have reached a crucial phase in which changes in the tempo and scale of the war are envisioned. . . . In sum, the one conclusion that can be drawn from all of this is that the war is probably nearing a turning point and that the outcome of the 1967-1968 winter-spring offensive will in all likelihood determine the future direction of the war.

CIA Saigon Station Dispatch, 8 December 1967[72]

[70]From Helms's statement to the President: "The new estimate is sensitive and potentially controversial primarily because the new strength figures are at variance with our former holdings. . . . I have considered not issuing this Estimate and after considerable consultation, believe this would be a mistake. . . . In short, the charge of bad faith or unwillingness to face the facts would be more generally damaging than the issuance of this document which can stand on its own feet." Helms, Memorandum for the President, 14 November 1967, (TS). CIA files, Job No. 80B01285A, DCI, Box 11, "DCI Helms," Folder 4.
[71]*The New York Times*, 22 November 1967.
[72]FVSA-24242, (S). CIA files, Job No. 80-00088A, Box 1, DO/EA, Folder 8: "Reporting on the Tet Offensive."

[This field study of 8 December quoted above] should not be read as the considered view of this Agency. . . . [The Station's assessment has been] predicated on certain assumptions whose validity seems questionable from our perspective here in Washington.

George Carver, Memorandum to the White House's Walt Rostow,
15 December 1967[73]

We will see (1) that three intelligence components, only, rang fairly sharp alerts prior to the Tet Offensive—the Army communications intelligence group supporting Maj. Gen. Frederick C. Weyand's 3rd Corps, National Security Agency Headquarters, and CIA's Saigon Station; (2) that their alerts barely registered outside the immediate tactical scene in Vietnam; and (3) that the rest of US intelligence, CIA Headquarters included, did little to prepare policymakers for the fact, scope, or significance of the Tet Offensive. The result was that the sudden, countrywide enemy attack stunned the Johnson administration and the American public and left an unbridgeable credibility gap between them.

Some postmortem judgments of the pre-Tet intelligence performance have been harsh, as witness the evaluation in a West Point textbook published a year later: "The first thing to understand about Giap's Tet Offensive is that it was an allied intelligence failure ranking with Pearl Harbor in 1941 or the Ardennes Offensive in 1944."[74] Or the judgment of former Secretary of Defense Clark Clifford: "The fact is that three months before the offensive both Westmoreland and Ellsworth Bunker . . . loudly proclaimed that enemy strength was decreasing. . . . [Their] telegrams contained not one word of warning about the possibility of large-scale, coordinated attacks in the future. On the contrary, they . . . must rank among the most erroneous assessments ever sent by field commanders."[75]

There were significant external influences on the failure of US intelligence, CINCPAC, MACV, the Saigon Embassy, and the White House to anticipate the 1968 Tet Offensive. Among them were the distractions of near-simultaneous foreign incidents, mostly in East Asia, that demanded the attention of intelligence analysts, diplomatic and military officers, national security strategists, and the President: North Korea's seizure of the USS Pueblo; a North Korean penetration of South Korean President Park Chung Hee's residence; Seoul's subsequent pressures on Washington to permit South Korea to withdraw some of its military units

---

[73]Carver, (Cover) Memorandum for the Hon. Walt W. Rostow, "Papers on Viet Cong Strategy," 15 December 1967, (S). CIA files, Job No. 80R01589R, DCI/ER Subject Files, Box 15, Folder 3.
[74]Lt. Col. Dave Richard Palmer (USA), *Readings in Current Military History* (West Point: Department of Military Art and Engineering, US Military Academy, 1969), pp. 103-104.
[75]Clifford, *The New Yorker*, 13 May 1991, p. 50.

from Vietnam; the Communist capture of a vital outpost in easternmost Laos; serious new pressures on the West Berlin air corridor by Soviet aircraft; and the crash of a US B-52 laden with nuclear weapons. A pervasive and probably more important contribution to the failure was Lyndon Johnson's preoccupation, as the presidential election year approached, with demonstrating success in Vietnam in the face of the sharply rising tide of public opposition to the war.

But the most important cause of American surprise was the deliberately optimistic mindsets key policymakers had adopted and continued to project in the runup to Tet. President Johnson, National Security Assistant Walt Rostow, Secretary of State Rusk, JCS Chairman Wheeler, CINCPAC Adm. Ulysses S. Grant Sharp, Ambassador Bunker, and MACV commander General Westmoreland all appeared confident that American ground and air operations were so grinding down Communist forces in Vietnam that they would not be able to maintain anything more than a limited war of attrition. The pronounced gulf between their beliefs and reality deserves representative highlighting:

Robert Komer, March 1967: Mr. Komer opened [the White House meeting] by exuding optimism on the current trend in Vietnam. . . . [He] expressed consider able disdain for MACV J-2, and particularly what he believes to be its *overall underestimate of enemy strength*. . . . Concluding, Mr. Komer recognized the possible trip-ups in the overall situation but anticipated that unless they occur, major military operations might gradually fade as the enemy began to fade away or put his emphasis on a protracted guerrilla level war. In either case, he said, the size of the problem in Vietnam will diminish, and fewer U.S. resources will be needed.[76]

Walt Rostow, mid-1967: Chaired by Mr. Rostow . . . the [concern of this White House] group . . . was with opinion manipulation and political persuasion, with the aim of altering perceptions to make them coincide with specific notions, whether those notions were supportable by evidence or not.[77]

Gen. Earle Wheeler, August 1967: In his prepared testimony, General Wheeler stated that the air campaign against North Vietnam is going well. . . . In some instances where he did present intelligence estimates, he made it clear that he did not agree with the conclusions of the Intelligence Community.[78]

Walt Rostow, September 1967: Mr. Rostow . . . commented that he was "outraged" at the intellectual prudishness of the Intelligence Community [concerning its evaluation of the lack of progress in pacification].[79]

---

[76] William E. Colby, Memorandum for the Record, "VIC Meeting, 1 March 1967," 3 March 1967 (S). CIA (DO) files, Job No. 78-646, Box 1, Folder 3, "Vietnam Interagency Committee (Komer Meetings), April 1966 - May 1967." (Emphasis added).

[77] As described by participant George Allen, "The Indochina Wars," pp. 299, 300.

[78] CIA memorandum (unsigned), commenting on General Wheeler's closed-door testimony to the Senate Armed Services Committee, 16 August 1967 (TS). CIA files, Job. No. 787S02149R, O/DDI, Box 3, Folder 20, "Stennis Committee (The McNamara Testimony on Air War in North Vietnam)."

[79] William E. Colby, Memorandum for the Record, "Meeting with Mr. Walt W. Rostow, 21 September 1967," 23 September 1967 (S). CIA (DO) files, Job. No. 78-646, Box 1, Folder 5.

Gen. William Westmoreland

Gen. W. C. Westmoreland, November 1967: Infiltration will slow; the Communist infrastructure will be cut up and near collapse; the Vietnamese Government will prove its stability, and the Vietnamese army will show that it can handle the Vietcong; United States units can begin to phase down.[80]

[80] Remarks to the National Press Club, Washington, DC, 20 November 1967. *The New York Times*, 21 November 1967.

Walt Rostow, January 1968: [Mr. Rostow criticized CIA for being "fixed on certain positions" and urged it to develop new analyses based on] certain totally different hypothetical key facts, e.g., . . . that the gentlemen in Hanoi see the equation . . . as tending to indicate that one year from now, they will be in a considerably worse bargaining position than they are today; so that settlement now might be to their advantage.[81]

General Westmoreland, January 1968: The year [1967] ended with the enemy increasingly resorting to desperation tactics in attempting to achieve military/ psychological victory; and he has experienced only failure in these attempts. . . . The friendly picture gives rise to optimism for increased successes in 1968.[82]

A "we are winning" consensus pretty much permeated the Saigon-Washington command circuit; intelligence reports and analyses that deviated from it tended to be discounted. The growing uneasiness about the course of the war expressed sporadically by a handful of senior statesmen[83] had little dampening impact on the pre-Tet convictions and pronouncements of the dominant administration officials.

Prior to the 1968 Tet Offensive, the quality of CIA officers' assessments of the situation in Vietnam was mixed. On certain questions their judgments were more accurate, overall, than those of the dominant policymakers. Those judgments have won kudos from a wide spectrum of observers. Notable among these is Gen. Bruce Palmer, Jr., who later wrote glowingly of "the extraordinarily good performance of the CIA" in its Vietnam analyses.[84] As we have seen, one of the questions working-level CIA officers had right was the enemy's order of battle. Despite the Agency's backdowns on this issue—in Saigon and in SNIE 14.3-67—most CIA analysts working on Vietnam continued to judge that the true totals of enemy forces were much higher than MACV had accepted into its O/B, and that local VC self-defense and irregular forces constituted a significant source of the enemy's effective strength. A representative example, contrasting sharply with the agreed language of the just-completed

[81] William E. Colby, Memorandum for the Record, "Meeting with Mr. Rostow, 6 January 1968" (S/ Eyes Only). CIA (DO) files, Job No. 78-646, Box 1, Folder 5.
[82] From Westmoreland yearend report, as cited in *Pentagon Papers* (Gravel ed.), Vol. IV, pp. 538, 539.
[83] The most significant such critic was now Robert McNamara, formerly a staunch supporter and key architect of the Johnson war effort, who was about to be replaced as Secretary of Defense. Among other senior critics at this time were Vice President Humphrey, George Ball, Clark Clifford, McGeorge Bundy, Robert Kennedy, Eugene McCarthy, some senior DoD civilians, and a scattering of doubters in the Congress.
[84] Palmer, Memorandum for DD/NFAC, "A Look at US Intelligence Assessments re SE Asia, 1965-1975," 5 October 1975, (S). Copy on file in History Staff. In this document General Palmer recommended that the CIA should "commission a special historical effort that would describe and objectively evaluate the Agency's performance (analytical side, *not* operational) during the Vietnam war." In his view, such an undertaking would "not only enhance the reputation of the Agency but also boost the pride and esprit of CIA personnel." The desired result, he wrote, "would be a fairly short publication, well documented, and if at all possible, unclassified." (Emphasis in the original).

SNIE, was a December 1967 CIA study which stressed that over and above the accepted enemy O/B, "the Communists make a strong effort to organize much of the total manpower under their control into various work forces and semimilitary organizations. Among the most significant of these organizations are the local 'self-defense' forces."[85]

Another area where CIA's assessments looked good was in the evaluation of allied bombing efforts. Here the themes stressed in studies prepared in 1967-68 for the President, Walt Rostow, and Secretary McNamara were (1) that, although ROLLING THUNDER and other bombing programs were seriously complicating the enemy's war effort, the level of supplies getting through to the Viet Cong was continuing to rise; (2) that US bombing of North Vietnam was not proving a significant limiting factor on enemy operations in South Vietnam; and (3) that the DRV's ability to recuperate from the air attacks was of a high order.[86] CIA's good batting average on these bombing questions has been acknowledged by a wide range of commentators. Among them is David Halberstam, not notably a booster of the Agency, whose view is that Secretary McNamara "pushed the CIA very hard for judgments on how effective the bombing had been and received in return what were considered some of the best reports ever done by the Agency."[87] In 1970, George Carver, still the DCI's Special Assistant for Vietnam, judged that these earlier CIA bombing studies were probably the Agency's "most important contribution" to President Johnson's post-Tet decision (of 31 March 1968) to curtail US bombings of the North.[88]

In the months before Tet, as they had consistently held since mid-1963, CIA officers continued to judge that bombing (no matter how unrestricted) could not render North Vietnam physically incapable of carrying on the struggle and that the Communists would almost certainly try to match any US escalation of the war. And Agency assessments persisted in the view, although not as consistently or clearly, that the enemy was

---

[85] CIA Memorandum (unsigned), "A Revision of the Situation in Vietnam," 8 December 1967, (S). CIA files, Job No. 80R01720R, O/D/NFAC, Box 5, "GAC Files (SAVA - NIO)," Folder 11.

[86] As we have seen, on 21 April 1967 Secretary McNamara had asked CIA to give him periodic assessments of the effectiveness of US air operations, as well as of the enemy's O/B and the progress of pacification. By mid-1967 the Agency and DIA were jointly preparing monthly bombing assessments. A few weeks before Tet, one of the customers of these reports, the JASON division of the Office of the Secretary of Defense, issued its own, similarly pessimistic assessment of the bombing programs, an assessment the authors of *The Pentagon Papers* later termed "probably the most categorical rejection of bombing as a tool of our policy in Southeast Asia to be made before or since by an official or semiofficial group." (Gravel ed.), Vol. IV, p. 222.

[87] Halberstam, *The Best and the Brightest*, p. 644.

[88] Carver, Memorandum for the Director, "The Bombing Decisions—31 March and 1 November 1968," 31 March 1970, (S/Sensitive). CIA files, Job No. 80R01720R, O/D/ NFAC, Box 3, "GAC Files," Folder 1.

not really interested in negotiating a settlement of the war and would use negotiating tactics only to provide breathers for the next round of warfare and to gain concessions from the US/GVN side.

Meanwhile, despite their routine disregard of the Agency's negative judgments, and in the midst of the Intelligence Community's embroilment with the SNIE on enemy military capabilities, the President and his advisers in 1967 continued to enlist CIA's help and participation on a wide range of Vietnam projects. The White House repeatedly asked O/NE and SAVA to estimate probable enemy reactions to various theoretical US courses of action. Policymakers involved the Agency in programs to help CORDS develop more accurate technical systems for quantifying success in Vietnam, and CIA officers led an NSC interagency task force seeking better ways to judge Vietnam data and trend indicators.

In September and October 1967, George Carver and Richard Lehman (Deputy Chief of the DDI's Office of Current Intelligence) helped the Pentagon's Assistant Secretary for International Security Affairs and his deputy (Morton Halperin) do a special study of Vietnam policy alternatives for Secretary McNamara. Carver later realized that in this study the Pentagon staffers planted the seeds that blossomed into President Johnson's switch to a negotiating strategy in March 1968 (below). Also in October, DCI Helms received a request from Under Secretary of State Katzenbach for an Agency assessment of what GVN reactions might be to various kinds of discussions between Washington and Hanoi.[89] The workload of outside requests in November 1967 was equally heavy: Secretary McNamara asked the Agency to give him "a comprehensive review of where we now stand in Vietnam" to help him prepare for a national television interview.[90] And President Johnson asked for a CIA estimate of Viet Cong losses and casualties, a task that George Carver fielded in concert with Secretary McNamara.[91]

[89] Katzenbach, letter to Helms, 16 October 1967, (TS/Sensitive). DDI prepared CIA's reponse: Memorandum, "The South Vietnamese View of Negotiations: Problems and Prospects," 27 October 1967, (TS/Sensitive). CIA files, Job No. 80B01721R, O/D/NFAC, Box 2, "Substantive Policy Files, DDI Vietnam Files," Folder 5.

[90] Carver, Memorandum for R. J. Smith, et al., "Request from Secretary McNamara," 21 November 1967, (S), attachment to Phil G. Goulding (Assistant Secretary of Defense for Public Affairs), Memorandum for George Carver, 21 November 1967, (S). CIA files, Job No. 80R01580R, DCI/ER Subject Files, Box 15, Folder 7. CIA's response to McNamara's 67 specific questions took the form of an Intelligence Report, "Questions and Answers Relating to Vietnam," 8 December 1967, (TS/Compartmented/NF). CIA files, Job No. 82S00205R, DDI/O/DDI, Box 3, Folder 19.

[91] Carver, Memorandum for The Director and R. J. Smith, "Memo Requested by the President," 21 November 1967, (U). CIA files, Job No. 80R01720R, O/D/NFAC, Box 5, "GAC Files (SAVA - NIO)," Folder 8.

Some of the White House demands on CIA went far beyond usual intelligence matters. One such example was that of roping the Agency into the Johnson administration's wide-ranging effort, begun in the summer of 1967, to stimulate public support of the President's policies and programs in Vietnam. George Carver usually represented CIA in these White House meetings, which were chaired by Walt Rostow—with Carver's deputy, George Allen, subbing for him when he was absent. Allen terms CIA's participation in those gatherings on manipulation of domestic opinion "the most distasteful and depressing meetings of my bureaucratic career."[92]

A second example of White House pressures: in September 1967, Rostow told the Agency that because President Johnson wanted some "useful intelligence on Vietnam for a change," the CIA should prepare a list of positive (only) developments in the war effort. According to George Allen, SAVA refused to prepare such a study; but, at Helms's request, the DDI did prepare one. Helms sent it to Rostow with a cover note protesting the exercise and pointing out that this special, limited study was not a true picture of the war; but Rostow pulled off that cover note and so was finally able to give the President a "good news" study from the CIA.[93] It was also at this time that President Johnson asked CIA to prepare a questionable (and therefore super-sensitive) study on "The International Connections of the US Peace Movement."[94]

Even though CIA's judgments were contributing to Secretary McNamara's change of heart, as we have seen, the White House found many of them so uncongenial that the President, Walt Rostow, and others occasionally growled at CIA officers during these months for not being "members of the team." For example, according to George Allen, Walt Rostow more than once assailed him with such questions as "Didn't I want to win the war? Whose side was I on, anyway? Why didn't I join the team?"[95]

---

[92] Allen later wrote that he was outraged by Rostow's "dishonesty" in misleading the President, and that the exercise "was an element of the public opinion campaign which was designed to peak with the visits to Washington in November [1967] of Ambassador Bunker and General Westmoreland, who were to pull out all stops . . . in beating the drum for the 'light at the end of the tunnel.'" Allen, "The Indochina Wars," pp. 302-304.

[93] Allen, p. 304.

[94] On 15 November DCI Helms replied that the CIA could find no evidence linking the peace movement to foreign support. See Helms cover memorandum (S/Eyes Only, later declassified and given to Congressional investigative groups in 1975). CIA files, Job No. 80B01285A, DCI, Box 11, "DCI Helms," Folder 3.

[95] Allen, p. 301. The same went for newsmen. Following the Tet Offensive, when asked by John Scali whether there had been an intelligence failure, Secretary of State Rusk is reported as having exploded, "There gets to be a point when the question is whose side are you on." Marvin Kalb and Elie Abel, *Roots of Involvement: The US in Asia—1784-1971* (New York: W. W. Norton, 1971), pp. 206-207.

Not all of CIA's judgments were displeasing to the White House, nor did they all prove accurate, nor do they justify any ringing endorsement of CIA's overall analytical performance in the months leading up to the Tet Offensive. One issue on which the Agency's performance can be questioned was the stability of the Government of Vietnam. In December 1966, an NIE commissioned to forecast the GVN's performance had simply catalogued Saigon's areas of strength and weakness, without providing a clear overall message or bottom-line assessment.[96] Three months later, George Carver wrote Rostow that, even though there were still many soft spots and weak areas in the GVN's situation, "the overall progress made in the last twenty-odd months is inescapable and overwhelming."[97] Spurred by Saigon Station reports, however, Carver modified this optimism in mid-January 1968, asking the Station to inform State's Philip Habib, then visiting Vietnam, that concern was rapidly mounting in Washington over the "disquieting air of malaise and lassitude permeating the GVN."[98]

CIA's assessments of the military balance in Vietnam during this period can also be questioned. On 13 January 1967, Carver had recommended that Congress be told that the buildup of friendly forces in Vietnam was proceeding well, that the relative advantage over enemy forces had reached about four to one, and that in terms of combat potential the rate of growth was "even more favorable."[99] Two months later, Carver privately assured Rostow that that "there is a considerably better than even chance that within a reasonable time frame, say eighteen months, the total situation in Vietnam will have improved . . . to the point where all but the willfully obtuse will be able to recognize that the Communist insurgency is failing."[100] According to Clark Clifford (chairman of PFIAB in 1967, later Secretary of Defense), in the spring of 1967 "the CIA's top Vietnam expert, George Carver, told the PFIAB that by the fall of 1968 the situation should be dramatically improved."[101] In July 1967, Helms gave President Johnson an evaluation by C/FE Bill Colby, following an

[96] NIE 53-66, "Problems of Political Development in South Vietnam Over the Next Year or So," 15 December 1966, (S/Controlled Dissem; declassified in November 1975). Copy on file with CIA's History Staff.

[97] Carver, letter to Rostow, 2 March 1967, (S/Sensitive), attachment to Carver, Memorandum for the Director, "Rostow-requested Memorandum, 3 March 1967, (S/Sensitive). CIA files, Job No. 80R01580R, DCI/ER Subject Files, Box 15, Folder 8.

[98] (Carver-drafted) DIR 66478 to Saigon, 13 January 1968, (S). CIA files, Job No. 80R01720R, O/D/NFAC, Box 5, "GAC Files (SAVA - NIO)," Folder 9.

[99] Carver, Memorandum for the Deputy Director, "Possible Congressional Questions," 9 January 1967, (S). CIA files, Job No. 80R01580R, DCI/ER Subject Files, Box 15, Folder 8.

[100] Carver, letter to Rostow, 2 March 1967 (S). CIA files, Job No. 80R01580R, DCI/ER Subject Files, Box 15, Folder 8.

[101] Clifford, *The New Yorker*, 6 May 1991, p.73.

inspection trip to Vietnam, which concluded that even though there were fragile elements present, "it is very clear that my Soviet and Chinese counterparts' reports must exhibit great concern over the Viet Cong's mounting problems and the steady improvement in the ability of both the South Vietnamese and the Americans to fight a people's war."[102] According to Clark Clifford, briefings given by George Carver and JCS Chief Gen. Earle Wheeler to the President's panel of "Wise Men" on 2 November 1967 "set an upbeat and optimistic tone."[103] And a few days later, DDCI Rufus Taylor wrote Helms that he felt strongly that the "great" progress made in the past year "could be emphasized in press interviews and comment by public officials," and that this "might be of considerable help in countering the peaceniks."[104]

As for giving warning that a major enemy offensive was in the making, it will be seen that the best that could be said of CIA was that it sounded a distant trumpet from the field that came to be muted at Headquarters. But, except for the National Security Agency, no other components of the Intelligence Community did any better.

South Vietnamese Intelligence: Eleventh-Hour Indicators

GVN intelligence collected a few indications, beginning about October 1967, that the enemy might launch an unprecedented winter offensive; and just hours before the Tet Offensive, the South Vietnamese produced at least two reports that proved extraordinarily accurate. The first was an intelligence report transmitted on 29 January 1968 to alert South Vietnamese tactical zone commanders that the Viet Cong would take advantage of the Tet Holiday in order to attack a number of provincial cities.[105] The second stemmed from the capture of an enemy soldier at 2100 hours on 30 January. He stated that Communist troops were going to attack central Saigon, Tan Son Nhut Airbase, and other installations in the capital city beginning at 0300 hours the next day—exactly the moment those attacks did start.[106]

[102] Colby, Memorandum, "Review of the Activities of the CIA's Vietnam Station," 25 July 1967 (S/ Sensitive), attachment to Helms, Memorandum for the President, "Transmittal of Vietnam Report," 27 July 1967, (S/Sensitive). CIA files, Job No. 80R01720R, O/D/NFAC, Box 5, "GAC Files (SAVA - NIO)," Folder 7.

[103] Clifford, *The New Yorker*, 6 May 1991, p. 77.

[104] Taylor, Memorandum for the Director, "Understanding the War in Vietnam," 7 November 1967, (U). CIA files, Job No. 80R01580R, DCI/ER Files, Box 15, Folder 3.

[105] CAS Saigon R 310742Z, (TS/Compartmented). CIA files, Job No. 80-00088A, Box 1, DO/EA, Folder 8, "Reporting on the Tet Offensive."

[106] As cited by GVN Col. Hoang Ngoc Lung, in his monograph, *General Offensives of 1968-1969* (Washington, D.C.: US Army Center of Military History, 1978), p. 37.

These reports came much too late in the game, however, to help very much. For the most part GVN intelligence on enemy intentions prior to Tet was scattered, incomplete, and ambiguous. On the very eve of the enemy's offensive, CIA's Saigon Station Chief observed that the GVN police had a few scattered reports of upcoming enemy operations but nothing which appeared to be very hard.[107] Moreover, according to South Vietnamese security chief Col. Lung, most GVN commanders believed that the enemy was incapable of launching a major nationwide offensive in the near future; he added that most GVN units did not even share their intelligence take with one another.[108] Nor, according to MACV's J-2 at the time, Major General Phillip B. Davidson, did they pass on their reports to MACV. GVN officials were clearly not prepared for this attack on the opening day of Tet, when large numbers of them were celebrating with their families.[109]

MACV Intelligence: Last Minute Precautionary Steps

MACV—and virtually everyone else—greatly underestimated the scope and intensity of the coming offensive and remained generally unaware of the enemy's overall intentions and timing, even though North Vietnamese newspapers were speaking rather freely of a coming campaign of "historic dimension." Nonetheless, by January 1968, MACV headquarters was persuaded by captured documents and other indicators that major shifts were occurring among many VC units. One of the clearest forecasts they had of a coming offensive was a VC document captured by US forces shortly before Tet which proclaimed that "the opportunity for a general offensive and general uprising is within reach," and that Viet Cong forces should undertake "very strong military attacks in coordination with the uprisings of the local population to take over towns and cities; troops should . . . move toward liberating the capital city, take power and try to rally enemy brigades and regiments to our side one by one."[110]

Enough such indicators reached General Westmoreland to prompt some concern and, almost at the last moment, some precautionary steps. On 25 January he cabled CINCPAC that that date seemed to be "shaping

[107] As cited in Carver, Memorandum for the Honorable Walt W. Rostow, "31 January Telephone Conversation with Saigon Station," 31 January 1968, (S/Sensitive). CIA files, Job No. 80R01720R, O/D/NFAC, Box 5, "GAC Files (SAVA-NIO)," Folder 9.
[108] Lung, *General Offensives of 1968-1969*, pp. 40-41.
[109] Davidson, *Vietnam at War: The History, 1946-1975* (San Francisco: Presidio Press, 1988), p. 480.
[110] As cited in Lt. Col. Dave Richard Palmer, *Summons of the Trumpet: U.S.-Vietnam in Perspective* (San Francisco: Presidio Press, 1978), pp.178-179. See also Clark Clifford, *The New Yorker,* 13 May 1991, p. 48.

up as a D-Day for widespread pre-Tet offensive action on the part of VC/NVA forces."[111] On 30 January Westmoreland cancelled a previous Tet ceasefire for US troops and ordered that "effective immediately all forces will resume intensified operations, and troops will be placed on maximum alert."[112] Finally, convinced by intelligence alerts given him by his III Corps commander, Maj. Gen. Frederick C. Weyand, Westmoreland reversed the orders he had just given Weyand's 25th Division to undertake offensive sweeps in the countryside: instead, some of its units were brought into and around Saigon, increasing the number of US maneuver battalions protecting the capital to some 27. These precautionary moves doubtless saved Saigon and the US presence there from disaster.

General Weyand called his alerts largely on the basis of his analysis of enemy radio traffic and his professional belief that MACV was greatly underestimating the number and military significance of local VC forces.[113] An experienced intelligence officer, Weyand respected CIA officers and thought they were "focused on one of the right ways to defeat the enemy"; but in the case of the Tet offensive he felt that CIA and MACV did not provide any warning intelligence "worth a damn."[114] Former CORDS Ambassador Robert Komer is similarly critical: "neither CIA nor MACV provided any warning at all of the magnitude or the targets of the enemy's Tet Offensive; we were all completely surprised."[115]

---

[111] COMUSMACV cable to CINCPAC, info to General Wheeler and Ambassador Bunker, 25 January 1968. Attachment to "Intelligence Warning of the Tet Offensive in South Vietnam," April 1968. (Initially classified, this postmortem was declassified and released to the House of Representatives' Pike Committee in 1975.) CIA files, Job No. 80R01720R, O/D/NFAC, Box 1, "GAC Files (SAVA-NIO)," Folder 8.

[112] MACV cable 300325Z Jan 1968, "Cancellation of TET Ceasefire," (initially Confidential, subsequently declassified and released to the Pike Committee). CIA files, as above.

[113] General Weyand, to author, 17 April 1991. The officer commanding General Weyand's communications battalion at the time, former Lt. Col. Norman Campbell, supports Weyand's accounts. Campbell, to author, 18 May 1992. For additional accounts of General Weyand's prescience, see Dave Richard Palmer, Summons of the Trumpet, p. 184; Don Oberdorfer, Tet (New York: Da Capo Press, 1984), pp. 137-141; and Neil Sheehan, A Bright Shining Lie: John Paul Vann and America in Vietnam, pp. 701-709. As of January 1968, Vann was attached to General Weyand's command. Weyand, who had previously held numerous military intelligence assignments, based his certainty of a coming major offensive largely on traffic analysis and radio direction finding; fomer Lt. Col. Campbell claims that their communications units were also reading some of the enemy's traffic. In March 1968, USMC Lt. Gen. Robert Cushman, then I Corps commander (and later DDCI), told visiting OCI officer Richard Lehman that the Marines in I Corps had had "ample forewarning" of the Tet Offensive, even though the enemy's specific targets had remained unknown. SAIG 0191 (IN 733895), 20 March 1968, (S). CIA files, Job No. 80B01721R, O/D/NFAC, Box 2, "Substantive Policy Files, DDI Vietnam Files," Folder 1.

[114] Weyand, to author, 17 April 1991.

[115] Komer, to author, 21 May 1990.

115

NSA

The National Security Agency stood alone in issuing the kinds of warnings the US Intelligence Community was designed to provide. The first SIGINT indicators of impending major enemy activity began to appear in the second week of January 1968. In the following days NSA issued a number of alerts, culminating in a major warning it disseminated widely in communications intelligence channels on 25 January, titled "Coordinated Vietnamese Communist Offensive Evidenced in South Vietnam."[116]

In the period 25-30 January, NSA issued a number of followup alerts for specific areas of Vietnam. Even so, as NSA stated later in its review of Tet reporting, SIGINT was unable to provide advance warning of the true nature, size, and targets of the coming offensive. This was due in large measure to the fact that the enemy's local and irregular forces, which played such a large role in the offensive, made only limited use of radio communications.

CIA Field Reports and Headquarters Publications

Beginning in October 1967, CIA's Directorate of Plans made some 15 disseminations prior to Tet which, in hindsight, provided scattered indications that preparations might be under way in individual provinces for possible major enemy offensives of some kind before, during, or after Tet. These disparate reports, by themselves, did not add up to a sharp alert that an unprecedented nationwide attack was in the offing.[117] When the Intelligence Community later conducted a postmortem on its pre-Tet reporting for the President's Foreign Intelligence Advisory Board, it concluded that CIA field reporting "did not . . . reflect the massive character of the preparations under way all over South Vietnam for simultaneous invasions of nearly all major cities and towns. Nor did this reporting impart a sense that 'all hell' was about to break loose."[118] This was still the conclusion in 1975 when a DO/Vietnam branch officer did a new survey of the CIA field reports prepared prior to Tet; in his view, the warning they had given was "zilch."[119]

---

[116] Classified NSA Historical Files, VIII, Box 19, "Tet Offensive, Jan/Feb 1968."

[117] The author's review of CIA/FE (EA) Division reporting for this period.

[118] *Intelligence Warning of the Tet Offensive in South Vietnam*, Section VII-1, "Indications Received in CIA, 15-30 January 1968," (S/later declassified and provided the Pike Committee in 1975), p.1. CIA files, Job No. 80R01720R, O/D/NFAC, Box 1, "GAC Files (SAVA-NIO)," Folder 8, "Intelligence Warning of the Tet Offensive in So. Vietnam." The CIA's DDI, R. Jack Smith, chaired this Intelligence Community postmortem.

[119] Handwritten comment by the Acting Deputy Chief, Vietnam Operations branch of EA Division in a Memorandum for Deputy Chief, East Asia Division, "Vietnam Reporting Prior to Tet 1968 Offensive," 18 September 1975, (S). CIA files, Job No. 80-00088A, Box 1, DO/EA, Folder 8, "Reporting on the Tet Offensive."

The current intelligence publications of CIA's Directorate of Intelligence distributed in the two months before Tet provided occasional intimations of impending Communist operations in the contested areas of northern South Vietnam, but no sharp warnings of a countrywide offensive. The treatment of East Asian matters by the Agency's premier publication, the *President's Daily Brief (PDB),* focused principally on South Vietnamese political developments; North Vietnamese and Communist Bloc attention to antiwar sentiment in the United States; the buildup of North Vietnamese military units just north of the Demilitarized Zone (DMZ); and especially the growing threat to the US outpost at Khe Sanh. From 23 January onward, North Korea's seizure of the USS Pueblo dominated the *PDB*'s reporting and analysis.[120]

The *PDB* at that time was primarily a vehicle for summarizing sensitive or late-breaking reports for the White House; lower-level White House officials and other consumers received the more inclusive *Current Intelligence Bulletin (CIB)* which, between 11 and 24 January, contained some eight reports on enemy activity, all confined to indications of scattered VC and NVA buildups in this or that local area, especially in the northernmost regions of South Vietnam. As Tet drew nearer, current intelligence publications did begin to focus on the possibilities of a large-scale enemy offensive. On 27 and 28 January the *CIB* replayed NSA's alerting memorandum of 25 January, reporting that communications intelligence had provided evidence of a widespread, coordinated series of attacks to be launched by the Communists. The 28 January *CIB* undercut that warning, however, by judging that the Communists intended to launch large-scale attacks on one or more fronts *soon after Tet,* and that it was not yet possible to determine if the enemy was indeed planning an all-out, countrywide offensive during, or just following, the Tet holiday period.[121]

The *CIB* for 29 January reported that North Vietnamese main force units were completing battle preparations in the western highlands of Pleiku and Kontum Provinces; that well-coordinated large-scale attacks may have been imminent there; and that the often mentioned "N-Day" may have been set for as soon as 30 January. The following day's current intelligence publications carried no reports or assessments of enemy intentions in Vietnam. On the 31st, as Communist assaults began to erupt all over the country, the DDI's published wrap-up of the situation characterized the enemy's attacks on US targets as harassments, and concluded

---

[120] The author's review of the PDBs of the eight months preceding Tet. CIA files, Job No. 79T00936A, NFAC/OCO, Boxes 53 to 58 (26 June 1967 - 20 February 1968)(TS/Compartmented).
[121] As cited in the Intelligence Community's postmortem, *Intelligence Warning of the Tet Offensive in South Vietnam, passim.* (Emphasis added).

that the enemy's operations to date might be preparatory to or intended to support further attacks in the Khe Sanh/DMZ/northern Quang Tri areas.[122]

The Intelligence Community's later postmortem described Washington's pre-Tet warning performance, overall, in these terms:

> "The urgency felt in Saigon was not, however, fully felt in Washington in the immediate preattack period. As a result, finished intelligence disseminated in Washington did not contain the atmosphere of crisis prevalent in Saigon. We do not believe this represents a failure on anyone's part. The information available was transmitted and fully analyzed, but atmosphere is not readily passed over a teletype circuit. Although senior officials in Washington received warnings in the period 25-30 January, they did not receive the full sense of immediacy and intensity which was present in Saigon. On the other hand, with Saigon alerted, virtually nothing further could be done in Washington that late in the game which could affect the outcome."[123]

True, little could have been done in Washington to affect the outcome in Saigon and elsewhere in Vietnam, but an alerted Johnson administration could at least have prepared the public for the sudden turn of events and better eluded the charge that it and the GVN had been taken by surprise. The sum of the Intelligence Community's pre-Tet assessments was clearly insufficient to alert policymakers or the public to what proved to be a devastating political upset.[124]

---

[122] *DDI Intelligence Memorandum*, "The Communist Tet Offensive," 31 January 1968, (TS/Compartmented). On file in OIR Document Library, CIA HQs.

[123] *Intelligence Warning of the Tet Offensive in South Vietnam*, pp. 5-6. This postmortem conclusion is less critical of the US intelligence performance than seems warranted, at least in hindsight. Its muted tone doubtless can be explained by an understandable reluctance to dramatize the shortcomings in the Intelligence Community's own record or to probe deeply the intelligence operations of a military command that was still fighting its way out of the consequences of its errors. When the postmortem evaluators formed a team to examine the performance of CIA, State, and military officers in the field, DCI Helms told the examiners that they should not "rock the boat"; they could be "critical but not inflammatory" in their report. The recollection of the team's chairman, Richard Lehman, to the author, 14 March 1995.

[124] A prime reflection of surprise is this incident related by CIA's George Allen. At CIA Headquarters he was in the process of giving a Vietnam briefing to State's Phil Habib and Nicholas Katzenbach when a CIA officer rushed in to tell them that the Embassy in Saigon was under attack. "Habib chuckled, suggesting that I have my troops knock off their horsing around . . . The officer earnestly persisted, exclaiming in his best 'Pearl Harbor' tones, 'This is no drill, sir; the wire tickers report that the embassy is under attack and the VC have penetrated the compound' . . . Habib's jaw fell, and he turned ashen gray; he realized immediately the significance of this development; that the wind had been taken out of the administration's sails, the 'light at the end of the tunnel' had been turned off, the administration's policies had been derailed from 'the right track.'" Allen, "The Indochina Wars," pp. 323-324.

CIA Alerting Appraisals From the Field

The CIA's field intelligence analysis prior to Tet was extremely good, but its alerting performance went largely for naught. In November and December 1967, Saigon Station sent in three major assessments, each of which warned that a powerful, nationwide enemy offensive was coming. The second and most substantial of these studies predicted that the impending offensive "would in all likelihood determine the future direction of the war," a judgment Gen. Bruce Palmer later termed "an uncannily accurate forecast!"[125] That assessment and its two companions stand out as the finest predictive performance by any CIA entity in the weeks leading up to Tet. Untainted by the packaged optimism of the MACV reporting channel, and arriving in Washington far ahead of the disturbing but too-late tactical intelligence reports of enemy troop movements, the judgments in these assessments could have made a profound difference — if only in bracing the administration for the Tet shock and giving it time to prepare the public. But, as we will see, the Saigon Station's assessments failed to shake the personal preconceptions of senior CIA and White House officials.

The three Saigon studies were the work of the Station's small assessments group headed by Bob Layton, an O/NE officer detailed to Saigon in mid-1967. The first two assessments (21 November and 8 December 1967) were produced as an apparently intentional overresponse to a request from the White House's Walt Rostow that the Station simply send in a list of its previous reports dealing with North Vietnamese/VC intentions. The November study included the requested wrap-up, but Layton and his colleagues added their own analytical estimate of the enemy's intentions in 1968 and promised a more thorough assessment in two weeks.[126]

Drawing heavily on prisoner interrogations and captured documents, this first field assessment concluded that the enemy seemed to be preparing an all-out effort to inflict a psychologically crippling defeat on allied forces sometime in 1968. The Station's analytic group called particular attention to numerous reports that enemy special action units had been directed to engage in widespread terrorism and sabotage in South Vietnam's major cities, coordinated with military attacks on the cities from without.[127] The Communists appeared to believe the time was ripe for such an effort, this assessment explained, because the GVN was perceived to be corrupt, unpopular, and incapable of gaining the allegiance of the bulk of South Vietnam's population and because the GVN's armed

[125] Palmer, *Studies in Intelligence* article, "US Intelligence and Vietnam," p. 55.
[126] Layton, to author, 18 February 1992.
[127] SAIG 4956 (IN 99377), (S). Copy given CIA History Staff by Layton and on file there.

forces were suffering from serious morale problems and were incapable of advancing or protecting the pacification program. At the same time, according to this assessment, the US administration was becoming increasingly isolated internationally, was facing rising internal dissension, and thus wanted to end the war before the fall of 1968.

The Station's follow-up assessment of 8 December pondered the recent evidence of Communist exhortations for an all-out offensive against US/GVN forces and bases and decided that this represented a deliberate departure from the existing strategy of a patient war of mutual attrition. This thinkpiece began with a careful sifting of the increasing references in North Vietnamese and Viet Cong documents to the necessity to launch "an all-out military and political offensive during the 1967-68 winter-spring campaign [the period beginning around Tet] designed to gain decisive victory." As described in captured enemy documents and in accounts by prisoners of troop indoctrination sessions, the offensive would include both "large-scale continuous coordinated attacks by main force units, primarily in mountainous areas close to border sanctuaries"— a strategy subsequently reflected in the enemy's major attacks on Khe Sanh—and "widespread guerrilla attacks on large US/GVN units in rural and heavily populated areas." All-out attacks by both regular and irregular forces would be launched throughout South Vietnam, designed to occupy some urban centers and isolate others.

Layton concluded that "the VC/NVN . . . appear to have committed themselves to unattainable ends within a very specific and short period of time," which included "a serious effort to inflict unacceptable military and political losses on the Allies regardless of VC casualties during a US election year, in the hope that the US will be forced to yield to resulting domestic and international pressure and withdraw from South Vietnam." The approaching winter-spring campaign was shaping up as a maximum effort, Layton judged, using all current VC/NVN resources "to place maximum pressure on the Allies" for a settlement favorable to the Communists. And if, as was likely, they failed to achieve this maximum goal, Layton reasoned, they would at least have hurt the US/GVN forces, knocked them off balance, and "placed themselves in a better position to continue a long-range struggle with a reduced force." He continued: "If the VC/NVN view the situation in this light, it is probably to their advantage to use their current apparatus to the fullest extent in hopes of fundamentally reversing current trends before attrition renders such an attempt impossible." "In sum," the study's final sentence read, "the one conclusion that can be drawn from all of this is that the war is probably nearing a turning point and that the outcome of the 1967-68 winter-spring campaign will in all likelihood determine the future direction of the war."[128]

The Station's third alerting assessment (19 December) reiterated, with additional evidence, that available indicators showed Viet Cong/North Vietnamese forces were preparing something very much like an all-out push. Layton's group conceded (as Headquarters analysts had argued) that these enemy themes might be only propaganda designed to sustain VC/VNA morale, but the group doubted this. And though the projected offensive would cost staggering losses, the enemy nonetheless was prepared to accept them in order to accelerate what Hanoi believed was a sharp decline in the American will to continue the war.[129]

These remarkably prescient alerts, with their postulation of the enemy's reasoning and probable actions, met an unfortunate fate. Special Assistant George Carver, the senior CIA official in closest constant touch with the White House on Vietnam matters, administered a coup de grace to Layton's warnings. On 15 December Carver sent the Station's second (8 December) warning study to Walt Rostow but distanced himself and CIA from it. In his cover note Carver told Rostow that the attached field assessment "should not be read as the considered opinion of this Agency;" that it omitted reference to "other [unspecified] materials" bearing on the subject; and that the Station's assessment was "predicated on certain assumptions whose validity seems questionable from our perspective here in Washington." Carver questioned the assessment's thesis that the enemy was about to make crucial new decisions on the course of the war, and he told Rostow in effect that the Communists would continue their strategy of a limited war of attrition.[130] It is difficult not to agree with Gen. Bruce Palmer's later conclusion that Carver's throwing of "cold water on the [field's] studies . . . no doubt contributed to the unprepared state of mind in Washington when Tet 1968 hit."[131]

Worse still, Layton and his colleagues were contending against the judgments not only of the influential Carver, but of virtually all the Vietnam analysts then at CIA Headquarters. On 2 December, two weeks before Carver sent his dissenting cover note to Rostow, the Directorate of Intelligence had prepared a quick critique of Layton's preliminary

---

[128] Saigon telepouch FVSA 24242, 8 December 1967, (S, subsequently declassified). CIA files, Job No. 80R01580R, DCI/ER Subject Files, Box 15, Folder 3.

[129] SAIG 5624 (IN 69402), 19 December 1967, (S). CIA files, Job No. 80B01721R, O/D/NFAC, Box 2, "Substantive Policy Files, DDI Vietnam Files, Folder 5.

[130] Carver (cover) Memorandum for the Hon. Walt W. Rostow, "Papers on Viet Cong Strategy," 15 December 1967, (S). CIA files, Job No. 80R01589R, DCI/ER Subject Files, Box 15, Folder 3.

[131] Palmer, "US Intelligence and Vietnam," p. 55.

(November) assessment; the analysts held that captured enemy documents did not indicate that the enemy was about to radically change his tactics, and did not suggest that the Communists thought they could really mount a decisive campaign.[132]

Doubly unfortunate for Layton and his colleagues was the timing of the second Headquarters product. On 8 December, the very day these field officers sent off their second (and most substantial) warning assessment, CIA Headquarters had just produced and distributed a major study—coordinated with all the Headquarters analytical offices—which differed sharply with Layton's conclusions. The 8 December Headquarters study told policymakers (1) because the war was not going well for the Communist forces, their present strategy was to hang on militarily and politically; and (2) the evidence suggested that for the present the North Vietnamese and the Viet Cong felt under no compulsion to abandon their basic objectives in the south or the means by which they were seeking to attain them.[133]

Thus, when Carver advised Walt Rostow on 15 December that, contrary to Saigon Station's warnings, the enemy was not likely to launch a sudden nationwide major offensive, he was speaking not only for himself but for CIA Headquarters—whose analysts of North Vietnamese strategy preferred their in-house expectations of rational behavior by Hanoi to radically new assessments from outside their ranks.

There was irony as well in the reception given Layton's warnings before and after Tet. At the beginning of 1968 no one exuded more confidence and less concern about the course of the war than President Johnson and his head cheerleader, Walt Rostow. Both men, however, later cited Layton's 8 December assessment as specific evidence that they had known all along the enemy's nationwide offensive was coming. In his memoirs, published in 1971, ex-President Johnson claimed that he had "agreed heartily with one prophetic report from our Embassy in Saigon [that the war was probably nearing a turning point and the outcome of the 1967-68 winter-spring campaign would in all likelihood determine the future direction of the war]. I was increasingly concerned by reports that the Communists were preparing a maximum military effort and were going to try for a significant tactical victory."[134] Similarly, writing in 1972, Walt Rostow quoted Layton's 8 December thinkpiece at some

[132] DDI (blind) memorandum, "Comments on SAIG 4956," 2 December 1967, (S). CIA files, Job No. 80B01721R, O/D/NFAC, Box 2, "Substantive Files, DDI Vietnam Files," Folder 5.
[133] CIA Memorandum, "A Review of the Situation in Vietnam," 8 December 1967, (TS/Compartmented), prepared jointly by the Office of Current Intelligence, the Office of Economic Research, O/NE, and SAVA. CIA files, Job No. 78T02095R, O/DDI, Box 1, Folder 1.
[134] Johnson, *The Vantage Point: Perspectives of the Presidency, 1963-1969*, pp. 371-372. According to Robert Johnson, who had been a colleague of Walt Rostow's in State's Policy Planning Staff, Rostow wrote much of the former President's autobiography. Robert Johnson, to author, 13 June 1992.

length, claiming that it indicated both the extent to which the structure of the Tet Offensive "was appreciated as early as December 8 and the kind of data available to Johnson at that time," and the fact that the President "had been receiving regularly and following closely the piecemeal evidence on which this summation was based."[135]

Tet, Its Aftermath, and CIA

> We have known for several months, now, that the Communists planned a massive winter-spring offensive. . . . The biggest fact is that the stated purposes of the general uprising have failed. . . . when the American people know the facts, when the world knows the facts and when the results are laid out for them to examine, I do not believe they will achieve a psychological victory.

President Lyndon Johnson, 2 February 1968[136]

> Gen. George Custer said today in an exclusive interview with this corresponden that the Battle of Little Big Horn had just turned the corner and he could now see the light at the end of the tunnel. . . . "We have the Sioux on the run . . . Of course we will have some cleaning up to do, but the Redskins are hurting badly and it will only be a matter of time before they give in."

Art Buchwald, 6 February 1968[137]

The Tet Offensive

Confounding the assurances CIA Headquarters had given the White House about the enemy's capabilities and intentions, 30 January 1968 brought the revelation that the Vietnamese Communists had changed their strategy, suddenly and radically. In the first two days of the Tet Offensive, enemy units attacked 39 of South Vietnam's 44 provincial capitals, five of six autonomous cities, 71 of 242 district capitals, some 50 hamlets, virtually every allied airfield, many other military targets, and Saigon itself. In the capital city, some 11 local force VC battalions struck the presidential palace, Tan Son Nhut Airbase, the Vietnamese Joint General Staff compound, and numerous other targets;

---

[135] Rostow, *The Diffusion of Power: An Essay in Recent History* (New York: MacMillan, 1972), pp. 464-465.
[136] *The New York Times*, 3 February 1968.
[137] *The Washington Post*, 6 February 1968.

Tet Offensive, 1968

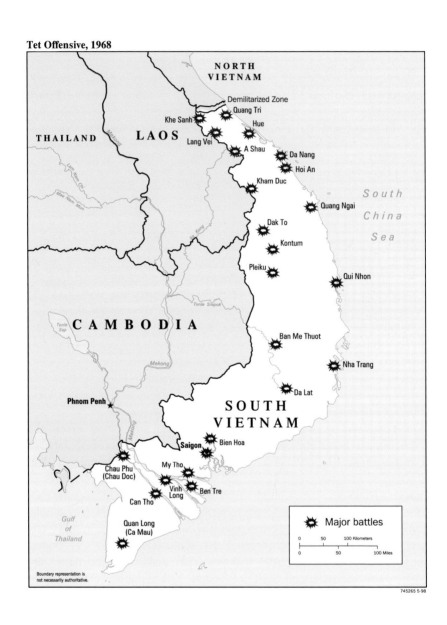

not least, they penetrated and for a while contested the grounds of the US Embassy.[138] According to CIA files, JCS Chairman Earle Wheeler candidly told President Johnson on 27 February that the enemy's initial attacks "nearly succeeded in a dozen places and the margin of victory— in some places survival—was very very small indeed."[139] Describing Wheeler's report some years later, Clark Clifford recalled that the JCS Chairman had told the President that the Tet Offensive was "a colossal disaster for us," that "we were in real peril," and that Lyndon Johnson consequently was "as worried as I have ever seen him."[140]

In many respects, the primary casualty of the Tet Offensive was President Johnson himself, who just two months later announced he would not stand for reelection. In the intervening weeks of February and March, the enemy's offensive continued in many areas. It included full-scale battles, the largest yet fought by US troops, at Hue and Khe Sanh. At home, the President's political position was weakening under sharpened attacks: Robert Kennedy entered the presidential field against LBJ, and on 12 March the antiwar candidate Eugene McCarthy captured a remarkable 42 percent of the Democratic primary vote in New Hampshire. Then, while many senior administration and military officials kept assuring the country that Tet had been a severe military defeat for the enemy, word leaked out that General Westmoreland was requesting 206,000 more troops.[141] And by this time not only Robert McNamara had come to doubt the President's course, but so also had his successor as Secretary of Defense, Clark Clifford, and a number of other senior

---

[138] *DDI Intelligence Memorandum*, "Communist Units Participating in Attacks During the Tet Offensive: 30 January Through 13 February 1968," (S/NF). CIA files, Job No. 80R01720R, O/D/NFAC, Box 2, Folder 14. The author of the present History Staff study was in Saigon during the first days of the Tet Offensive and witnessed the Embassy compound minutes after it was secured.

[139] Wheeler, Memorandum for the President, "Military Situation and Requirements in South Vietnam," 27 February 1968, (TS). CIA files, Job No. 80R01720R, O/D/NFAC, Box 3, Folder 2, "March 1968 Review Commissioned by Pres. Johnson." In the body of his report, attached to his cover letter to the President (from which the quotations above are taken), General Wheeler described the Tet Offensive as "a very near thing." Report of Chairman, Joint Chiefs of Staff, Gen. Earle G. Wheeler, on the Situation in Vietnam, 27 February 1968, as cited in Gareth Porter (ed.), *Vietnam: The Definitive Documentation of Human Decisions*, Vol. II, p.502. Wheeler's description, "it was a near thing," is also cited in the Gravel edition of *The Pentagon Papers*, Vol. IV, p. 547; and by former MACV J-2 Gen. Phillip Davidson, who describes Wheeler's report as "the blackest possible evaluation of the battlefield situation in Vietnam." Davidson, *Vietnam at War*, p. 504.

[140] Clark Clifford, to interviewer John B. Henry II, 22 June 1970. Henry, "February 1968," *Foreign Policy*, Fall 1971, p. 23.

[141] The news story was broken by *The New York Times* on 10 March, presumably leaked by someone who opposed General Westmoreland's request. The manner in which this news item hit the country —with Westmoreland calling for thousands more troops just after having supposedly inflicted a major defeat on the enemy—obscured the particular circumstances of Westmoreland's message. The 206,000 additional troops were a contingency requirement in the event the United States decided to change its basic ground force strategy in Vietnam from defense to offense.

defense advisers. Prominent among the latter were DoD's Paul Nitze and Paul Warnke, who in those weeks of February and March made extremely gloomy assessments of the situation. On 1 March, Nitze told Secretary Clifford that the overall national security interests of the United States demanded that we should stop bombing North Vietnam and give General Westmoreland no more than 50,000 additional troops. Warnke has been quoted as later recalling that Tet exposed the fact that "what we had thought was political progress was just so thin as to be illusory," and that the United States could go on winning battles but it would not make any difference because there was no way in which we could "bring about political progress in South Vietnam."[142]

CIA: Post-Tet Assessments

During these weeks Agency officers, often working against impossible deadlines, made substantial inputs to the administration's efforts to devise military and political responses to the Tet-inspired crisis. In addition to providing a steady stream of current intelligence, CIA officers supported executives and strategists with numerous studies and assessments, both requested and volunteered, and participated in senior policy forums. The range of their inputs was wide and at times went considerably beyond strictly intelligence boundaries.

One of the broadest tasks requested of CIA intelligence producers was a list of cosmic questions Vice President Humphrey asked the Agency on 20 February to answer, which added up to assessing whether the United States should abandon its basic strategy in Vietnam. This proved too touchy a question even for George Carver; he advised DCI Helms to duck Humphrey's request. Carver argued that it was not the Agency's business "to tell the Vice President what U.S. strategy in Vietnam is or ought to be," and that he (Carver) was "edgy" about providing a CIA answer to the Vice President's staff "which is not noted for its discretion or good security practices."[143] Carver and other CIA officers did, however, respond to the numerous other difficult questions asked them.

The Department of Defense levied several requests on CIA at this time, including some cosmic questions of its own: what the likely course of events in South Vietnam would be over the rest of 1968; what the enemy's military strategy would be; how North Vietnam, China, the Soviet Union, and "other key countries" might respond to a US troop increase in Vietnam of 200,000; and what terms Hanoi would be willing

[142] Warnke, to interviewer John B. Henry II, 12 August 1970, Henry, "February 1968," p. 29.
[143] Carver, Memorandum for the Director, "Request from [Vice President Humphrey's aide] George Carroll," 21 February 1968 (S). CIA files, Job No. 80R01720R, O/D/NFAC, Box 5, "GAC Files (SAVA-NIO), " Folder 9.

to accept if the United States halted its bombings of North Vietnam. According to CIA files, Paul Warnke's Office of International Security Affairs dropped such blockbusters on George Carver on 29 February, requesting that CIA reply "if possible, by tomorrow noon."[144] CIA was hit at the very same time by somewhat similar questions from the President's "Clifford Group," a set of senior advisers then headed by the President's personal counselor, Clark Clifford. The group included Maxwell Taylor, Robert McNamara, Paul Nitze, Walt Rostow, Phil Habib, Paul Warnke, and Nicholas Katzenbach. In three studies prepared on 29 February, 1 March, and 2 March, the Agency's answers fed directly into the efforts of these senior counsellors—sharply divided among themselves—to advise President Johnson on what basic post-Tet courses he should adopt. Among the specific questions the Clifford group asked CIA were (1) whether Hanoi had concluded that it must abandon its strategy of protracted conflict and risk all-out offensive efforts; (2) what Hanoi's basic views were toward negotiations; and (3) what the course of political/military events was likely to be in South Vietnam, assuming no change in US policy or force levels. CIA's responses to these requests were, in sum, that the enemy had no serious interest in negotiations except as a tactical means to gain temporary relief and reciprocal advantages; that it was not likely to gamble on an all-out try for military victory; and that the most likely outlook in Vietnam was continued stalemate.[145]

The State Department, too, asked for quick CIA answers to very difficult questions. CIA files record that on 8 March Assistant Secretary William Bundy sent DCI Helms a "no dissemination" memo asking the Agency to estimate the effects of four different bombing options, several possible increased US ground force packages, and possible US mining of North Vietnam's Haiphong harbor. Bundy's memo asked for immediate answers and explained that he wanted the Agency's views alone, without bringing DIA into the exercise.[146]

O/NE answered this request on 13 March, judging (1) that the enemy would probably persist and seek to match any US escalations of the war; (2) that increased US bombings of North Vietnam would have no significant effect on North Vietnamese capabilities or determination, given the assumption that this US course did not include major urban attacks on Hanoi and Haiphong or the mining of the latter; (3) that

[144]Carver, Memorandum for the Director, "DOD Estimate Request," 29 February 1968, (S). CIA files, Job No. 80R01720R, O/D/NFAC, Boc 3, "GAC Files," Folder 2.
[145]*Pentagon Papers* (DoD ed.), Book 6-IV-C-7-b, "The Air War in Vietnam, Vol. II, pp. 149-153. Also, O/NE Memorandum, "Questions Concerning the Situation in Vietnam," 1 March 1968, (S). CIA files, Job No. 80R01270R, O/D/NFAC, Box 1, "GAC Files (SAVA-NIO)," Folder 6.
[146]Bundy, Letter to Helms, 8 March 1968, (TS/NODIS). CIA files, Job No 79R01012A, O/D/ NFAC, Box 240, Folder 2, "March 1968 Review Commissioned by Pres. Johnson."

intensified bombing would not be likely to cause China or the USSR to intervene directly in the war; and (4) that US mining of Haiphong would be the action most likely to cause the Soviets to prompt serious retaliations against the United States, though probably in areas outside Southeast Asia.[147]

The President himself asked CIA for several studies during these weeks. One concerned "Future Communist Military Strategy in Vietnam"; another, "Communist China's Troubles and Prospects."[148] In March President Johnson asked the Agency for an assessment of North Vietnamese strength and infiltration into South Vietnam. George Carver fielded that request, writing Walt Rostow that in the past three or four months there had been a "dramatic increase" in the movement of regular NVA units into the South, that the net increase totaled some 35,000 to 40,000 troops, and that available evidence suggested that even more such deployments were under way.[149]

The Intelligence Community's Postmortem

The most notable of the White House requests was for a governmentwide postmortem covering prior indicators of the Tet Offensive, warnings given, and the military response, which was levied through the President's Foreign Intelligence Advisory Board (PFIAB). The PFIAB Chairman, Gen. Maxwell Taylor, asked DCI Helms for a response by 1 April.[150] Helms tasked his Deputy Director for Intelligence, R. Jack Smith, with heading a combined effort by representatives from CIA, DIA, INR, NSA, and the Joint Chiefs of Staff. After studying the record and sending an interagency examining team to Saigon which, in conjunction with CINCPAC and MACV, interviewed a large number of senior US and South Vietnamese officials, Smith's group submitted an interim report to PFIAB on 3 April and a final report on 7 June.

---

[147] O/NE, Memorandum for the DCI, "Communist Reactions to Certain US Courses of Action," 13 March 1968, (TS/Sensitive). CIA files, Job No. 80R01580R, DCI/ER Subject Files, Box 15, Folder 2.

[148] DCI Helms: "These two studies were requested by Walt Rostow on behalf of the President. I thought you would be interested in seeing them." Helms, cover note to Secretary of State Rusk, 23 February 1968, (TS). CIA files, Job No. 80B01285A, DCI, Box 11, 'DCI Helms," Folder 5.

[149] Carver, Memorandum for Rostow, 26 March 1968, (TS/Compartmented). CIA files, Job No. 80R01580R, DCI/ER, Subject Files, Box 15, Folder 2.

[150] Taylor, Letter to Helms, 23 February 1968, (TS/Compartmented). CIA files, Job No. 80R01580R, DCI/ER, Subject Files, Box 16, Folder 6. Taylor: "President Johnson directed the President's Foreign Intelligence Advisory Board of which I was chairman to investigate the charges that American forces had been surprised by the Tet offensive." Taylor, *Swords and Plowshares* (New York: Norton, 1972), p. 383.

The principal findings of this postmortem were:

• That there had been evidence (especially communications intelligence) that some attacks might occur during Tet, as a result of which field military commanders took various actions that reduced the impact of the enemy offensive.

• That better intelligence performance was harmed by (a) the lack of high-level clandestine penetrations of the Communist hierarchy; (b) the "blare of background noise"; (c) the great pains the enemy had taken to conceal his intentions; (d) the fact that few US or GVN officials believed the enemy would attack during Tet; and (e) the view of most commanders and intelligence officers "at all levels" that the enemy was incapable of accomplishing the objectives stated in propaganda and in captured documents.

• That "prevailing estimates of attrition, infiltration, and local recruitment, reports of low morale, and a long series of defeats had degraded our image of the enemy."

• And that the urgency felt in Saigon was not fully felt in Washington, where finished intelligence "did not contain the atmosphere of crisis present in Saigon."[151]

Attached to the postmortem were several detailed annexes. These included Saigon Station's (Layton's) warning of 8 December that the outcome of the enemy's winter-spring offensive would in all likelihood determine the future direction of the war. The postmortem, however, made no mention of other key elements that had been added to the intelligence equation by CIA: (1) George Carver's 15 December cover memo to Walt Rostow belittling Layton's warning assessment; (2) the DDI-O/NE study of 8 December which held that North Vietnam and the Viet Cong felt under no compulsion to abandon their basic objectives in the south or the means by which they were seeking to attain them; (3) the DDI's 2 December disagreement with Layton's first alerting assessment in November; and (4) Saigon Station's 19 December warning that something like an all-out push was in the offing.

As observed above, it is difficult not to conclude that, even though this postmortem made some criticisms of the pre-Tet US intelligence performance, it was not complete or fully candid, and that had it been, its tone and judgments would have been more severe. Indeed, even before

---

[151]*Intelligence Warning of the Tet Offensive in South Vietnam, passim.* In the process of producing this estimate, chairman R. Jack Smith met several times informally with the PFIAB.

PFIAB requested its community postmortem, SAVA had made an in-house assessment that was more candid than the postmortem turned out to be. On 15 February SAVA told Director Helms (1) that MACV's method of bookkeeping on enemy O/B had "unfortunately been designed more to maximize the appearance of progress than to give a complete picture of total enemy resources," and thus the "very system has a built-in bias for a persistent underestimate of enemy capabilities"; and (2) that "the US Intelligence Community believed the Communists were wedded to a protracted war strategy—which indeed they were, until they changed it, *probably sometime late last summer.*" [152]

CIA's Dark View

Many of the assessments CIA officers volunteered to policymakers at this time took a dark view of the Vietnam situation and clearly went beyond strictly intelligence matters. One of the first such offerings following Tet, dated 2 February 1968, was a thinkpiece, "Operation Shock," which volunteered the policy recommendation that the GVN be told to shape up, or else. Its authors, William Colby (then Chief of the DDO Far East Division), George Carver, and former Saigon Station Chief John Hart, concluded (1) that the Tet Offensive had "forcefully demonstrated" that the GVN lacked some of the principal attributes of sovereignty because it could not "defend its frontiers without a half million U.S. troops"; (2) that there had been a lack of popular resolution to fight the Viet Cong; (3) that the GVN must make a number of immediate reforms, including the dismissal of key officials; and (4) that if "positive results" were not shown within 100 days, President Thieu should then "be advised that the United States will reserve its position" with regard to the GVN. [153]

For his part, DCI Helms gave the President CIA's collective opinion that the United States lacked an integrated strategic plan for Vietnam and should develop one. The genesis of this voluntary excursion beyond

[152] SAVA Memorandum for the Director, "PFIAB Request," 15 February 1968, (S). CIA files, Job No. 80B01710R, O/D/NFAC, Box 1, "Substantive Policy Files, DDI Vietnam Files," Folder 5. (Emphasis added).

[153] Blind memorandum, "Vietnam Operation SHOCK," 2 February 1968, (S), attachment to Helms, Memorandum for Undersecretary of State Nicholas Katzenbach, Deputy Secretary of Defense Paul Nitze, Chairman of the Joint Chiefs Gen. Earle Wheeler, and Special Assistant to the President Walt Rostow, "An Immediate Program for Vietnam," 2 February 1968, (S). CIA files, Job No. 80B01285A, DCI, Box 11, Folder 5. Helms distributed "Operation Shock" widely to key policymakers, and it became the basis for an advisory cable later addressed to Ambassador Bunker by the State Department. CIA's Saigon Station did not fully share these pessimistic views of the GVN. In March the Station observed to Headquarters that the GVN had passed a great trial by fire and might well emerge with a stronger temper, and it emphasized what it felt were some of the positive factors present. SAIG 0357 (IN 86842), 24 March 1968, (S). CIA files, Job No. 80B01721R, O/D/NFAC, Box 2, "Substantive Policy Files, DDI Vietnam Files," Folder 1.

intelligence was a wide-ranging examination conducted by Helms on 11 February with a dozen of the Agency's Vietnam specialists (from SAVA, DDI, O/NE, and DDP). With one notable exception these officers took a markedly pessimistic view of the post-Tet situation. Among their assertions (according to Helms's handwritten notes):

- The United States had no strategic concept or coherent policy in Vietnam.

- The outlook there was for five or six more years of continuing war.

- GVN troops had performed poorly during Tet.

- The United States should avoid further set-piece battles like Khe Sanh.

- It would be pointless for Washington to send more US troops to Vietnam.

- If the GVN proved unable to make its way, the United States "ought to get out."[154]

The sole dissenter in this case was George Carver, who complained to Helms afterward about the discussion's atmosphere of malaise and general disquiet, in which participants expressed opinions that contained "many more adjectives than nouns" and "ranged from despondency to despair." He distanced himself from the group's views, writing Helms that "I am apparently very much out of phase with the current thinking of most of my colleagues."[155] Despite Carver's dissent, and acknowledging that it was not the Agency's function to advise on military or political strategy, Helms nonetheless proposed to President Johnson in late February that "an appropriate task force" be urgently formed "to develop a comprehensive U.S. strategy to guide us during the weeks and months ahead."[156]

During the Johnson administration's post-Tet search for new policies to meet the changed situation, CIA volunteered a number of additional studies, including an assessment of the continuing Communist military threat in the northern regions of South Vietnam;[157] a study

[154] Helms notes, "Session with '12' Vietnamese experts, mid-February, 1968." CIA files, Job No. 80B01285A, DCI, Box 11, Folder 5.

[155] Carver, Memorandum for the Director, "Agency Vietnam Discussion," 15 February 1968, (S). CIA files, Job No. 80R01720R, O/D/NFAC, Box 5, "GAC Files (SAVA-NIO)," Folder 9.

[156] (Carver-drafted) Helms, Memorandum for the President, "Vietnam Strategy," 28 February 1968, (S/Sensitive). CIA files, Job No. 80R01720R, O/D/NFAC, Box 1, "GAC Files (SAVA-NIO)," Folder 6, "Alternative Strategies in Vietnam."

[157] Helms, Memorandum for the President, 13 March 1968, (TS/Compartmented). CIA files, Job No. 80R01580R, DCI/ER, Subject Files, Box 15, Folder 2.

(jointly with DIA) which found that available manpower was not a limiting factor on the DRV's ability to continue the war;[158] an R&D proposal designed to inhibit the enemy's use of tunnel warfare;[159] a proposal that CIA-directed paramilitary units in South Vietnam be re-equipped with a new assault rifle being developed by CIA;[160] and a number of O/NE assessments of the enemy. Two years later the Office of National Estimates judged that, whereas prior to Tet its estimates of enemy capabilities and intentions had been overly sanguine, after Tet its judgments were more accurate.[161]

The Agency's most significant contribution to post-Tet policy formulation, however, was doubtless the face-to-face counsel provided to the President and his chief strategists by senior Agency officers, notably the Director and his Special Assistant for Vietnam Affairs, George Carver, but also by William Colby (the Far East operations chief) and R. Jack Smith, (the Deputy Director for Intelligence). Of these, the most active player was Carver, who during February and March met almost daily with senior administration officials and consultants and ultimately came to be credited with directly influencing President Johnson's decision, announced at the end of March, to abandon the effort to win in Vietnam.[162] Carver's influential role of course predated these weeks; as this study makes clear, he had enjoyed remarkable access to senior Vietnam decisionmakers for some time.

---

[158]"The Attrition of Vietnamese Communist Forces, 1968-1969," 30 March 1968, (S/Sensitive). CIA files, as above.

[159]Carver, Memorandum for Maj. Gen. William E. DePuy, "Tunnel Denial by Means of an Electrical Field Emplaced in the Soil," 21 March 1968, (S). CIA files, Job No. 80R01580R, DCI/ER Subject Files, Box 15, Folder 6.

[160]Carver, Memorandum for the Director, "M-14 Discussion with General Wheeler," 21 March 1968, (S). CIA files, Job No. 80R01720R, O/D/NFAC, Box 5, "GAC Files (SAVA-NIO)," Folder 9.

[161]O/NE Staff Memorandum No. 27-70, "National Intelligence Estimates on the Vietnam War Since October 1964," 11 August 1970, (S/Sensitive/Internal ONE Distribution Only). Copy on file in CIA History Staff.

[162]Carver himself dated the roots of the President's decision to the product of a "quiet quartet" commissioned by Defense Secretary McNamara, back in September 1967, to "canvass possible alternative strategies in Vietnam." The Assistant Secretary of Defense for International Security Affairs, Paul Warnke, and his deputy, Morton Halperin, worked through the fall of 1967 with Carver and with Helms's Deputy Director of Current Intelligence, Richard Lehman, to produce "An Alternative Fifteen-Month Program for Vietnam." Carver later recalled that "the paper basically argued for a curtailment, if not suspension, of the bombing plus the opening of negotiations"; "the final effort . . . was much more Warnke and Halperin's paper than it was Lehman's and mine." Although Carver and Lehman thought the paper had "quietly died" after its delivery to McNamara, when Carver re-read his copy in 1970 he found that "its ultimate function becomes clearer. . . . It contains in well developed outline almost all the arguments Warnke—and Halperin—successfully urged on [Clark] Clifford during March 1968." Found in Carver, Memorandum for the Director, "The Bombing Decisions—31 March and 1 November 1968," 31 March 1970, (S/Sensitive). CIA files, Job No. 80R01720R, O/D/NFAC, Box 3, "GAC Files (SAVA-NIO)," Folder 1.

George A. Carver, Jr.

Carver had been briefing Secretary McNamara on Vietnam every Monday since 1966, meeting with Walt Rostow almost as frequently, and had been representing or accompanying the DCI at major interagency meetings on Vietnam since the beginning of Helms's tenure as DCI. During the late fall of 1967, Carver and Helms participated in informal discussions of a group of distinguished administration officials and consultants, including Dean Rusk, Nicholas Katzenbach, Robert McNamara, Walt Rostow, McGeorge Bundy, William Bundy, Clark Clifford, Cyrus Vance, Dean Acheson, George Ball, Douglas Dillon, Arthur Dean, Robert Murphy, Omar Bradley, Matthew Ridgway, Maxwell Taylor, Abe Fortas, and occasionally others. Carver typically briefed this group on enemy capabilities and intentions, with the Chairman of the JCS presenting the overall military situation and an Assistant Secretary of State covering the political dimension.

Following the Tet debacle, Helms detailed Carver to join a smaller panel at former Secretary of State Dean Acheson's home for "a frank, full discussion inventorying post-Tet 68 positions, problems and prospects" to help Acheson in advising the President. According to Carver's later account, the participants represented "the entire spectrum of informed official opinion" and "the arguments got pretty brisk." Then in early March, Lyndon Johnson convened a panel termed his "Wise Men" under the chairmanship of Clark Clifford, McNamara's successor as Secretary of Defense (whom Carver had prepped for his Senate confirmation hearings). The President directed them to review the entire Vietnam situation *de novo* and develop their own policy recommendations. Helms and Carver participated in two of that body's early meetings, on 2 and 3 March 1968.

But it was Carver's later briefing of the "Wise Men" on 25 March and of the President himself on 27 March that has been cited as CIA's most direct and telling contribution to President Johnson's decision to seek negotiations with Hanoi and retire from office, which he announced on 31 March.[163] On the 25th, Carver, Philip Habib from State, and Gen. William E. DePuy briefed the "Wise Men." When DePuy, leading off, asserted that the enemy had suffered a crushing military defeat, he ran into a buzzsaw. Pointing out the numerical contradiction between MACV's understated enemy order of battle on the one hand, and its claims of enemy killed and wounded on the other, in order to demonstrate that there could be few if any NVA/VC troops left, senior US jurist and diplomat Arthur Goldberg asked DePuy, "Who, then, are we fighting?"[164]

Phil Habib gave what Clark Clifford later called "the most important briefing," full of "hard facts and honest opinions." It was a grim presentation of the Tet Offensive's destructive effects on the GVN political-administrative structure, the pacification program, and rural development. Clifford elicited from Habib the opinion that the war could not be won under present circumstances and that the best US course would be to stop the bombing and negotiate.[165]

Carver, speaking from notes, dwelt first on the origins of the shift in Communist strategy represented by the offensive in an analysis very similar to Layton's pre-Tet reasoning. He observed that, although the Communists now controlled much of the countryside and ringed most of the cities and major towns, they had expended a great deal of their human, material, and psychological assets without achieving their maximum objectives of defeating the ARVN, discrediting the GVN, and forcing a US withdrawal. He thought there would be more major attacks and continuing pressure on allied forces; the Communists, meanwhile, would exploit the political and economic advantages of their widened control in the countryside. Noting the major setback the pacification program had suffered, the enemy's unchanged objectives, and the GVN's fragility, he concluded that the next three months were likely to be decisive, with the

---

[163]Numerous observers attest to the impact these briefings produced on their hearers. See Lyndon B. Johnson, *The Vantage Point*, pp. 416-418; Clark Clifford, *The New Yorker*, 13 May 1991, pp. 75-79; Maxwell Taylor, *The Uncertain Trumpet*, pp. 390-392; Gen. Phillip Davidson, *Vietnam at War*, pp. 524-525; George Allen, "The Indochina Wars, pp. 324-325; *Pentagon Papers* (Gravel ed.), Vol. IV, pp. 266-268, 591-593 (which mistakenly state that Carver gave these briefings on 18 and 19 March); Stuart H. Loory, *The Washington Post*, 31 May 1968 (which similarly misdates Carver's briefings and was perhaps the source of the *Pentagon Papers'* later misdating); Henry Brandon, *Anatomy of Error: The Inside Story of the Asian War on the Potomac, 1954-1969* (Boston: Gambit Incorporated, 1969), pp. 132-135; Kalb and Abel, *Roots of Involvement*, pp. 244-248; and Carver, Memorandum for the Director, "The Bombing Decisions--31 March and 1 November 1968," 31 March 1970, (S/Sensitive). CIA files, Job No. 80R01720R, O/D/NFAC, Box 3, "GAC Files (SAVA-NIO)," Folder 1.

[164]Clark Clifford, *The New Yorker*, 13 May 1991, pp. 75-76; and David Halberstam, *The Best and the Brightest*, pp. 653-654.

[165]Clifford, *The New Yorker*, 13 May 1991, p. 76; and *Pentagon Papers* (Gravel ed.), Vol. IV, p. 592.

primary burden of coping with the enemy falling on the GVN; its response would be the prime determinant of the war's eventual outcome.[166]

Following discussions with Clark Clifford and among themselves the next day, the "Wise Men" met with the President, and most of them now advised him that the United States should stop the bombing of North Vietnam and seek negotiations. The President, shocked by the sudden turnaround of men who had previously shared his views and supported his strategy, demanded to know if the briefers had "poisoned the well." The authors of *The Pentagon Papers* attribute Johnson's shock to the fact that "throughout much of 1967 he had discounted 'negative analyses' of the US strategy by the Central Intelligence Agency and the Pentagon offices of International Security Affairs and Systems Analysis," and had instead "seized upon the 'optimistic reports' from General Westmoreland to counteract what many Pentagon civilians sensed was a growing public disillusionment with the war."[167]

President Johnson's own account is similar: "The net effect [of the daily reports received during March 1968] was positive and this was one reason for my growing confidence in the situation. These reports help account for the surprise I felt every time I encountered otherwise knowledgeable people who seemed to be sunk in gloom." The President's account is also strange: "I think the explanation [for the presumably gloomy assessments given the "Wise Men" on 25 March] was in part that the briefers, in passing on some judgments about Vietnam, especially concerning the situation in rural areas, had used outdated information."[168]

President Johnson then asked that the three briefers meet personally with him and repeat their presentations. Phil Habib, who appears to have been the most gloomy of the three, was out of town (in Canada), but Gen. DePuy and George Carver met with the President on Wednesday afternoon, 27 March, in the Cabinet Room of the White House. Also present were Vice President Humphrey, Walt Rostow, Gen. Creighton Abrams, Gen. Earle Wheeler, and DCI Helms. DePuy and Carver repeated the briefings they had given the "Wise Men" two days before. According to Carver's later account of that meeting, the President paid close attention to his briefing (even though interrupted repeatedly by

---

[166] Carver, "Notes for Establishment Briefing II - 25 January 1968," (5 pp. typscript, no classification indicated). CIA files, Job No. 80R01720R, O/D/NFAC, Box 5, "GAC Files (SAVA-NIO)," Folder 9. Also "Where We Stand in Vietnam," (apparently a backup for the above notes, typescript, 28 pp., no date or classification). Above CIA file, Box 1, Folder 8.

[167] *Pentagon Papers* (*The New York Times* ed.), p. 203.

[168] Johnson, *The Vantage Point*, pp. 414, 416. It will be recalled that Walt Rostow was the principal screener of the President's daily information on Vietnam at this time and, according to at least one source, the principal drafter of his memoirs.

phone calls), asked Carver a number of questions, and, shaking off the lengthy interruptions "with a grin," told him to complete his full presentation. Then, as Carver later recalled:

> If President Johnson was upset or distressed, he certainly did not show it. In fact he started to walk out of the room then turned to walk its full length to where I was standing, pumped my hand, thanked me warmly for my presentation, and made some very flattering and gracious remarks about my overall work and contribution to the national effort.[169]

At the End, Carver Shifts His Position

It is apparent that the tone of Carver's briefings of 25 and 27 March were markedly different from the generally more optimistic views of the situation he had been expounding right up to that time.[170] As we have seen, a few weeks before Tet he had told Rostow that he did not share Saigon's concern that the enemy might be about to launch a nationwide offensive. Not long after the offensive, he had told Helms that he did not share the more pessimistic views of most of his CIA colleagues. Three weeks later, commenting on a bleak characterization of the GVN by Saigon Station, Carver told Helms that "We get the impression, perhaps unfairly, that our colleagues (like the rest of the US Mission) are tired and a trifle defensive in their response to Washington's needles."[171]

Indeed, Carver had long been viewed as a "true believer," one who tended to emphasize the positive in his assessments and go along with the administration's "we are winning" philosophy. Journalist David Halberstam summed it up this way: " . . . in savvy Washington circles it was said that there were two CIAs: a George Carver CIA, which was the CIA at the top, generally optimistic in its reporting to Rostow; and the rest of the CIA, which was far more pessimistic."[172] Helms's biographer Thomas Powers: "Perhaps the clearest expression of the CIA view came from George Carver, who remarked that 'intelligence is not written for history; it's written for an audience'—meaning that it's useless if the audience for whom it's written refuses to read it. If the White House

---

[169]Carver, Memorandum for the Director, "The Bombing Decisions--31 March and 1 November 1968," 31 March 1970, (S/Sensitive). CIA files, Job No. 80R01720R, O/D/NFAC, Box 3, "GAC Files (SAVA-NIO)," Folder 1

[170]George Allen says he implored Carver, when briefing the President following his session with the Wise Men, "...to resist the temptation to plug his personal views, to give a balanced presentation. He tended, even after Tet, to take a somewhat more hopeful view of the situation than I did." Allen, "The Indochina Wars," p. 334.

[171]SAIG 9460 (IN 62464), 3 March 1968, (S); and Carver, Memorandum for the Director, "Station Comments on GVN Actions and Performance," 4 March 1968 (S). CIA files, Job No. 80R01720R, O/D/NFAC, Box 2, Folder 13, "DIR/SAVA Field Query and Answers, Feb '68;" and Box 3, Folder 9.

[172]Halberstam, *The Best and the Brightest*, p. 638.

absolutely insists on an enemy OB under 300,000, that is what it is going to get."[173] One of the sharpest such criticisms is voiced by a former NSC staff officer: "Within a few weeks after Carver became head of SAVA he had changed from an independent analyst into a courtier . . . I felt that as long as Carver held the SAVA job, we'd never get the right picture of the war."[174]

Then, suddenly, in his White House briefings on the 25th and the 27th of March, Carver, in the words of his SAVA deputy, George Allen, "uncharacteristically leveled with the 'Wise Men' and President Johnson."[175] Others also thought that Carver's candor had a significant effect on the Wise Men. Former Assistant Secretary of State William Bundy believed that Carver's late-hour shift "undoubtedly had a tremendous influence on his hearers because they knew his usual optimism."[176] No one made the point about Carver's impact more explicitly, however, than Vice President Humphrey. Writing Carver a letter of thanks on 19 April 1968, Humphrey congratulated him for "holding your ground and telling us about the situation as you saw it in Vietnam. It was a brutally frank and forthright analysis. The President's speech of March 31 indicated that your briefings had a profound effect on the course of U.S. policy in Vietnam."[177]

Whatever the degree to which Carver deserted his previous more optimistic assessments, his—and the CIA's—influence upon President Johnson was clearly less than that of many other forces above and beyond the inputs of CIA's intelligence: the shock of the Tet offensive itself; the sharply rising tide of antiwar sentiment among the Congress and the public; the candid, very grim post-Tet assessments given by JCS Chairman Earle Wheeler, Paul Nitze, and Paul Warnke; and the sudden defections of Clark Clifford and most of the other "Wise Men" who had previously backed Johnson's war effort. Nonetheless, to these causes of the President's change of heart must be added the late-March assessments given him by State and CIA officers.

The Author's Assessment

In preparing this episode of CIA performance, the author subscribes to the thesis that the outcome of the Tet Offensive was a military defeat for the enemy: Communist forces suffered crippling losses; contrary to

---

[173] Powers, *The Man Who Kept the Secrets*, pp. 189-190.
[174] Former NSC staff officer (name on file in CIA History Staff), to author, 12 April 1990.
[175] Allen, to author, 11 April 1990. Ambassador Robert Komer recalls that when he learned of what Carver had told the "Wise Men" and the President, "He sent me though the roof because he was so pessimistic." Komer, to author, 21 May 1990.
[176] Bundy, to author, 4 October 1990.
[177] A copy of this letter is in CIA files, Job No. 80R01720R, O/D/NFAC, Box 1, "GAC Files (SAVA-NIO)," Folder 7. Carver later kept the original proudly on display in his office at 18th and K Streets.

the apparent expectations of their leaders, the South Vietnamese country-side did not rise in their support; and it took the Communists seven more years to gain victory in Vietnam.

Nonetheless, the author shares the preponderant view of historians that the Tet Offensive was an overwhelming political victory for the enemy. The psychological shock of the offensive, which swept away the remaining optimism about the war that the White House and MACV had been at such pains to generate, helped destroy the Johnson administration and was instrumental in causing Presidents Johnson and Nixon to begin the process of negotiating the best US backdown in Vietnam that they could.

Retrospect

Recent events indicate that we should reopen the question of excluding from numerical military order of battle holdings all Communist components other than main and local force . . . We strongly suspect that much of recent urban excitement was caused by personnel drawn from secret self-defense components, perhaps the assault youth, and other elements currently written out of the record by J-2 MACV on the grounds that they "have no military significance."

George Carver, 13 February 1968[178]

The Central Intelligence Agency has concluded that the enemy's strength in South Vietnam at the beginning of the winter-spring offensive was significantly greater than U.S. officials thought at the time . . . the two categories excluded by Gen. Westmoreland, the political cadres and the hamlet-level irregulars . . . played a major role in the assault on the cities, military and civilian sources say.

The New York Times, 19 March 1968

Tragically, the Tet Offensive validated three significant judgments CIA officers had previously tried to sell their superiors. The enemy's sudden nationwide offensive made manifest the November-December assessments Saigon Station had sent in, warning that the NVA/VC were about to launch just such attacks. The offensive's scope validated the long-held certainty of most CIA analysts that the enemy's total O/B was substantially greater than MACV's intelligence managers and commanders—and the unfortunate November NIE—had been willing to admit. And the enemy's commitment of substantial numbers of irregular forces to the

---

[178] (Carver-drafted) DIR cable 75802, 13 February 1968, (S). CIA files, Job No. 80R01720R, O/D/NFAC, Box 3, "GAC Files (SAVA-NIO)," Folder 9.

Tet Offensive brought home the truth of many CIA analysts' earlier arguments that such forces were militarily significant and justifiably part of a total O/B. That these judgments had not been bought by top intelligence and policymaking officers can legitimately be termed an additional casualty of the Tet Offensive.

Following the Tet Offensive, the sharply different O/B assessments CIA and MACV officers had championed resurfaced with new vigor. Less than a month afterward, CIA began deserting the compromise O/B positions it had agreed to with MACV in November. On 21 February a *CIA Intelligence Memorandum* stated that there was now sufficient evidence to support a judgment that in his offensive the enemy had committed numerous irregular forces, of various types.[179] Two days later, in response to a query from the White House, DCI Helms reported that available evidence did not support the US military's claim of an enemy decimated by Tet.[180] On 1 March OCI and OER sharply questioned MACV's continuing claims that the enemy had suffered a very high percentage of losses: "the dilemma with respect to the casualties arises when the reported enemy KIA (38,600) is considered against the total offensive force estimated [by MACV] to have been involved (77,000). Taken at face value, this means that approximately one half of the attacking force was killed in the offensive and its aftermath."[181] This OCI-OER study concluded that these figures were exceedingly difficult to accept, given the continuing current high level of enemy activity throughout the country.[182] An OER officer shortly thereafter ridiculed MACV's claims, pointing out that if the 1.5 to 1 ratio of wounded to killed in action were applied, the resultant casualty total exceeded the forces committed.[183]

---

[179]"Communist Units Participating in Attacks During the Tet Offensive, 30 January Through 13 February 1968," (S/NF/prepared jointly by SAVA, OCI, and OER). CIA files, Job No. 80R01720R, O/D/NFAC, Box 2, Folder 14.

[180]Helms, Memorandum for Secretary of State Rusk, "Future Communist Strategy in South Vietnam," 23 February 1968 (TS/Compartmented). CIA files, Job No. 80R01580R, DCI/ER Subject Files, Box 15, Folder 2.

[181] George Carver's deputy, George Allen, had just reported from Saigon that "MACV's J-2 is quite unrealistic. Its recent assesssment of 'net losses' for the VC since 1 January was absurd; they listed 14,000 VC troops as participating in the Tet Offensive in III Corps, of which they killed 12,000, another 2,050 died of wounds, and 784 were detained—a total loss of 14,838 out of 14,000 committed!" (Here Allen presaged the White House scene, just a month later, when Justice Goldberg asked General DePuy, "Who, then, are we fighting?") From Allen, letter to Carver, 25 February 1968, (U). CIA files, Job No. 80R01720R, O/D/NFAC, Box 5, "GAC Files (SAVA-NIO)," Folder 9.

[182]OCI-OER Memorandum, "The Communists' Ability to Recoup Their Tet Military Losses," 1 March 1968, (S/NF). CIA files, as above. This memorandum also reported that the enemy employed large numbers of civilian irregulars as "shock troops in many of the urban assaults."

[183]Smith, Memorandum for DD/OER, "The Communists' Ability to Recoup Their Tet Military Losses," 19 March 1968, (S/NF). CIA files, Job No. 78T02095R, O/DDI, Box 2, Folder 22.

Nevertheless, US military officers clung to their previous O/B estimates despite the contradiction created with their claims of enemy losses. Negotiations over the enemy strength estimates between CIA and the military, reminiscent of the previous year's work on the NIE, dragged on for weeks but failed to bridge the gap. In April DCI Helms had to admit to Gen. Maxwell Taylor in the White House that he had "become increasingly concerned that the strength of enemy forces was underestimated and that there were serious errors in the way the forces were characterized and in the way attrition was handled."[184]

Finally, in May 1968, Helms, who six months before had accepted the contested MACV O/B figures rather than send a split estimate to the President, told the White House that the two sides had thus far been unable to reach agreement: MACV, DIA, and CINCPAC still held enemy strength in South Vietnam to be between 280,000 and 330,000, he reported, whereas CIA now believed the figure to be somewhere between 450,000 and 600,000. Helms added that, of those totals, CIA accepted some 90,000 to 140,000 enemy irregulars, whereas MACV and CINCPAC still maintained that such forces could not and should not be quantified.[185] And there the matter rested.

Clearly, MACV's O/B estimates remained much too low. It is also clear that MACV's reluctance to accept higher enemy O/B figures all along had a corrupting effect on the conduct of US intelligence analysis and presentation. Perhaps the premier exemplar of such flaws was one of MACV's chief intelligence officers, later DIA Director Lt. Gen. Daniel O. Graham, who testified in 1975 to Congress that MACV had not been surprised by Tet; that all the previous MACV, DIA, and CIA estimates of the enemy's O/B had been "*too high* in terms of total VC combat strength available; and that the worst estimate around was Mr. [Sam] Adams's 600,000."[186] As noted earlier, in 1967 then Col. Graham had confided to George Allen that "of course" he did not believe MACV's lower O/B figures, but "it's the command position and I'm sticking with it."[187]

---

[184] Helms, Memorandum for Gen. Maxwell Taylor, Special Consultant to the President, "Status Report on Resolution of Estimates of VC/NVA Strength," 9 April 1968. (S/NF). CIA files, Job No. 80R01580R, DCI/ER Subject Files, Box 15, Folder 2.

[185] Helms, Memorandum for Walt W. Rostow, Special Assistant to the President, "Estimates of Enemy Strength in South Vietnam" 2 May 1968, (S/Compartmented). CIA files, Job No. 78T02095R, O/DDI, Box 1, Folder 2.

[186] Graham (at the time Director of DIA), testimony to Representative Otis Pike's investigating committee, "Intelligence on Enemy Order of Battle at the Time of the Tet Offensive," November 1975 (Emphasis added). Copy on file in CIA History Staff.

[187] Allen, "The Indochina Wars," pp. 317-318.

Summing Up

In sum:

• Senior intelligence and policymaking officers and military leaders erred on two principal scores: for having let concern for possible political embarrassment derail objective assessments of the enemy order of battle, and for ignoring NSA's alerts and Saigon Station's warnings that did not accord with their previous evaluations of probable enemy strategy.

• The least astute performance, clearly, was MACV's. Its O/B positions misled planners and policymakers, distorted intelligence reporting and analysis, contributed directly to the psychological shock the Tet Offensive inflicted on the public and the White House, and thus caused serious damage to the national interest. One military element did work well, at the last moment, when General Westmoreland responded to field communications intelligence alerts and approved certain changes in US troop dispositions that limited the scope of the enemy's depredations in Saigon and General Weyand's III Corps sector.

• The best Tet Offensive alerts were those provided by NSA and by General Weyand's units cited above. Communications intelligence often afforded a better reading of the enemy's strength and intentions (and was better heeded by command elements) than did agent reports, prisoner interrogations, captured documents, or the analytic conclusions derived from them. But in Washington the SIGINT alerts apparently made little impression on senior intelligence officers and policymakers.

• CIA's performance in the O/B and Tet episodes was mixed—better than MACV's in the former, less perceptive than NSA's in the latter. The best CIA performances were by a few working-level officers who tried to sell their judgments that the enemy had thousands of irregular forces that were militarily significant, and that the enemy was about to launch a major nationwide offensive. But the Agency's most senior Vietnam intelligence officers gave in to MACV's stonewall defense of its O/B estimates, enshrined that position in a definitive NIE, downplayed Saigon Station officers' warnings, and so left administration officials unprepared for the shattering of their illusions of progress in Vietnam. To the intelligence managers' credit, after Tet they did level with the President on the facts of the situation, abandoned their earlier O/B compromises with MACV, and acknowledged to the White House that the Intelligence Community's assessments of the enemy's numbers, capabilities, and intentions had been in error.

The Three Episodes in Perspective: Lessons To Be Learned About the Intelligence/ Policymaking Relationship[1]

The mixed picture of CIA performance illustrated in these episodes should not obscure the generally good analytic record the Agency chalked up on Vietnam in the years under review. From the early 1950s onward, CIA's assessments in the main proved more accurate than those of any other US Government entity, and CIA's analytic record on Vietnam compares favorably with its endeavors in the counterinsurgency field. CIA officers fairly consistently insisted their analyses showed that military force alone would not win the war; that our South Vietnamese creation, the GVN, was not proving adequate to the political-military task; that we should not underestimate the enemy's covert presence throughout South Vietnamese society; that we should not underestimate the enemy's staying power; that US bombing efforts were not appreciably slowing the enemy's progress in the South; that the enemy would try to match US escalation rather than meaningfully negotiate; and that ill-founded official claims of great progress distorted reality to the detriment of policy objectives.[2] CIA's record of candor is all the more remarkable because CIA officers often had to brave pressures from senior political and military officers to "get on the team" and to support the war effort with more optimistic findings and estimates.

That overall record must be tempered, however, by the fact that on the three occasions under review in which Agency assessments had a chance to affect key US decision points in Vietnam—how to assess and deal with a failing Diem regime, whether and how to "go big" in Vietnam, and how to assess the enemy's subsequent capabilities and intentions—the character of CIA's intelligence input was mixed.

In our first episode, 1962-63, because DCI McCone brought heavy pressure on the Board of National Estimates and the Intelligence Community to produce a more optimistic National Intelligence Estimate than they felt the evidence supported, because the Board caved in to that pressure, and because that NIE fed the confidence of policymakers that the war effort was going fairly well, those policy managers were wholly

---

[1] The author recognizes that gauging such intangibles as the quality of intelligence and its impact is an inexact science, and is also the refracted product of the particular gauger's lenses.

[2] That CIA's doubts ultimately contributed to Secretary McNamara's fading vision of light at the end of the tunnel is illustrated in his *In Retrospect*, where he publishes (pp. 321-323) a list of his and others' misconceptions about the Vietnam War; certain of these match counterarguments CIA officers had long tried to sell higher authorities.

unprepared to deal with the sudden collapse of political stability in South Vietnam only days after the definitive NIE was issued. The judgment must be made, as we have seen in the statements of the authors of *The Pentagon Papers*, that in the case of that NIE senior decisionmakers *were* influenced by an Intelligence Community product; the problem was that, thanks to the intervention of policymakers and program managers, this particular input was misleading.

Director McCone's subsequent cautions concerning the wisdom of overthrowing Diem proved well taken, but they failed to counter the original impetus or the momentum that gathered around that impulse. Equally unfortunate, the sorry outcome of the unilateral Harriman-Hilsman-Lodge initiative had the ironic result of leaving CIA with much of the blame for the disaster, obscuring the fact that the CIA Director had tried his best to persuade the White House that that course would breed disaster.

In no period during the Vietnam conflict did the conclusions of CIA's working-level officers prove more accurate in retrospect than in the second episode we have examined, when they consistently argued in 1963-65 that substantially increasing US combat operations in Vietnam would not solve US problems there because the war was essentially a political-military struggle which had to be won in the South and primarily by the South Vietnamese. Those arguments unfortunately made little if any dent in policymakers' increasing certainty that the war in the South could be won only by committing US forces to combat there and by consistently bombing the North. One of the reasons the impact of those assessments was dulled was because the Agency spoke with two voices at the time, with Director McCone giving the President's circle his personal assessments which at times did not agree with those of his analysts and officers. But as we have seen, other, more potent forces also caused policymakers to shrug off CIA assessments they found uncongenial. In only a slow, cumulative sense did the Agency's generally pessimistic analyses find resonance among some senior consumers and contribute to the growing uncertainty of Robert McNamara, George Ball, Hubert Humphrey, Clark Clifford, and the civilian heads of the Pentagon's International Security Affairs bureau that there was light at the end of the tunnel.

In our third episode, 1967-68, a few working-level CIA officers developed and championed accurate assessments that enemy strength in South Vietnam was perhaps twice what the US military was willing to acknowledge, and that the enemy was about to change strategy radically by launching a nationwide offensive. Many hazards, however, undercut those judgments. Political pressure from the White House, MACV, and the US Embassy to understate the number of enemy forces caused DCI Helms, Special Assistant George Carver, and the Board of

National Estimates to override the conclusions their analysts had derived from available evidence. Then Headquarters analysts themselves refused to accept new field estimates of the enemy's intentions for Tet because these did not jibe with their own published estimation of the enemy's likely conduct.

Last but not least, CIA's offerings to senior managers of Vietnam policy generally had to filter through one particularly influential Agency officer, George Carver, who until two months after the Tet Offensive generally supported the Johnson administration's view that things in Vietnam were looking up. To his credit, in the end Carver did level with the President and his "Wise Men"—and so helped influence the radical changes Lyndon Johnson began to make in his domestic and Vietnam policies at the end of March 1968.[3]

In our three episodes, why were CIA's published analytical judgments so often more pessimistic than the positions of the rest of the government? By and large, CIA's analysts had no special sources of intelligence not available to others; the difference was in the interpretations they gave existing evidence. In this they had certain advantages over other US Government analysts. They were much freer at that time from pressures to produce judgments supporting the operational offices' enthusiasms that the tide in Vietnam was being turned by the efforts of the US Mission and MACV. Also, CIA reporting from the field was generally more rigorously conducted and more candidly transmitted than that of most other USG elements, and it gave Headquarters analysts unique insights into political developments in South Vietnam. Compared with their colleagues in the military, DDI and O/NE officers had usually been at their jobs longer and were more experienced at interpreting and calling developments in Indochina. And many of CIA's Vietnam analysts of this period were the recipients of occasional confidences from working-level field officers, civilian and military, about the difficulties and distortions they were encountering in their attempts to get candid reporting past their superiors in Saigon. By 1966, improved CIA field reporting—especially overhead imagery—and new analytical methods enabled CIA officers to quantify North Vietnam's continuing ability to support its forces in the South despite the US bombing campaign. It was these methods and judgments that at last helped convince the Defense Intelligence

<hr>

[3] Equally to his credit, Carver not only continued to have considerable impact with top policymakers in the years following those studied here, but also is credited with having generally contributed candid intelligence inputs during that period.

Agency and Defense Secretaries Robert McNamara and Clark Clifford that America's expanded efforts were not causing the enemy to slack off, and probably would not do so.[4]

The advantages enjoyed by CIA officers deserved greater respect from decisionmakers than they received. And the credentials CIA's analysts brought to bear on Vietnam issues were impressive. Many of these officers had not only been studying East Asia questions for years, but also had racked up fairly strong estimative batting averages. They had correctly warned that the difficulties the French were encountering in combating the Communist-led Viet Minh's military and political advantages would force Paris to call it quits in Indochina—and so confront the United States with a very weak South Vietnam and very difficult policy decisions on whether and how to take up the anti-Communist burden there. CIA officers had accurately gauged the limits of Communist China's boldness in the Quemoy-Matsu offshore island crisis of 1958. DDI and O/NE officers, moreover, had led the way within the Intelligence Community in trying to alert decisionmakers that Moscow and Beijing would split—a development of immense consequence that had become clearly evident by 1963-65, the key years in which President Johnson and his advisers were wrestling with the question of whether to go big in Vietnam.

Questionable on several scores is former Secretary of Defense Robert McNamara's present complaint that "there were no Vietnam experts" to whom policymakers could turn for advice. That charge not only reveals that he and his colleagues were ignorant of the credentials which Agency and other Intelligence Community officers brought to their tasks; it also contradicts the several acknowledgements McNamara himself makes in his *In Retrospect* to the positive contributions DCI Helms and other CIA officers gave him.

During the years under review here, the dangers of offering heretical expert counsel were repeatedly demonstrated. Senior policymaking officers often put pressure on analysts to make their assessments rosier, or placed political lids on objective estimates of the enemy's strengths, or warned doubters to shape up and join the team. Especially illustrative in these respects was the fate of State Department expert Paul Kattenberg who, after telling President Johnson and other senior officers that available evidence did not support the optimism they were expressing, was relieved of his Vietnam responsibilities and thereafter given backwater assignments.

[4]It should be noted, however, that despite its rigorous methods, ORR, joined by other CIA analysts, later discounted and underestimated the magnitude and significance of North Vietnamese support reaching the Viet Cong through Cambodia's port of Sihanoukville.

Thus, although there were ranks of competent CIA Vietnam experts ranged behind John McCone, Richard Helms, George Carver, Bill Colby, and the few others who dealt with top Administration officials, they were perceived as juniors of unknown quality by most senior decisionmakers. Perhaps contributing to this perception was the fact that, at least until 1967-68, CIA's views on Vietnam were generally uncongenial to most policy planners. Not only did many CIA officers question the progress so many top officials were claiming, they also did not accept the widespread assumption that Vietnamese Communist aggression was essentially one thrust of a global campaign of conquest masterminded in Moscow and Beijing. Not least, O/NE's officers had the audacity to doubt the core belief of the American political-military establishment that the fall of Saigon would necessarily lead to an inexorable Communist takeover of all Southeast Asia. Of such elements was the judgment made that there were "no experts at hand."

It must nevertheless be emphasized that the analysts of CIA's O/NE, OCI, and the Office of Research and Reports did not fully agree among themselves on all questions about Vietnam. Though they shared a generally more pessimistic view of events there than did most Vietnam analysts elsewhere in the government, there were differences on various questions among offices and analysts. The least pessimistic tended to be officers of the North Vietnam Branch of the Office of Current Intelligence, who were by definition analysts of global Communism and had served in Soviet-related offices.

In any case, among the principal intelligence concerns these episodes illustrate is the mischief that can be done by stubbornly held preconceptions, and by the unwillingness of senior consumers of intelligence to entertain new data or judgments that do not support their own analyses or that threaten their political commitments. Such hazards clearly were important factors in the refusal of policymakers to buy the working-level intelligence officers' warnings in early 1963 that all was not well in South Vietnam; and later, in CIA's insistence that going big in Vietnam would not do the trick; and still later, in Saigon Station's warning that the enemy was about to launch a major nationwide offensive.

These episodes also show that preconceptions are not the monopoly of policymakers. Intelligence analysts and managers, too, can be unreceptive to new, different stimuli. This certainly occurred in early 1963, when John McCone refused to credit O/NE views which challenged policymakers' optimism; and in the winter of 1967-68, when George Carver and CIA Headquarters analysts preferred their existing estimates of likely enemy behavior to Saigon Station's new and different interpretations.

We have also seen that preconceptions were at times more firmly held and resistant as one went up the lines of command in CIA, in somewhat similar fashion to the hesitance of senior military and Embassy officers in the field to accept their junior officers' more candid reporting and assessments.

Then, too, these episodes show also that intelligence facts ultimately are no match for political considerations. Such concerns distorted intelligence in early 1963. They accounted later for the deaf ear that policy managers turned to CIA officers' skepticism about "going big" as a cure-all in Vietnam. Political considerations distorted intelligence again in 1967 when fear of political embarrassment dictated that only so many enemy troops could be counted and that the Viet Cong's additional, irregular forces could not be counted at all.

CIA officers who serve at the interface of intelligence and policy are no less subject to the inherent conflicts between the two, and when a policy problem lasts as long as the Vietnam War did, the infection of intelligence estimates by policy concerns is inevitable. At crucial points in the three episodes studied, some senior CIA officers felt they had to adjust what might be called "pure" intelligence judgments to "practical" political considerations, as did the Board of National Estimates in its 1963 NIE on the outlook for Vietnam; DCI Helms in the 1967 faceoff with MACV's Order-of-Battle estimators; O/NE and the Intelligence Community in the subsequent NIE on the enemy's O/B and combat capabilities; and Vietnam Special Assistant Carver in both the O/B controversy and the Tet offensive forecasts.

These episodes also illustrate that one reason CIA's inputs did not have greater impact is that the Agency's officers often defined their intelligence roles rather narrowly. Policymaking customers have often complained that intelligence officers, by being too shy about intruding into policy matters, fail to offer up the helpful policy-relevant ideas of which they are capable. There is indeed a fine line that intelligence officers must follow in order to retain their essential credibility as policy-free advisers.

Yet it seems clear that when CIA officers did volunteer policy critiques in 1967-68, their arguments definitely contributed to the diminishing certainty among Administration officials—including Secretaries McNamara and Clifford, and belatedly President Johnson himself—that a military solution in Vietnam was possible. One of the most remarkable of these, one that went considerably beyond the strict lines of intelligence matters, was a sensitive assessment sent "Eyes Only" to the President by DCI Helms well before Tet, in September 1967. As cited by Robert McNamara in his retrospective book, that memorandum concluded that, although an unfavorable outcome in Vietnam would of course have many very damaging effects, "The risks are probably more limited and controllable than most previous argument has indicated."[5] Observing that the assessment showed that "CIA's most senior analysts believed we could have withdrawn from Vietnam without any permanent damage to U.S. or Western security," McNamara states that the CIA authors were expressing the same view he himself was giving to Senator John Stennis's subcommittee at the time, "supported by CIA/DIA analyses," that "we could not win the war by bombing the North."[6]

Similarly, certain of the candid policy prescriptions pushed forward by CIA officers in February and March 1968 doubtless added to the post-Tet recognition by policymakers that US policies sorely needed re-examination. As we have seen, such CIA assessments certainly included Bill Colby's "Operation Shock" recommendation in February 1968: that if the GVN did not shape up, President Thieu should be advised that the United States would reserve its position with respect to South Vietnam. Even more frank were the views of CIA analysts given to President Johnson by DCI Helms that same month: that the United States had no strategic or coherent policy in Vietnam, and that if the GVN proved unable to make its way, the United States ought to get out. And we have seen also that George Carver was in constant contact with Lyndon Johnson's closest advisers throughout February-March 1968, and that in the end he gave them candid appraisals of the limited prospects in Vietnam.

Another facet of intelligence-policy interplay illustrated in these episodes is the key influence that individuals often exert on either side of the equation. John McCone was much less hesitant to offer up policy-relevant inputs than were DCIs before and after him. George Carver, though a middle-level officer, enjoyed extraordinary entree and influence with top policymakers. Assertive, strategically placed officers in the policy hierarchy, notably Robert McNamara, Walt Rostow, McGeorge Bundy, Roger Hilsman, and Robert Komer, often overrode competing arguments. And Lyndon Johnson's hardly subtle influence was paramount.

We have seen, too, that the views individual officers hold may differ from time to time, depending on what responsibilities they hold and whether they are speaking privately or for the record. Among intelligence officers this was shown especially in the degrees of candor displayed by George Carver when he was an O/NE officer remote from the policy arena and when he was the DCI's Special Assistant for Vietnam Affairs.

---

[5] Mr. McNamara italicizes this concluding phrase from the assessment. *In Retrospect*, pp. 292-294. He adds that he did not see this unique Agency document until discovering it in Johnson Library files in the course of researching his book.

[6] *In Retrospect*, p.294.

Policy officers' statements (illustrative examples are in the Appendix) could be influenced by the office they happened to hold at the time, and by whether they were giving higher authority their private views or publicly conforming to the official line of the moment. Once they were out of office, moreover, hindsight could alter an earlier view.

Salient in these episodes is the fact that the intelligence and policy worlds often were widely separated, their respective officers ignorant of the other's world. If policymakers were at times unappreciative of how Intelligence Community experts could help them, it was equally true that intelligence officers might have carried more weight if they had been closer to the decisionmakers. Most of the CIA officers who earnestly offered up their assessments on Vietnam were separated by a figurative and literal river from the policymaking arena. And rarely, if at all, did they factor in the many broader questions with which their seniors had to wrestle or consider the many inputs other than intelligence which of necessity influence the determination of policy. The intelligence officers' task studied in our episodes was a narrowly focused one, and their vision was largely confined to Vietnam and Southeast Asia, whereas policymakers saw the Vietnam problem as one of many in much broader perspectives, both foreign and domestic.

Indeed, these episodes demonstrate that the impact of intelligence on policymaking consumers is clearly secondary to that of broader, outside forces. CIA's pessimism regarding proposals for sending US forces directly against Hanoi and its expeditionary forces was offset by Lyndon Johnson's determination to succeed in Vietnam. It seems clear that John McCone almost instinctively deep-sixed the challenged draft of NIE 53-63 because his confidence in his Board of National Estimates had been shaken by the Board's earlier miscalling of the emplacement of Soviet missiles in Cuba, and because he was still under fire on that issue from the President's Foreign Intelligence Advisory Board. Richard Helms's acceptance of the too-low estimates of enemy O/B produced by MACV and endorsed by DIA was doubtless influenced by his desire not to damage his equities with the military on other issues; a similar consideration was his need to keep DIA aboard the joint CIA-DIA assessments that told the Johnson Administration its bombing campaign was not seriously damaging the enemy's capabilities or will to persist. The O/B positions insisted upon by MACV and the Saigon Embassy were dictated by the perceived need to avoid the public relations damage a suddenly larger O/B estimate would cause. And Walt Rostow's belief in and dedication to the prospect of victory led him to gloss over such troubling intelligence as Saigon Station's pre-Tet warnings, which ran against the administration's public affairs campaign to bolster flagging confidence in its Vietnam strategy.

A principal reason why CIA's data and judgments may have had so little influence on policymaking was that decisions on what to do in Vietnam were not being made in a political vacuum, but had to be developed by leaders whose political party had long been accused of "losing" China and not winning in Korea. Presidents Kennedy and Johnson each affirmed repeatedly that he was not going to be the President who lost Vietnam and the rest of Southeast Asia. Told by CIA that "you can't win in Vietnam," they might well have told themselves, "I can't *not* win in Vietnam."

Finally, these episodes illustrate yet again the dilemma DCIs and senior intelligence professionals face in cases when they know that unvarnished intelligence judgments will not be welcomed by the President, his policy managers, and his political advisers. At such times intelligence officers must decide just what balance to make between the ever-present contradictory forces of whether to tell it like it is (and so risk losing their place at the President's advisory table), or to go with the flow of existing policy by accenting the positive (thus preserving their access and potential influence). In these episodes from the Vietnam era, we have seen that senior CIA officers more often than not tended toward the latter approach. DCI McCone did so in early 1963 when he chose the policy managers' interpretations of intelligence over the judgments of his own professional staff. So did DCI Helms in 1967 when he struggled to avoid a sharp dispute with MACV on the O/B dispute. And so did CIA's senior Vietnam professional, George Carver, on many occasions.[7] But on at least one occasion, over a period of months in 1964-65, DCI McCone preferred sticking with his own judgments on how the United States should prosecute the war in Vietnam, refusing to ratify the views of other advisers on the course President Johnson was setting. The result was that his persistent candor left him frozen out of the President's inner circle.

In the end, the story of intelligence and the Vietnam conflict is one of competing forces: many potent influences on policy, some of the most significant of them extraneous to Vietnam, versus the obligation CIA's officers had to present their findings candidly, to try to "tell it like it is." As a working-level participant in some of this history, the author can attest to the frustration CIA officers experience when they find no one listening to them downtown. It may be ever so, when intelligence comes up against committed policymakers grappling with intractable, highly charged crisis situations. But the obligation to present candid intelligence

---

[7] As we have seen, however, it is notable that as an O/NE analyst prior to becoming CIA's chief Vietnam affairs officer, Carver had been a champion of candor, whatever the views of policymaking consumers; and that at the end of March 1968 he did give the White House the kind of bad news that earlier he had often played down.

findings still applies. One balm for such frustrations when they do occur is the fact that since CIA's founding, every US President, Republican and Democrat alike, has asked for, received, and often benefited from the input of dispassionate, professional intelligence. It is a safe bet that Presidents will continue to need and even welcome such inputs, whatever their ultimate influence on policy decisions.

It is also the author's view that in these episodes Agency officers performed their greatest service when they maintained CIA's professional intelligence integrity without regard to whether candor would or would not prove congenial to their DCIs and to policymaking consumers. To the degree that CIA officers withheld or modified their judgments, they were not only distorting intelligence but also undercutting CIA's very raison d'etre.

There remains an underlying question of whether all the events in this study of producer-consumer relations were taking place within a context of foreordained US failure in Vietnam. Nothing is inexorable; given much stronger South Vietnamese administrations, an earlier and more determined "Vietnamization" effort, and a sharper sensitivity among US policymakers that the war's outcome hung more on political considerations than on body count, the outcome in Vietnam might have been different. Nevertheless, the basic necessity for victory was probably a total American determination as fierce as that of the enemy's to sacrifice and persevere. Successive US administrations and Congresses, and American society at large, were unable to sustain such a degree of determination.

Finally, US policymakers could have acted more wisely, and might have had more successes in Vietnam than they did, had they been more receptive to more of the bald facts and probing interpretations CIA analysts gave them along the way. But the war's outcome was determined by historical considerations far broader than those examined here, and no firm estimate can justifiably be formed of what weight and impact CIA judgments had—or could have had—among the sum of those considerations.

Annex: Examples of . . .

I. Expectations

September 1953: [An unidentified American official in Saigon said] A year ago none of us could see victory. There wasn't a prayer. Now we can see it clearly—like light at the end of a tunnel.[1]   —*Time* magazine

9 September 1953: [Adm. Arthur Radford, Chairman of the Joint Chiefs of Staff, told an NSC meeting] that this was the first time that the political climate had actually improved to a point where military success could be achieved. With aggressive implementation of the Navarre Plan, Admiral Radford predicted that the war in Indochina could be reduced in scale to mere guerrilla operations in the course of a single season of fighting—certainly in two such seasons.[2]

November 1953: I attended his [Gen. John O'Daniel's] briefing of the Joint Chiefs of Staff, which he opened by stating that he was "encouraged by the prospects of victory in Indochina in the next twelve to fifteen months.[3]   —George Allen

21 January 1954: Admiral Radford . . . was inclined to feel that the press had exaggerated the emergency in French Indochina, and that things were not as bad as they were presented.[4]

11 February 1954: [DCI Allen Dulles told the NSC meeting that] The surrounding force [of Viet Minh troops] which remained at Dien Bien Phu was now sufficiently reduced so that a frontal attack on the French strongpoint appeared unlikely.[5]

12 October 1960: If ever there was a war where we would have been engaged in a hopeless struggle without allies, for an unpopular colonialist cause, it was the 1954 war in Indochina.[6]   —John F. Kennedy

---

[1] From *Time* magazine, as cited in U.S. Congress, Congressional Research Service, Library of Congress, *The U.S. Government and the Vietnam War: Executive and Legislative Roles and Relationships,* Part I, 1945-1961, p. 141. Written by Dr. William Conrad Gibbons. Printed for the use of the Committee on Foreign Relations, U.S. Senate, 98th Congress, 2d Session, 1984. (Hereafter cited as Gibbons).

[2] U.S. Department of State, *Foreign Relations of the United States, 1952-1954, Indochina, Part I, p. 784. (*Hereafter cited as *FRUS).*

[3] George Allen, "The Indochina Wars," p. 61.

[4] Memorandum of Discussion, 181st meeting of the NSC. *FRUS,* pp. 988-989.

[5] Memorandum of Discussion, 184th meeting of the NSC. *FRUS,* p. 1036.

[6] US Senator and Presidential candidate John F. Kennedy, remarks to Democratic National and State Committees, New York. U.S. Congress, Senate Committee on Commerce, Subcommittee of the Subcommittee on Communications, *Freedom of Communications,* Part I, as cited in Chester L. Cooper, *The Lost Crusade,* p. 162.

7 April 1962: The following considerations influence our thinking on Vietnam: 1. We have a growing military commitment. This could expand step by step into a major, long-drawn out indecisive military involvement. 2. We are backing a weak and, on the record, ineffectual government and a leader who as a politician may be beyond the point of no return. 3. There is consequent danger we shall replace the French as the colonial forces in the area and bleed as the French did.[7]   —John Kenneth Galbraith

30 January 1963: Adm. Harry D. Felt, Pacific commander, predicted today that the American-backed Government of Vietnam would win its war against communist guerrillas within three years.[8]

—The New York Times

Spring 1963: . . . barring greatly increased resupply and reinforcement of the Viet Cong by infiltration, the military phase of the war can be virtually won in 1963.[9]   —DIA

Spring 1963: We are winning, this we know.
General Harkins tells us so.
In the delta, things are rough.
In the mountains, mighty tough.
But we're winning, this we know.
General Harkins tells us so.
If you doubt that this is true,
McNamara says so too.[10]

April 1963: [At the Secretary of Defense's conference in Honolulu] General Harkins said the war would be over by Christmas.[11]

6 May 1963: A Pentagon spokesman said today that "the corner has definitely been turned" toward victory in South Vietnam and Defense officials are hopeful that the 12,000 man U.S. force in Vietnam could be reduced in one to three years.[12]   *—The New York Times*

---

[7] Ambassador John Kenneth Galbraith, Memorandum for the President, as cited in *Pentagon Papers* (DoD ed.), Book 12, V-B-4, "U.S. Involvement in the War, Internal Documents, The Kennedy Administration, January 1961-November 1963," Book II, p. 461.

[8] *The New York Times,* 31 January 1963

[9] DIA "Summary of Highlights," as cited in *Pentagon Papers* (DoD ed.), Book 3, IV-B-4, "Phased Withdrawal of U.S. Forces in Vietnam, 1962-1963," p. 11.

[10] Ditty being sung in Saigon at the time by newsmen, as cited in Arthur Schlesinger, *A Thousand Days: John F. Kennedy in the White House* (Boston: Houghton Mifflin Co, 1965), p. 983.

[11] George Herring, *America's Longest War: The United States and Vietnam, 1950-1975,* 2nd ed. (New York: Knopf, 1986), p. 93.

[12] *The New York Times,* 7 May 1963.

31 August 1963: [Secretary of State Rusk added] that he believes we have good proof that we have been winning the war, particularly the contrast between the first six months of 1962 and the first six months of 1963.[13]

—Unidentified NSC principal

14 March 1964: The military tools and concepts of the GVN-US effort are generally sound and adequate. . . . Substantial reductions in the number of US military training personnel should be possible before the end of 1965.[14]

—Robert McNamara

10 September 1964: *Senator Wayne Morse*: Is it presently contemplated as you survey the problems of the next 6 to 12 months that it will be necessary to send additional military personnel to South Vietnam?

Gen. Maxwell Taylor: No. The present authorized strength is about 20,000, which, in General Westmoreland's estimate, would last him. He foresaw no requirement beyond that in the coming year.[15]

1 March 1967: Mr. [Robert] Komer opened by exuding optimism on the current trend in Vietnam. . . . [he] expressed considerable disdain for MACV J-2, and particularly what he believes to be its over-estimate of enemy strength. . . . Concluding, Mr. Komer recognized the possible trip-ups in the overall situation but anticipated that unless they occur, major military operations might gradually fade as the enemy either began to fade away or put his emphasis on a protracted guerrilla level war. In either case, he said, the size of the problem in Vietnam will diminish and fewer U.S. resources will be needed. He felt that the enemy threat had peaked out, and that we may be facing a Malaya-type run-down.[16]

—William Colby

2 March 1967: The contrasts between the situation existing then [spring of 1965] and that existing today were dramatic and striking. There are many soft spots and weak areas in the present situation but the overall progress made in the last twenty-odd months is inescapable and over-

---

[13] Statement made at a meeting of NSC principals at the State Department, Vice President Johnson present, as cited in *Pentagon Papers* (Gravel ed.), Vol. II, p. 742.

[14] McNamara, Memorandum for the President, cited in CIA/IG Report, p. 55.

[15] Statements at executive session of the Senate Foreign Relations Committee. U.S. Senate, 88th Congress, 2d Session, 1964, *Executive Sessions of the Senate Foreign Relations Committee, Together with Joint Sessions of the Senate Armed Services Committee* (Historical Series). Made public December 1987 (USGPO, 1988), p. 332.

[16] William E. Colby, Memorandum for the Record, "VIC Meeting, 1 March 1967," 3 March 1967 (S). CIA/DDO files, Job No. 72-233R, Box 1, Folder 3, "Vietnam Interagency Committee (Komer Meetings), April 1966 - May 67."

whelming. . . . It would be too much to say that our side scents victory, but there is certainly no atmosphere of defeat or impending disaster.[17]

—George Carver

January 1968: Westmoreland's summary of 1967 had reached Washington just four days before the Tet offensive began. Like nearly every official, the general was optimistic. He confidently reported: "In many areas the enemy has been driven away from the population centers; in others he has been compelled to disperse and evade contact, thus nullifying much of his potential. The year ended with the enemy resorting to desperation tactics in attempting to achieve military/psychological victory, and he has experienced only failure in these attempts."[18]

—Col. Dave Palmer

March 1968: Three days after the New Hampshire primary [in which antiwar candidate Eugene McCarthy had gained a stunning number of votes], on March 15, Acheson sat down to lunch alone with the President and told him what he had found. Johnson, already shaken by the wobbly attitude of one renowned hawk, Clark Clifford, was thunderstruck by Acheson's apparent defection. Acheson told the President that his recent Vietnam speeches were so far out of touch with reality that no one believed him, at home or abroad.[19]

—Marvin Kalb and Elie Abel

II: Distortions of Intelligence

In the June [1962] *BBC Listener*, Martin Harrison discusses the role of the press in war. "Freedom of information," he writes, "was an early victim of the Algerian War. At the root of the chronic failure of Algerian policy lay an irrational insistence on taking wish for reality. Governments assiduously cultivated fictions of which they were as much the prisoners as the public. . . . To close the gap between myth and reality," Harrison concludes, "progressively tighter control of information seemed essential." Without the change of a syllable, the lesson can be applied in South Vietnam.[20]

---

[17] George A. Carver (assessing the situation after a two-week visit to South Vietnam), Memorandum, "Comments on Vietnam," 2 March 1967. (S) On 14 March Carver sent a copy of his memo to the DDI, R. J. Smith, indicating that he had prepared it at the request of Walt Rostow but had told Rostow it was a personal paper, not an official CIA memorandum. CIA files, Job No. 80B01721R, O/D/NFAC, Box 1, "Substantive Policy Files, DDI Vietnam Files," Folder 7, "Special Assistant for Vietnam Affairs (SAVA) Jan-June 1967." George Allen told the author on 1 December 1995 that Carver had asked O/NE and DDI officers for a draft memo for Rostow but had then "rosied up" the judgments provided.

[18] Col. Dave Richard Palmer, *Summons of the Trumpet*, p. 263.

[19] As cited in Marvin Kalb and Elie Abel, *Roots of Involvement: The U.S. in Asia, 1784-1971* (New York: W. W. Norton, 1971) p. 236.

[20] *The Nation*, 14 July 1962, p. 1.

1979: As the last operational chief of (MACV) collection in Vietnam, I encountered problem areas and restrictions on my ability to report that I feel worthy of note. . . . All reports generated by my office (approximately some 1,200 per month) were passed to the Ambassador. . . . My attempts to bring some qualitative dimension to RVNAF reporting came to his attention quickly, and his displeasure was voiced to [the DAO] in clear and unmistakable terms. . . . In the earlier experiences reports were severely edited, refused approval, or delayed to the point that [they] were no longer of value. In the latter months most reports simply disappeared into the great Embassy maw never to be seen or heard. . . . To their credit, and particuarly because of their justifiable feeling that the DAO operation was amateurish, the CIA did not interfere with DAO operations. . . . From my earliest associations with Vietnam (1961) I have been concerned about US handling of information from that area. . . . This included deliberate and reflexive manipulation of information, restrictions on collection, and censorship of reporting.[21]   —Henry Shockley

29 November 1975: [Col. Shockley's memorandum] is a fascinating document of considerable intrinsic interest and importance. It points up a problem that was particularly acute in Vietnam but occurs world-wide, especially in areas where there is a close relationship between a US advisory establishment and the local government's armed services. It is a piece of paper I commend to your perusal and believe will be of interest to the other recipients of this memorandum.[22]   —George Carver

Every military man with whom I talked [during my recent Southeast Asia tour] privately admitted that we are losing the war.[23]
                                                              —Richard M. Nixon

The United States mission in Saigon is under instructions from Washington to get along with President Ngo Dinh Diem's regime come hell or high water and forget about political reforms. . . . American officials who "leak" stories unflattering to the Saigon Government or who depart from the Washington line of "cautious optimism" are tracked down by the embassy and muzzled. Correspondents who send gloomy dispatches are apt to be upbraided for lack of patriotism.[24]   —Homer Bigart, *The New York Times*

1969: The men to watch as the pressure of events grew, he [John Mecklen, USIA chief in Saigon] said, were the two who were at the fulcrum, William Trueheart, the Deputy Chief of Mission, and Brig. Gen. Richard Stilwell, the new chief of staff to Harkins . . . .[Stilwell] became

---

[21] Lt. Col. Henry A. Shockley, Memorandum for House Select Committee on Intelligence, 1975. Col. Shockley had had several tours in Vietnam, was a Ph.D., and had been a Vietnamese language officer.

[22] George Carver, cover memorandum to DCI Colby. "Lt. Col. Shockley's Critique of the Collection of Intelligence on the ARVN," 29 November 1975 (S). CIA/DDI files, Job No. 80R01720R, O/D/NFAC, Box 1, Folder 9.

[23] Richard M. Nixon, "Needed in Vietnam: The Will to Win,"*Reader's Digest*,August 1964, p.38.

[24] Homer Bigart, *The New York Times*, 3 June 1962.

the hatchet man for Harkins, the man who personally quashed the report-ing of the dissenting colonels, who challenged all dissenting views, and who, though he was not in the intelligence operation, went through the intelligence reports, tidying them up.[25]   —David Halberstam

One area we failed to investigate during those early years of the American buildup was the growing gap between the optimistic reports of progress that were coming in through the official chain of command and the increas-ingly skeptical reporting by some of the journalists covering the war. . . Even though these skeptical reports were based in part on the views of many junior American officers serving as advisers to the South Vietnamese Army, the Administration viewed the reports as a public-relations nui-sance rather than as something that needed to be looked at carefully.[26]

—Clark Clifford

1 October 1963: The restrictive US press policy in Vietnam . . . unques-tionably contributed to the lack of information about conditions in Vietnam which created an international crisis. Instead of hiding the facts from the American public, the State Department should have done everything possi-ble to expose the true situation to full view.[27]   —House Subcommittee

I was summoned to Ambassador Taylor's office to go over the estimate [drawn up in response to a Washington request that the field submit a coor-dinated assessment]. . . . The Ambassador at first wanted to omit the con-clusions entirely. . . . Then he suggested eliminating those parts of the concluding paragraphs which attempted to assess future trends. . . . Finally, he directed that I omit two of the five concluding paragraphs, on the grounds that they painted too dark a picture. . . . So the estimate was sent off to Washington without those paragraphs assessing ARVN's diminishing effectiveness and future prospects.[28]   —George Allen

1984: [In late 1963, my own cursory on-the-spot impression of the sorry state of the strategic hamlet program in the Delta] was confirmed in a more extensive survey conducted by Earl Young, the senior U.S. representative in the province. He reported in early December that three quarters of the two hundred strategic hamlets in Long An had been destroyed since the summer, either by the Vietcong or by their own occupants, or by a combi-nation of both. He also contradicted the American and South Vietnamese optimists in Saigon, who had been heralding the decline in enemy activity, by pointing out that Vietcong attacks in the province had subsided prima-rily because there were no longer any strategic hamlets worth attacking. "The only progress made in Long An Province," he concluded, "has been by the Vietcong."[29]   —Stanley Karnow

[25] David Halberstam, *The Best and the Brightest,* p.251.

[26] Clark Clifford, *The New Yorker,* 6 May 1991, p. 46.

[27] Report, House Subcommittee on Foreign Operations and Government Information, 1 October 1963, as cited in Gibbons, Part II, fn., p. 111.

[28] George W. Allen, "The Indochina Wars," pp. 236-237.

[29] Stanley Karnow, *Vietnam: A History,* p. 324.

June 1966: I must admit that unless I maintained some degree of optimism it was hard to get out of bed in the morning. One tended, I think, to magnify those points which made the situation a little promising and tended to discount a little the things that made it less so. . . . Basically the fellows who are optimistic are not so much those in the field, as the chaps in headquarters in Washington and Saigon who . . . tend to take a happier view than perhaps the objective circumstances might indicate.[30]

—Chester Cooper

III: The Domino Thesis

June 1949: . . . the extension of Communist authority in China represents a grievous political defeat for us . . . If Southeast Asia is also swept by communism, we shall have suffered a major political rout the repercussions of which will be felt throughout the rest of the world, especially in the Middle East and in a then critically exposed Australia . . . the colonial-nationalist conflict provides a fertile field for subversive Communist movements, and it is now clear that Southeast Asia is the target for a coordinated offensive directed by the Kremlin. (NSC 48/1).[31]   —*Pentagon Papers*

27 February 1950: It is recognized that the threat of Communist aggression against Indochina is only one phase of anticipated Communist plans to seize all of Southeast Asia. . . . The neighboring countries of Thailand and Burma could be expected to fall under Communist domination if Indochina were controlled by a Communist-dominated government. The balance of Southeast Asia would then be in grave hazard. (Report by the Natonal Security Council).[32]   —*Pentagon Papers*

31 January 1951: [Military assistance for Indochina is essential because] it is generally acknowledged that if Indochina were to fall under control of the Communists, Burma and Thailand would follow suit almost immediately. Therafter, it would be difficult, if not impossible for Indonesia, India and the others to remain outside the Soviet-dominated Asian Bloc.[33]

—Dean Rusk

17 March 1951: General de Lattre is to be here in a few minutes (at 8:45) to see me reference his request for reinforcement for Indochina: the French have a knotty problem on that one—the campaign out there is a

---

[30] Chester L. Cooper, former O/NE and NSC staffer, Oral History given to the John Fitzgerald Kennedy Library, June 1966. Cooper has provided a copy to CIA's History Staff.

[31] As cited in *Pentagon Papers* (Gravel ed.), Vol I, p. 82.

[32] "The Position of the United States with Respect to Indochina." *Pentagon Papers* (Gravel), Vol. I, pp. 161, 162.

[33] Then Assistant Secretary of State Dean Rusk. *FRUS*, 1951, Vol. VI, pp. 20, 22.

draining sore in their side. Yet if they quit and Indochina falls to Commies, it is easily possible that the entire Southeast Asia and Indonesia will go, soon to be followed by India.[34]   —Dwight D. Eisenhower

13 February 1952: Communist domination of Southeast Asia, whether by means of overt invasion, subversion, or accommodation on the part of the indigenous governments, would be critical to United States security interests. . . . The fall of Southeast Asia would underline the apparent economic advantages to Japan of association with the Communist-dominated Asian sphere. . . . In the long run the loss of Southeast Asia, especially Malaya and Indonesia, could result in such economic and political pressures in Japan as to make it extremely difficult to prevent Japan's political accommodation to the Soviet Bloc.[35]   —NSC Staff Study

16 January 1954: In the conflict in Indochina, the Communist and non-Communist worlds clearly confront one another on the field of battle. The loss of the struggle in Indochina, in addition to its impact in Southeast Asia and in South Asia, would therefore have the most serious repercussions on US and free world interests in Europe and elsewhere.[36]   —NSC 5404

12 March 1954: Should Indochina be lost to the Communists and in the absence of immediate and effective counteraction on the part of the Western Powers which would of necessity be on a much greater scale than that which could be decisive in Indochina, the conquest of the remainder of Southeast Asia would inevitably follow. . . . Orientation of Japan toward the West is the keystone of United States policy in the Far East. In the judgment of the Joint Chiefs of Staff, the loss of Southeast Asia to Communism would, through economic and political pressures, drive Japan into an accommodation with the Communist Bloc. The communization of Japan would be the predictable result.[37]
     —Adm. Arthur Radford, Chairman, Joint Chiefs of Staff

6 April 1954: [President Eisenhower stated that] Indochina was the first in a row of dominoes. If it fell its neightbors would shortly thereafter fall with it, and where did the process end? If he was correct, said the President, it would end with the United States directly behind the 9-ball: "in certain areas at least we cannot afford to let Moscow gain another bit of territory. Dien Bien Phu itself may be such such a critical point."[38]

---

[34] As cited in Robert H. Ferrell (ed.), *The Eisenhower Diaries* (New York: W.W. Norton, 1981), p. 190. At the time General Eisenhower was President of Columbia University.

[35] "United States Objectives and Courses of Action with Respect to Communist Aggression in Southeast Asia." *Pentagon Papers* (Gravel ed.), Vol. I, p.375.

[36] "United States Objectives and Courses of Action with Respect to Southeast Asia." *FRUS, 1952-1954*, Vol. XIII, Indochina, Part 1, p. 971.

[37] Memorandum for the Secretary of Defense, "Preparation of Department of Defense Views Regarding Negotiations on Indochina for the Forthcoming Geneva Conference," *Pentagon Papers* (Gravel ed.), Vol. I, pp. 449-450.

[38] Memorandum of Discussion, 192nd Meeting of the NSC. *FRUS*, 1952-1954, Vol. XIII, Part 1, p. 1261.

7 April 1954: In a press conference on April 7, 1954, Eisenhower . . . [applied] what might be called the falling domino principle; he compared Indochina to the first of a row of dominoes which is knocked over, making the fall of the last one a certainty. The fall of Indochina would lead to the fall of Burma, Thailand, Malaya and Indonesia. India would then be hemmed in by Communism and Australia, New Zealand, the Philippines, Formosa and Japan would all be gravely threatened.[39]

—Sherman Adams, President Eisenhower's Special Assistant

19 January 1961: President Eisenhower opened the discussion on Laos by stating that the United States was determined to preserve the independence of Laos. It was his opinion that if Laos should fall to the Communists, then it would be just a question of time until South Vietnam, Cambodia, Thailand and Burma would collapse. He felt that the Communists had designs on all of Southeast Asia, and that it would be a tragedy to permit Laos to fall.[40]

—Memorandum of Conversation, Eisenhower-Kennedy meeting on Laos

19 January 1961: As I listened to him [Eisenhower] in the Cabinet Room that January morning, I recalled that it was President Eisenhower who had acquainted the public with the phrase "domino theory" by using it to describe how one country after another could be expected to fall under Communist control once the process started in Southeast Asia.[41]

—Clark Clifford

8 November 1961: The Secretary of State, the Secretary of Defense and the Joint Chiefs of Staff agree: 1. The fall of South Vietnam to Communism would lead to the fairly rapid extension of Communist control, or complete accommodation to Communism, in the rest of mainland Southeast Asia and in Indonesia. The strategic implications, world-wide, particularly in the Orient, would be extremely dangerous.[42]

13 January 1962: It must be recognized that the fall of South Vietnam to Communist control would mean the eventual Communist domination of all of the Southeast Asian mainland. . . . Of equal importance to the immediate losses are the eventualities which could follow the loss of the Southeast Asian mainland. All of the Indonesian archipelago could come under the domination and control of the USSR and would become a Communist base posing a threat against Australia and New Zealand. The Sino-Soviet Bloc would have control of the eastern access to the Indian Ocean. The Philippines and Japan could be pressured to assume, at best, a neutralist

---

[39] Adams, *Firsthand Report: The Story of the Eisenhower Administration* (New York: Harper & Bros., 1961), p. 120.

[40] Porter, Gareth, *Vietnam: The Definitive Documentation of Human Decisions, [The Pentagon Papers]* (Earl M. Coleman Enterprises, 1979), Vol. II, p. 90.

[41] Clifford, "A Viet Nam Reappraisal: The Personal History of One Man's View and How it Evolved," *Foreign Affairs*, Vol XXVII, No. 4 (July 1969), p. 605.

[42] Draft Memorandum for President Kennedy. *FRUS*, 1961-1963, Vol. I, Vietnam, p. 561.

role, thus eliminating two of our major bases of defense in the Western Pacific. Our lines of defense then would be pulled north to Korea, Okinawa and Taiwan resulting in the subsequent overtaxing of our lines of communications in a limited war. India's ability to remain neutral would be jeopardized and, as the Bloc meets success, its concurrent stepped-up activities to move into and control Africa can be expected. . . . It is, in fact, a planned phase in the Communist timetable for world domination.[43]

        —Gen. Lyman Lemnitzer, Chairman, Joint Chiefs of Staff

10 May 1962: Eisenhower dwelt at length on the danger to South Vietnam and Thailand as both will be outflanked if Laos is in Communist hands and concluded that such a situation would be so critical to Southeast Asia and so important to the U.S. that most extreme measures, including the commitment of U.S. forces to combat in Laos, were justified. . . . Finally Eisenhower warned of the consequences of losing Southeast Asia, pointing out that if it is lost, nothing would stop the southward movement of Communism through Indonesia and this would have the effect of cutting the world in half.[44]   —John McCone

September 1963: [Upon being asked by Chet Huntley whether he believed in the "domino theory," he replied] I believe it, I believe it. I think that the struggle is close enough. China is so large, looms so high just beyond the frontier, that if South Vietnam went, it would not only give them an improved geographic position for a guerrilla assault on Malaya, but would also give the impression that the wave of the future in Southeast Asia was China and the Communists. So I believe it.[45]

        —President Kennedy, on NBC/TV

17 March 1964: We seek an independent non-Communist Vietnam. . . . Unless we can achieve this objective in South Vietnam, almost all of Southeast Asia will probably fall under Communist dominance (all of Vietnam, Laos, and Cambodia), accommodate to Communism so as to remove effective U.S. and anti-Communist influence (Burma), or fall under the domination of forces not now explicitly Communist but likely then to become so (Indonesia taking over Malaysia). Thailand might hold for a period without help, but would become shaky, and the threat to India on the West, Australia and New Zealand to the South, and Taiwan, Korea, and Japan to the North would be greatly increased.[46]

        —NSC Action Memorandum (NSAM) 288

---

[43] Memorandum for the Secretary of Defense, "The Strategic Importance of the Southeast Asia Mainland," *Pentagon Papers* (DoD ed.), Book 12, V-B-4; U.S. Involvement in the War, Internal Documents, The Kennedy Administration: January 1961-November 1963, Book II, pp. 448-450.

[44] McCone, Memorandum for the Record, "Discussion with General Eisenhower." (S/Eyes Only). CIA/DCI files, Job No. 80B01285A, DCI McCone, Folder No. 2.

[45] *Public Papers of the Presidents, John F. Kennedy, 1962*, p. 659, as cited in Gibbons, Part II, p. 163.

[46] "U.S. Objectives in South Vietnam." *Pentagon Papers* (*The New York Times* Edition: Bantam Books, 1971), pp. 283, 284. The above statement, incorporated into the NSAM, was a verbatim repeat of a Memorandum for the President the Secretary of Defense, Robert McNamara, had prepared the previous day, 16 March 1964. *Ibid.*, p. 278.

9 June 1964: A formal question the President [Lyndon Johnson] submitted to the C.I.A. in June also indicated what was on his mind. "Would the rest of Southeast Asia necessarily fall if Laos and South Vietnam came under North Vietnamese control?" he asked. The agency's reply on June 9 challenged the domino theory, widely believed in one form or another within the Administration. "With the possible exception of Cambodia," the C.I.A. memorandum said, "it is likely that no nation in the area would quickly succumb to Communism as a result of the fall of Laos and Vietnam. Furthermore, a continuation of the spread of Communism in the area would not be inexorable, and any spread which did occur would take time—time in which the total situation might change in any number of ways unfavorable to the Communist cause." The C.I.A. analysis conceded that the loss of South Vietnam and Laos "would be profoundly damaging to the U.S. position in the Far East" and would raise the prestige of China "as a leader of world Communism" at the expense of a more moderate Soviet Union. But the analysis argued that so long as the United States could retain its island bases, such as those on Okinawa, Guam, the Philippines and Japan, it could wield enough military power in Asia to deter China and North Vietnam from overt military aggression against Southeast Asia in general. Even in the "worst case," if South Vietnam and Laos were to fall through "a clear-cut Communist victory," the United States would still retain some leverage to affect the final outcome in Southeast Asia, according to the analysis. It said that "the extent to which individual countries would move away from the U.S. towards the Communists would be significantly affected by the substance and manner of U.S. policy in the period following the loss of Laos and South Vietnam."[47]   — *Pentagon Papers*

February-March 1968: Also, I could not free myself from the continuing nagging doubt left over from that August [1967] trip, that if the nations living in the shadow of Viet Nam were not now persuaded by the domino theory, perhaps it was time for us to take another look.[48]

—Clark Clifford, then Secretary of Defense

[47] *The New York Times* Edition, pp. 253-254. The CIA memorandum was prepared by the Office of National Estimates. President Johnson's request for CIA's views on the validity of the domino thesis came some 12 weeks after he had already made that thesis a part of formal US policy (NSAM 288, of 17 March 1964). Former Secretary of Defense McNamara, referring to the O/NE memorandum but omitting the language cited, claims that it supported the domino thesis. *In Retrospect*, pp.124-125.

[48] Clifford, "A Viet Nam Reappraisal," p. 612.

Index

165

166